SPIRITUAL HIGH TREASON

BY JIMMY SWAGGART

Jimmy Swaggart Ministries
P.O. Box 2550
Baton Rouge, Louisiana 70821-2550

TABLE OF CONTENTS

FOREWORD

In 1982, the Lord spoke to my heart and told me that I was to deliver a message that He would give me to the nation, to the Catholics, to the denominational world, and to the Pentecostals and Charismatics. He told me that the latter would be the hardest of all. The exact words of the Spirit to my heart were, "Your own will turn against you."

In spite of everything I can do to assuage my "own" turning against me (Pentecostals and Charismatics), I have not been successful. Actually, we are facing opposition such as we have never faced before in this Ministry. However, I am doing my very best to deliver what God has told me to say.

I believe this is the most dangerous hour the church has ever known. Much of the false teaching that is pervading the airwaves and pulpits today is coming under the guise of Pentecostal and Charismatic faiths. (Actually, it is not Pentecostal.) It seems that if a preacher laces what he says with shouts of "praise the Lord" and speaking in tongues, this somehow makes it all very spiritual.

Many, sad to say, are being deceived with such theology as is put out by the "Kingdom Agers," the "Power of Positive/Possibility Thinking" people, and the "Power of Positive Confession" crowd. (There is a *true* biblical positive confession, but it is not what is being promoted today.) Then there is the Counseling/Psychology teaching which is rife in our Bible Colleges and churches, leading people and future preachers away from a dependence on God and His Word.

In the early '60s, I preached a series of camp meetings with A.N. Trotter, one of the greatest men of God I have ever had the privilege of knowing. He had a profound impact upon my ministry. He made this statement to me one day: "Brother Swaggart, the Pentecostal fellowships have gone so far down the road to backsliding that it is already too late. They won't make it back."

I'll be frank with you. At that time, I did not understand what he meant. Then (in the '60s) it seemed to me that the spiritual world was on a roll; there was no place to go but up. If I had been forced to comment on his statement, I would have had to say (in honesty) that I did not believe him. He was seeing things that were too subtle for me to perceive in my youth and enthusiasm. But, oh, how right he was.

The Pentecostal message is unquestionably the message of the hour. It is the message of power and love that God is using to take His Word to a world that has lost its way. It is the *only* vehicle that God is using effectively to get His work accomplished today. This does not mean that people outside of the Pentecostal fold can't be saved or that other lives can't be touched. Certainly they can. But as a whole, it is the power of the Holy Spirit that is accomplishing things. Without this, precious little will be done.

Today is Pentecostalism's finest hour. Inroads are being made as never before. Its great message (Jesus saves, Jesus baptizes in the Holy Spirit, Jesus heals, and Jesus is coming again) is girdling the globe at an *unprecedented* rate. However, even in the midst of such glad tidings, there are ominous clouds gathering on the horizon. That is what this book is all about.

The messages contained herein will possibly make you angry, but perhaps they will make you think. And, if they do, the anguish I have experienced in delivering them will not have been in vain.

Jimmy Swaggart

CHAPTER 1

ROCK AND ROLL MUSIC IN THE CHURCH

 The August 25, 1986, issue of *U.S. News and World Report* contained a story on the advent of "contemporary gospel music" — which is a less sinister phrase than "rock and roll in the church."

Before that article was written, the author called and requested an interview, which I granted. He quoted me, and, interestingly, I was the only one cited in the article as being opposed to rock and roll music in the church.

To be sure, there *are* others out there who are less than enchanted with contemporary gospel music, but there are precious few — at least among those who are willing to stand up and be counted.

However, even though I frequently feel alone in this situation, I am not completely discouraged. I am confident that truth and reason will finally prevail. And for the sake of the youth of this age — for whom I have a deep and abiding concern — I will gladly bear whatever stigma might be attached to protesting against it.

1

A MEETING

Some months back, several "religious rock stars" requested a meeting with me, and a number of prominent rock names attended. Others — who have become household words in the area of sacred music — came, and these too have begun dabbling in the rock and roll style. In addition, several ministers of the gospel were present. This chapter is a result of that meeting.

Up front, I would like to say that I have nothing but Christian love and goodwill for every single individual who attended — and that would include all who are involved in the rock music world. I pray for them. Above all, I pray that God will open their eyes and show them the *real* road they are traveling.

Fundamentally, I don't blame or condemn those who are performing this kind of music, although God will be the final judge of their actions. Basically, I place the greater blame at the doorsteps of the church as a whole. There was a day when members were sufficiently attuned to God that such deviations wouldn't even have been *entertained* as suitable activity within the church. But today? *I believe this is an example of the spiritual decline infecting the leadership of the Pentecostal and Charismatic fellowships.* Standards have deteriorated to a point where just about *anything* goes.

One of the preachers present that day stated, "Very shortly, the heaviest rock will be the norm in all of our churches." Now this preacher is not a youngster just starting out in the ministry. He is a man in his early '70s, with the highest degrees our universities and seminaries can bestow. He has served as president of Bible colleges and is considered to be a noted Bible authority.

I will cite no specific names of rock performers, except in passing. As we have noted, while God will certainly judge their motives, I feel it is those in positions of spiritual leadership who will bear the heaviest burden of responsibility when the time comes for the accounting — *and that time will come.*

THE ARGUMENT

Contentions of legitimacy fly thick and fast when the question of religious rock music is raised:

- "It is the music of this generation."
- "It is a tool for winning young people to Christ."
- "It is the message of the young."
- "All music is the same."
- "It's the lyrics that count."
- "Music is like a platter: it's what you put *on* it that matters."
- "God gave rock and roll to the world."
- "If we don't have rock and roll, the young people will not come to our churches."
- Ad infinitum.

THE CHURCH'S WORST PROBLEM?

A pastor wrote the other day. "Brother Swaggart," he said, "the greatest problem in our churches today is rock and roll music."

Now I am not sure if that is absolutely correct. While rock and roll music is *among* our greatest problems, with Satan utilizing such a broad spectrum of devices, it is hard to point to any one as being the *worst* problem of all. But rock and roll is a severe and destructive force. To show just how bad the situation has become, I will quote a part of the letter this good pastor wrote.

I am concerned with the activities of our state leaders — the so-called *Christian* entertainment being sponsored and promoted by our district and youth leaders. There seems to be no rational approach that will reach them and change their direction.

Last year at our youth convention, there was a group called [name deleted], and about 3,000 young people attended. I do not exaggerate when I say that it was literally a punk rock concert, with only a *veneer* of Christianity to lend it legitimacy.

The singers were on a three-level stage, in boxed cubicles. On the last evening of their show, a young man dressed in skintight white jeans (and carrying a shield and sword "representing Jesus Christ") strutted across the stage. All the lights were out except for a spotlight on this performer. Swinging his pelvis out toward the audience, he brought everything to a halt. The band leader then yelled, "Let's party!"

A blast of gold dust was shot out toward the audience, and everything went wild as punk rock dancing, stomping, screaming, and whistling filled the hall. Our state youth director sat on the side of the stage smiling approval.

This *supposedly* depicted the resurrection of Jesus. Through it all, our district leaders sat watching, doing nothing. It was supported and defended by most of the youth representatives in the state.

It was suggested (sometime back) that we have Rich Wilkerson address our youth convention. The state youth director turned this down, stating that Rich Wilkerson was "too holiness."

You can see the deception is much greater than most of us realized. It is going to require a mighty move of God's Spirit and the supernatural intervention of God to set things right again. I feel, at the same time, as if the devil is sneering and saying, "It's too late, forget it."

Brother Swaggart, worldly entertainment is beginning to overwhelm the Pentecostal world. Our Bible colleges, churches, and districts are promoting this as "success" in the ministry. There are so many worldly individuals representing themselves as Christians who promote all this.

One youth evangelist related to me that at a youth convention he received $700 for preaching the gospel several days and nights. The rock group providing the music was paid $7,000.

I wonder, are the Church of God, the Pentecostal Holiness, the Word of Faith, the Foursquare, and the Independents all following suit?

WHERE ARE OUR PRIORITIES?

It should reveal something to us when in a state youth convention the speaker preaching the gospel of the living Christ is given barely enough to meet his expenses, while a rock band with little understanding of the Bible is paid many times that amount. This is an abomination as far as I am concerned, and I suspect that it is an abomination in God's eyes as well.

Some of the most vituperative letters I receive come from youth pastors in Pentecostal and Charismatic churches. The tone, spirit, and statements of their letters are very revealing.

Oh, a few of these individuals write with a gracious and kind spirit. But most think nothing of calling me stupid, a preacher of hate, and many other derogatory names.

They ignore the fact that God has imposed a responsibility on me to reach the world for the cause of Christ and that our telecast is aired in 145 countries around the world.

It makes no difference that the message entrusted to us has enough Holy Spirit anointing that over a million people have written (during the last two years) to tell us of their coming to Jesus Christ.

These individuals seem to have no fear of God. They seem to be totally lacking in biblical understanding (not to mention common courtesy). They treat us just about as the pornographers and rockers from *Playboy, Penthouse,* and *Hustler* do. *Could it be that all these are responding to the same spirit?* But these are youth pastors from some of our own Assemblies of God, Church of God, Foursquare, and Word of Faith churches. God help us!

Oh, yes, it is a problem in our churches — a serious problem — a problem that threatens to destroy an entire generation of Pentecostal and Charismatic youth, not to mention Baptists, Methodists, etc.

The simple fact is that the Spirit of God works in only one way — and that is *His* way. He will never deviate from His scriptural method and resort to accepting the methods of the world.

WHAT CAN THE HOLY SPIRIT USE?

This question is plaguing the church today. Many claim that the Holy Spirit can use psychology, inner healing, possibility thinking, etc. They say that just because "they're not mentioned in the Bible doesn't rule them out as useful tools." But what does the Word of God say?

> *"And have no fellowship with the unfruitful works of darkness, but rather reprove them. For it is a shame even to speak of those things which are done of them in secret. But all things that are reproved are made manifest by the light: for whatsoever doth make manifest is light"* (Eph. 5:11-13).

> *"And when he is come, he will reprove the world of sin, and of righteousness, and of judgment . . . Howbeit when he, the Spirit of truth, is come, he will guide you into all truth . . . He shall glorify me"* (John 16:8, 13, 14).

Would God use alcohol for His glory? What about gambling or illegal drugs? Would He use jealousy, envy, or malice? Is it possible for the Lord to take rock and roll — which has long promoted drugs, alcohol, illicit sex, perversion, Satan worship, and every other deviate satanic ploy — clean it up a little, and use it for His glory? Can you clean up alcohol? Drugs? Can you clean up envy, malice, hate, gambling, or sexual abuse? *The church of the living God is falling into a terrible trap by binding the Holy Spirit into an untenable position. In other words, it is trying to make Him a part of a nefarious worldly scheme.*

It is difficult enough to get the Spirit of God to use us after we have sought God's face earnestly, cleansed ourselves from all filthiness of the flesh, sanctified ourselves unto God, and (to the very best of our abilities) walked holy and clean before Him. Even then He often refuses to use us. But to think that we can clothe ourselves in the "spirit of the age" and *then* believe the Spirit of God will utilize us is spiritual insanity.

David Wilkerson said this:

> What God deplores is the mixture being introduced into Charismatic circles. "Mixture" is synonymous with lukewarmness.
>
> You find this mixture everywhere you look today. Attend a so-called Christian rock concert, for example. What an incredible mixture. They usually begin with, "We are here only to minister Jesus — to glorify His name." You will hear sweet talk about holiness, repentance, and giving up all for Jesus.
>
> But suddenly, as the spirit of Elvis takes over, they are transformed before your eyes into rollicking, unabashed, sensuous hard-rockers. Before the event is over, you will hear them boast, "We are going to take Jesus where the church never goes — into bars, secular concerts, MTV! We are praying God will give us the ear of the world. We want to get the same crowd the world gets."
>
> If I am to believe what Jesus taught, they would be

stoned with tomatoes and hooted off the stage by that worldly bunch. That is, if they *truly* ministered in the Spirit.

The more they sang for Jesus, the more they would be hated and despised. Gospel singers who are praised and accepted by the world have lost the presence of Jesus — the very thing that *causes* rejection.

"And ye shall be hated of all men for my name's sake" (Mark 13:13).

Meg Greenfield, in the July 28 issue of *Newsweek*, said, "We don't seem to have a word for 'wrong' anymore in the moral sense, as in 'theft is wrong.' "

James Chute, music editor for the *Milwaukee Journal*, said that Amy Grant, along with other Christian performers, does not overtly mention the Lord for fear of turning off a big portion of her audience. As an example, he cited the use of "you" in the song, "You Light Up My Life." It is left to the discretion of the listener to determine if the "you" is the Lord, a spouse, a lover, a parent, or a pet.

In his article, Chute went on to note that Grant uses "all the commercial weapons available, including sex, to promote her music."

Admitting that the devil didn't own all the good tunes, the columnist cautioned that the answer to developing "Christian" music is not in the wholesale adoption of musical styles that "overwhelm the message" of Christian musicians.

He concluded by saying that if Christian music is to survive, it must "forge a musical style with a content rooted in Christians' own experiences and in their own communities; a style where the words and the music are inseparable."

"This style will probably never play the 'Tonight Show,' " Chute wrote, "but at least it should be honest about its intentions — rather than masquerading as an angel who borrows the worst clothing."

How interesting that individuals who don't even claim *to know Jesus should sense more accurately the ways of the Holy Spirit than some who claim His name.*

THREE TYPES OF MUSIC

* **Sacred, or Christian**
* **Worldly, which includes most pop, ballad, country and western, rhythm and blues, folk, etc.**
* **Modern rock**

Until a couple of centuries after the resurrection, most of the music in the world was written in a minor key. All the psalms were sung in a minor key. As a matter of fact, our Jewish and Arab friends still utilize the minor key in their music.

However, after the resurrection of Jesus Christ, *music gradually changed from the minor to the major key.* It was as if the resurrection reversed the direction of an upside-down world.

Basically, with the exception of modern rock, all music today springs from gospel music — whether it be country and western, ballad, rhythm, traditional, or otherwise. The chord structures are basically the same. In other words, the melody to "Amazing Grace" could be exchanged for "Your Cheating Heart."

It must be realized, however, that the spirit of the world rapidly infiltrated the *music* of the world — which immediately brought it under the sway of Satan and of the world system.

So just because chord systems are the same, this doesn't make it right for the child of God to participate in this type of music; the *lyrics* differ greatly in their orientation.

The music of the world, even though structurally and basically the same — except for the lyrics — is infected and infested by the spirit of the world. *This is why Christians should not embrace any types of songs other than those which glorify the Lord Jesus Christ.* In John 16:14 (quoted previously), the Word tells us:

"He [the Holy Spirit] shall glorify me."

There is no way you can glorify the Lord Jesus Christ (through the power of the Holy Spirit) by listening to any type of worldly song, no matter how innocuous the lyrics might seem.

I am amazed that some "Christian" television shows perform worldly songs such as "Chattanooga Shoeshine Boy" or "I Left My Heart in San Francisco." Apparently, they believe that because these do not *overtly* promote adultery or perversion, they are "acceptable." This is totally untrue. The child of God is to glorify the Lord Jesus Christ *continually*.

To participate in anything reflecting the spirit of the world — no matter how innocuous — demonstrates only ignorance of God and His Word. Why should any well-intentioned Christian choose to do so?

Many "Christian" songs, even though they are considered to be "sacred" or "spiritual," are also infected by the spirit of the world and should be excised as well.

Only the Lord knows the number of songs we reject in rehearsal as we prepare for our crusades. Why?

Because the Lord reveals to us that they promote some element of the spirit of the world and are therefore unsuitable for those who wish to worship God.

I watched a very popular "Christian" television show. The host introduced the singers and said they would sing some "Broadway tunes." Then for nearly ten minutes they buck-danced their way through these numbers. He then called them back for more, and I wondered, "How is this supposed to glorify God?"

No, it not only doesn't *glorify* God, it, in effect, *blasphemes* Him.

If these people had any idea of the holiness of God, they would flee in terror. Even if they were not struck down on the spot — as was done in Old Testament days — they are still dying *spiritually*. The church is literally overrun with "walking corpses" who rush about mouthing the name of Jesus as they demonstrate no awareness of what He is and what He stands for.

ROCK AND ROLL

America was first exposed to what we call *"modern rock"* in the '60s. It was music unlike anything our nation had ever heard before. It was accompanied by smoke pots and strobe lights — and with a spirit that promoted drugs, illicit sex, and perversions.

In the middle '60s, the Beatles journeyed to India to sit at the feet of Indian gurus. Sometime later, George Harrison wrote the song, "My Sweet Lord." This song glorified a demon-possessed spiritualist Indian guru with Satan as his master. From that moment, rock music took a turn downward. What previously was bad became literally dominated by Satan. Modern rock started with the plunge into hell itself.

I maintain that these anthems of rebellion (and that's precisely what they are) were fathered by Satan. Rock doesn't have its roots in any other type of music in the world today — except perhaps the music of the Eastern cultures. And remember, these are undergirded with the philosophies of Hinduism, Buddhism, and the occult.

Purely and simply, this is the music of Satan.

ROCK AND ROLLER

The other day I heard a so-called "Christian" rock artist say, "I'm just a rock and roller." I wonder if he knew what he was saying. Does he even understand the meaning of the term?

The phrase "rock and roll" was coined by Alan Freed, a Cleveland disc jockey in the middle '50s. It is a street term denoting a sexual climax — do I have to fill in the blanks?

It has since added rebellion, illicit sex, perversion, Satan worship, homosexuality, and drugs — plus every other darkness that hell can promote.

It has become a theme song for multitudes of the young who have od'd on drugs. It speaks for two million teenagers *per year* who attempt suicide. It represents tens of thousands of young *pregnant* girls — who are only children themselves. It is a dirge for endless rows of caskets, for death and dying, and for millions upon millions now eternally relegated to hell.

Why would anyone who names the name of Jesus want to classify himself as being under this banner? I guess people do so because they are woefully ignorant — or perhaps because they really *are* rock and rollers. I suppose, of the two, woeful ignorance is much to be preferred.

GOSPEL MUSIC DOVE AWARDS

The crowd was large. It was a star-studded event, not only with so-called gospel favorites, but with country and western and rock stars as well.

I guess the "gospel" scene has really arrived, now that it can assemble country and western artists, rock and roll superstars, and Broadway luminaries all under one roof.

The show (and that's what it was) was hosted by a country and western performer. Oh, to be sure, he claims to be a Christian — a popular title to adopt today. One just tacks Christianity onto whatever long list of philosophies already subscribed to.

A group called "Stryper" was brought out. They are heavy metal — of the type Lester Bangs describes as "most closely identified with violence and aggression, rapine and carnage . . . a fast train to nowhere."

I knew what was going to happen by the audience's greeting of this group. When their jack-hammer, technological nihilism came to an end, the crowd (supposedly representing the Lord Jesus Christ and the love and grace of the Holy Spirit) was on its feet, screaming and applauding. Gospel Music *Dove* Awards? More appropriately, Religious Music *Buzzard* Awards.

James Chute went on to say in the *Milwaukee Journal*:

> The CCM movement has gone far beyond a few musicians strumming guitars in harmony. Tune in to any of the Christian cable programs and you won't have long to wait before some band, dressed in sequins and tuxedos — looking for all the world as if its last gig was at Caesar's Palace — will praise Almighty God in the same way Las Vegas praises the almighty dollar.

Then he said:

> They all make the same fatal mistake: that somehow the lyrics change the music's context, its subliminal message. More likely, the very opposite happens. The Las Vegas/Wayne Newton lounge-act style is sanctified through its Christian associations.

James Chute is right. It is a *fatal* mistake. The lyrics do not change the music's content nor its subliminal message. Actually, it is the music that converts the Christian message into a nightclub format. And when this happens, we come very close to blaspheming the Holy Spirit.

ARE THE ARTISTS TO BLAME?

Certainly, insofar as we will all have to give account when we stand before God.

But in the broader perspective, I think the majority of the artists are doing what they do because of our so-called "spiritual leadership." A legitimacy is extended to this whole sordid mess by the preachers who approve it — whether through ignorance on their part or through an overt selling out for the traditional mess of pottage.

I was shocked to hear one preacher in the meeting I mentioned. He said, "God gave us rock and roll."

What an appalling statement! In other words, God gave us grapes, so wine is a commodity for good. God gave us barley, so whiskey benefits mankind. God gave us sexuality, so rape, perversion, and child molestation are from God. How warped can a person allow his thinking to become?

Another preacher at this meeting told me he had been to Africa and that after natives were saved, they continued to perform their primitive, demonic dances: the same weird contortions, the same abandonment of the flesh.

I said, "Yes, that may well have been the case *immediately* after they were saved, but I would venture a guess that it stopped as soon as they began to learn even a little bit about the Lord." He lowered his eyes and admitted that this was true.

One of the basic characteristics of Christianity is that it changes the cultures it contacts. Look at the world. The only cultures really worth living in are those produced by Christianity. It is not our business (God forbid) to *succumb* to the culture of the ungodly, reprobate, worldly system. Rather, it is our business to *change* the culture of the world. Pray tell me how we can hope to change it by wallowing in the lowest elements within it.

Yes, the rockers *are* to blame. But the *greater* blame (and the greater sin) must be placed on the shoulders of ministers and district officials of Charismatic and Pentecostal fellowships who choose to avert their eyes as Satan destroys an entire generation.

"BUT THE END JUSTIFIES THE MEANS"

Stories of rock concerts drawing fabulous crowds of unsaved youths, and of the great camp meeting atmosphere prevailing, with great altar work resulting . . . is a crock! It just isn't happening that way.

Sitting in that meeting with the rockers, they continually returned to this very claim: "It's the only way to attract the unsaved youth. They just won't come any other way."

Well let's look at this contention. Glen Berteau, leader of one of the largest youth groups in the nation at Family Worship Center in Baton Rouge, turned to one of them and said, "There is no truth in what you're saying. I've attended many of these concerts and there are precious few, if any, unsaved young people there."

Glen went on to say, "In a youth meeting of 900 young people, I asked how many had been saved at a religious rock concert. Only one raised his hand — and he had been saved five years ago when his cousin witnessed to him on the way to the concert! It had nothing to do with the concert itself." The rocker he was addressing had to admit this was true.

But he wasn't yet willing to admit that his way was unproductive — despite the evidence. "What we're going to have to do," he persisted, "is to make it even more heavy metal in order to attract the unsaved young people."

If we are to follow this ludicrous logic, the Pentecostal and Charismatic communities should be running bars and porno shops in order to bring the church and Christians into wider contact with the unsaved.

Ridiculous? Yes, but that is no less rational than his contention.

I maintain that there are precious few young people who are being saved at these "sell-outs to Satan." Rather, an entire generation of Pentecostal and Charismatic youth are being systematically exposed to a spirit of rebellion as a consequence of being encouraged to listen to rock music. And this spirit of rebellion is precisely what we are discussing here.

I maintain that "Christian" rock concerts are *worse* than their worldly cousins. The conventional ones are obvious in their intent while the "Christian" ones are insidious in their action. Regrettably, the hell they both promote is the same.

"STAR AURA"

The other day a rock star wrote me to say, "I'm in the same work you're in — winning souls to Jesus."

I wonder if this poor individual has even the *foggiest* idea of what he's talking about. I'm sure he doesn't. It's reminiscent of the incident (Acts 8:9-24) where Simon the Sorcerer suggested to Simon Peter that they were in the same line of work. (And please don't misunderstand, I could not stand in Simon Peter's shadow.)

As we have repeatedly stated, the Christian rock scene is in the mode of the spirit of this world. The "star aura" is there — diametrically opposed to the spirit of the Man of Galilee.

And, once again, please don't misunderstand. Preachers of the gospel can succumb to this same temptation — as can anyone else in the work of God. But it will bring quick ruin to the preacher while it (temporarily) brings only fame to the rock star. And again it demonstrates Satan's typical response to following him: a *momentary* reward as compensation for *eternal* punishment.

WHAT CAN SAVE OUR YOUTH?

Young people today are facing problems I never had to face in my youth. All the problems of my day are still present, but in addition they have to contend with drugs, illicit sex, perversion, Satan worship, and every conceivable bondage of death and destruction. Think of this:

- Over half of our kids today are living in broken homes.
- Hundreds of thousands are being sexually molested by lust-filled libertines as a result of the "spirit of the age" — fostered by pornography, Hollywood, the television industry, and that ultimate destroyer, Satan.
- Two million a year are attempting suicide, with all too many succeeding.
- The problem of preteen alcoholism is acute.
- Despite rampant abortion, hundreds of thousands of infants are being born to teenage girls. In a disposable society, we now have "throw-away" children. No one wants them.

Does anyone care? How can we reach them, morally and spiritually? There is only one way — not two, three, or four. And that is the method laid down in God's Word and proven over the centuries by results.

"And I, if I be lifted up from the earth, will draw all men unto me" (John 12:32).

"Come unto me, all ye that labour and are heavy laden, and I will give you rest. Take my

*yoke upon you, and learn of me; for I am meek
and lowly in heart: and ye shall find rest unto
your souls. For my yoke is easy, and my burden
is light"* (Matt. 11:28-30).

The answer is Jesus. And we bring *all* to Him —
including young people — only by the Holy Spirit.

What *methods* does the Holy Spirit use?

To begin with, He does *not* use the spirit of this world.
He will use only the Word of God as conveyed by a clean
vessel which has *"come out from among them [the
world]."*

At Family Worship Center in Baton Rouge, as we have
mentioned, our youth department (Crossfire, headed by
Glen Berteau) is one of the largest such organizations in
the nation. Many of the young people in Crossfire are
former drug addicts, alcoholics, Satan worshipers — and
just about anything else one might imagine.

They were lost and hopeless, thinking that there was no
answer and that no one cared. But then someone invited
them to Crossfire. And with nothing but songs that truly
glorified Jesus Christ (along with the Word of God), they
were offered hope. They found the Lord Jesus Christ as
their personal Saviour and they were delivered by the might
and power of God.

Some say that deliverance cannot be effected in this
manner. Of course, anyone who would make such a statement has no knowledge of the Word (and power) of
Almighty God. Jesus plainly said it (and we quoted it
earlier):

"If I be lifted up, [I] will draw all. . . ."

And "all" here certainly must include teenagers.

Modern "Christian" rock is not drawing teenagers to Jesus. It is drawing them to rock concerts. The greatest thing that could happen within the church today would be for all rock artists to consecrate themselves to God and *abandon* their obsession with contemporary music.

The pastors? They should forsake this "deception of darkness" and banish it from their churches.

It is almost as though Satan wasn't accomplishing his destruction of a generation on his own, so pastors and church elders are volunteering to do his job for him.

Satan is rocking and rolling with laughter.

How can all this be done "in the name of God" when the hand of the destroyer is so evident?

"For the time will come when they will not endure sound doctrine; but after their own lusts shall they heap to themselves teachers, having itching ears; And they shall turn away their ears from the truth, and shall be turned unto fables" (II Tim. 4:3, 4).

"Behold, I stand at the door, and knock: if any man hear my voice, and open the door, I will come in to him, and will sup with him, and he with me" (Rev. 3:20).

CHAPTER 2

SHIELDS OF GOLD AND SHIELDS OF BRASS

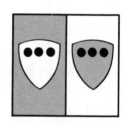

"And it came to pass in the fifth year of king Rehoboam, that Shishak king of Egypt came up against Jerusalem: And he took away the treasures of the house of the Lord, and the treasures of the king's house; he even took away all: and he took away all the shields of gold which Solomon had made. And king Rehoboam made in their stead brasen shields, and committed them unto the hands of the chief of the guard, which kept the door of the king's house. And it was so, when the king went into the house of the Lord, that the guard bare them, and brought them back into the guard chamber" (I Kings 14:25-28).

THE GOLDEN AGE OF ISRAEL

Solomon's reign has been properly called (and for more than symbolic reasons) the Golden Age of Israel. The forty years during which he ruled was a period of unprecedented national prosperity and power. At that time Israel was unquestionably the dominant nation of the earth.

Because of David's devoted consecration to God, his forty-year reign (which immediately preceded that of Solomon) saw Israel expand from a small community of tribes into a powerful nation. All enemies were subdued and prosperity prevailed. When David's son Solomon assumed the throne, it was simply a matter of allowing David's momentum to bring it to full stature as the "superpower" of its day.

The Bible wonderfully illustrates the degree to which God's blessings had exalted Israel. *"Silver,"* it says, *"was as rocks on the ground."* As a matter of fact, the overwhelming percentage of all the gold mined throughout the world to that day had come to reside in Israel. And Solomon, as the personification of the nation, controlled that incredible, golden hoard.

Now one might logically expect, knowing the wisdom of Solomon as described in II Chronicles 1:11 and 12, knowing that he grew up seeing his father as a living example of piety and devotion to God, and knowing that he was more abundantly blessed (in the material and intellectual sense) than any person in history, that Solomon would — if anything — outdo even his father, David, in his commitment to God.

But was this the case? Standing before the exquisite temple he built, a strange sight would have greeted the eye. Let's set the scene:

The Mount of Olivet lay directly before the temple with the beautiful Brook Kidron separating Olivet from the

Temple Mount. But — if you were to stand looking at Olivet from the Temple — a bizarre sight would have greeted your eye.

Greasy plumes of smoke writhed sinuously skyward, hour after hour and day after day. These came from altars built — not by a small, hard-core fringe element of malcontents, but — by the very *wives* of Solomon. They were altars to heathen gods and deities: Moloch (Milcom, Molech), Baal, Beelzebub, Astarte (Ashtoreth), Chemosh, and just about any pagan god one might ever think to mention. And inseparably intertwined with their heathen worship was its age-old partner-in-sin — religiously sanctioned prostitution.

One can't help but wonder in shocked bewilderment, "How could this have happened? Surely, if any person in history must have been aware of God's bounty and blessings, it should have been Solomon." Solomon's wives turned away his heart from God.

> *"For it came to pass, when Solomon was old, that his wives turned away his heart after other gods: and his heart was not perfect with the Lord his God, as was the heart of David his father"* (I Kings 11:4).

God, because of David, promised to withhold judgment from Solomon. But when Solomon died after this forty-year reign, Rehoboam took the throne. God had stated that judgment would come and, as surely as eternity, judgment *did* come.

Just five years after Rehoboam assumed the throne, Shishak, the powerful and ambitious king of Egypt, came to lay siege upon Jerusalem. Again, the Bible says:

*"Then Asa took all the silver and the gold
that were left in the treasures of the house of
the Lord"* (I Kings 15:18).

EGYPT A TYPE OF THE WORLD

The analogy here is clear. Either we commit ourselves
wholeheartedly to God, or "Egypt-Shishak" (a type of the
world) will come to overwhelm us. This is the ageless,
never-ending confrontation.

The beloved John wrote almost 2,000 years ago:

*"Love not the world, neither the things that
are in the world. If any man love the world, the
love of [for] the Father is not in him"* (I John
2:15).

This Scripture merits particular attention by today's
Pentecostal and Charismatic bodies. Obviously, while
individuals have an infinite *capacity* for love, conflicting
avenues of love cannot coexist. For example: A man cannot
juggle contradictory relationships involving a decent and
loving spouse, while he concurrently maintains a mistress
on the side — without one or the other relationship being
eventually destroyed. A man cannot balance an affection
for a peaceful and serene home with a love for the
neighborhood tavern. Sooner or later he must choose
which will direct, or dominate, his life.

And so it is today that the *world* is the greatest problem
in the Pentecostal and Charismatic communities.

We are, sad to say, in the process of trading our shields
of gold for shields of brass. The Bible states that Shishak
took away the shields of gold. And it says that at this point,
King Rehoboam replaced them with *brazen* shields.

"And king Rehoboam made in their stead brasen shields, and committed them unto the hands of the chief of the guard, which kept the door of the king's house" (I Kings 14:27).

Now let's look at this for a moment from a metallurgical point of view. There are "noble" metals and there are "base" metals. Noble metals (gold and platinum as examples) do *not* react with oxygen to oxidize or "rust." On the other hand, base metals *do* oxidize — to the point where oxidation will eventually *destroy* them completely.

The shields of the temple were originally of gold, which was eternal and never-changing. But when Shishak removed these, what did Rehoboam do? Some previous Israelite leaders, when defeated by enemy forces, would don sackcloth and ashes and seek God's face to reveal to them where they had gone astray.

Rehoboam chose not to do this. Instead he *replaced* the gold (eternal and faithful) shields with *imitations* of brass. Brass is an alloy of copper and zinc which *looks* a great deal like gold. The *difference* is that brass *does* oxidize and rapidly loses the *appearance* of gold — unless constantly repolished. When burnished, it offers a fair imitation of gold — on the surface — while internally it is rotting away.

So with this in mind, let's get back to the condition of today's church.

It's the same old story repeated again and again. The Spirit of God moves and there is great revival. But then those affected succumb to the temptations of the world, which can be buffed and burnished to temporarily and superficially give the *appearance* of gold.

Pentecostal denominations — the Assemblies of God, the Church of God, Pentecostal Holiness, the Foursquare, the Open Bible, plus all the Charismatic groups — are at this spiritual crossroads today. We trust it hasn't already gone beyond this to where the gold shields are long since gone, and their brass replacements well into the process of internal decay.

Some months ago I wrote to the leader of one of the most powerful Pentecostal fellowships in the world. He had just been elected to its highest office.

"You are," I said, *"going to face problems and difficulties never before encountered. These problems will be different, infinitely greater, than any your predecessors have faced. And the overtures of Satan will so subtly tempt your fellowship that I'm concerned that most members won't even recognize its source."*

In the past, the false doctrines Satan would try to introduce into the work of God could take months, even years, before their influences might be felt. But today it can happen in a matter of weeks or even days — *due almost totally to television's impact.*

So-called Christian television is now bringing the world into the church as never before. *Christian TV is the horse Shishak is riding toward our contemporary Jerusalem.* If the Pentecostal and Charismatic fellowships cease to exist, or lose their effectiveness, it is "Christian" television that must shoulder the major part of the blame.

SATAN'S TACTICS

"And the serpent said unto the woman, Ye shall not surely die: For God doth know that in the day ye eat thereof, then your eyes shall be opened, and ye shall be as gods, knowing good and evil. And when the woman saw that the tree was good for food, and that it was pleasant to the eyes, and a tree to be desired to make one wise, she took of the fruit thereof, and did eat, and

*gave also unto her husband with her; and he did
eat"* (Gen. 3:4-6).

Note here the three-pronged attack by Satan. The
beloved John readdressed this subject in I John 2:16. He
expanded the lesson of the above Scripture when he said:

> *"For all that is in the world, the lust of the
> flesh, and the lust of the eyes, and the pride of
> life, is not of the Father, but is of the world."*

There you have it: The three appeals (to the body, to the
eyes, and to the ego) that Satan used to bring about the
downfall of Adam and Eve are still his methods of choice
today. Let's look at these three avenues to spiritual ruin:

- The lust of the flesh.
- The lust of the eyes.
- The pride of life.

THE LUST OF THE FLESH

This is a relatively obvious list. Paul gives the specifics
(and they are self-explanatory) in Galatians 5:19-21. We
would do well to heed them, for Paul warns that falling prey
to them will disqualify anyone from inheriting the kingdom of God:

> *"Now the works of the flesh are manifest,
> which are these; Adultery, fornication, unclean-
> ness, lasciviousness, Idolatry, witchcraft, ha-
> tred, variance, emulations, wrath, strife,
> seditions, heresies, Envyings, murders, drunken-
> ness, revellings, and such like: of the which I
> tell you before, as I have also told you in time*

past, that they which do such things shall not
inherit the kingdom of God" (Gal. 5:19-21).

THE LUST OF THE EYES

This category is far more subtle. Under this heading
comes *"the little foxes, that spoil the vines"* (S. of Sol.
2:15). Everyone recognizes the obvious dangers of the lusts
of the *flesh,* so few (if any) Christians wander naively into
situations that will involve them with adultery, witchcraft,
murder, or drunkenness.

Ah, but the lusts of the eyes. These are sins that are far
less easily recognized — especially in ourselves. Is it
really good Christian concern for the image our brother is
projecting with his new possessions — or is it overt *envy?*
Do we offer advice to a brother because we're concerned
with his immortal soul — or is it sheer *malice* that prompts
our action? Is it for the good of the church that we discuss a
sister's shortcomings — or is it a simple love of *gossip?*
*The lusts of the eyes are, for some reason, exceedingly
difficult to recognize and root out — especially in ourselves.*

THE PRIDE OF LIFE

And if the lusts of the eyes are hard to define, let's look
at a truly insidious problem — *"the pride of life"* as John
phrased it, or *"the desire to be wise"* as it is described in
the Scripture on the downfall of Adam and Eve. Today, in
our time of preoccupation with psychological jargon, this
will be more readily recognized as egotism or concern for
self-image. The Bible refers to it repeatedly in Ecclesiastes
as *vanity.*

TEMPTATION: UPWARD AND DOWNWARD

The first two categories (lust of the flesh and lust of the eyes) might be classified as *downward* temptations. In other words, it is obvious that succumbing to them will draw us *down* morally. But, uniquely, the pride of life is an *upward* temptation. That is, falling prey to this equally sinister sin can *seem* to be justified by a "highly moral" Christian ambition to improve our situation, our reputation, or our position.

THE PRIDE OF LIFE
IS THE SIN OF THE PENTECOSTAL CHURCH

It should be obvious that Satan's wiles never change. He lured Adam and Eve with appeals to the eyes, to the body, and to the ego. The fruit was *"pleasant to the eye,"* *"good to eat,"* and would *"make one wise."* Today he lures *us* with appeals to these same lusts, and critical as we might be of *Eve's* naiveté — *we fall for the same old lures*.

To be sure, the sins of lust of the flesh and lust of the eyes are not totally unknown within the body of Christ. Most churches will not countenance, nor compromise with, the lusts of the flesh. Any church accepting the tenets of faith would take quick action against a minister involved in adultery, fornication, or homosexuality.

There is, however, far less recognition of the lusts of the eyes. Greed, covetousness, jealousy, envy, etc. *are* present in many church bodies, just as they are in the world. The problem, of course, is that the lusts of the eyes are insidious. They provide instant gratification, and they are easy to paper over with excuses — even when the conscience reminds us that we're wandering off course. So they're a real and continuing problem in many church bodies. Can they be rooted out? Yes, but only by preaching the Word of God and by praying that the Holy Spirit will point up our personal shortcomings.

But when it comes to the pride of life, we are dealing with a far more sinister situation.

Not only does the body of Christ seldom recognize this terrible sin, in many quarters it is even *applauded and encouraged.*

All the while it is at *least* as destructive as the first two, and oftentimes more so, just because of its subtlety.

This is the sin that has played a major role in destroying the denominational world, and is well on its way to neutralizing the effectiveness of the Pentecostal and Charismatic fellowships as well.

The pride of life is commonly seen today masquerading under several disguises: psychology/psychotherapy, inner healing, the fourth dimension, positive confession, dream your own dream, possibility or positive thinking, and ever-higher education.

No, higher education, in and of itself, is not inherently wrong. But when an individual sees this as an end in itself or as *the* road to spiritual growth, that person has substituted man's ways for God's ways. He has yielded to human vanity, despite the fact that God's way is *always* the moving and operation of the Holy Spirit within a yielded vessel.

These are all elements conducive to entrapment by "upward sin." By engaging in, or subscribing to, these particular philosophies, one must first set aside the true ways of God — which are the cross of Jesus Christ, the Word of God, and the operation of His Holy Spirit in our lives. All too many Pentecostal and Charismatic churches are replacing these, however, with man-made philosophies.

Instead of our efforts being God-centered, they are becoming man-centered.

As mentioned, the sin of the pride of life is more often applauded, eagerly sought, and even rewarded. It is the replacement of a shield of gold with one of brass and an error that will lead the church of the living God into captivity.

Preachers have been brought before church officials (and properly so) for the lusts of the flesh. But rarely (if ever) is one brought before an official body for the lusts of the eyes. And when it comes to the pride of life, those who indulge in this equally pernicious sin are more often than not brought up for *commendation!*

Men write books on "possibility thinking" — which demeans the cross and the will of God. And what happens? These books are applauded, given rave reviews, and consumed voraciously by the church body (led by the preacher oftentimes). Preachers are lauded and congratulated for promoting such philosophies when, in reality, they have committed sins that are perhaps *worse* than adultery or fornication.

The other day I was preaching in our college chapel and said this:

> Everyone who has received a degree in psychology
> (psychotherapy) has received a certificate in what amounts to
> a bald-faced fabrication — in other words, a lie.

Modern-day psychology is steeped in heathenistic attempts to meld its ungodliness with the Word of God. This is impossible. It can only draw people away from the true help available through the Word of God. And then its proponents are congratulated and exalted.

In reality, they are guilty of the sin of the pride of life. Shields of brass have been substituted for shields of gold.

SHISHAK TOOK AWAY THE TREASURES OF THE HOUSE OF THE LORD

The Bible tells us that Shishak (the world) came in and took away the treasures of the house of the Lord. The Bible says he took away *all*, and he took away the shields of gold. Now what are the treasures of the house of the Lord and the shields of gold?

Tragically, the Lord's "treasures" are a complete mystery to most Christians today. They've never seen the real thing so they're persuaded that brass replicas are the norm. *The treasures of the house of the Lord are the anointing of the Holy Spirit, the power of Almighty God, the flow of the Spirit within our hearts and lives, the operation of the gifts of the Spirit, the convicting power of the Holy Spirit, the utilization of discernment, and the Word of God utilized in all its strength and glory in righteousness and holiness.*

These are shields of gold. These are what Shishak (the world) is *stealing* away from our churches and out of the hearts and lives of our people.

SERVICE IN SANTO DOMINGO, DOMINICAN REPUBLIC

It was a Saturday night and the site was the stadium in Santo Domingo. Nearly sixty thousand people were present. (The following night there would be nearly seventy thousand). And right in the middle of the message it began raining. As I said, nearly sixty thousand people sat there. The stadium was packed to capacity and thousands were seated on the ground of the infield. But even though the rain was pouring down, I didn't see a soul leave the stadium. I was, of course, praying that the rain would stop and I'm sure everyone else was too. And in a few minutes, the rain did stop.

It seemed then as though the Lord grew impatient with Satan's attempt to disrupt the service, because suddenly an anointing fell upon that audience. You could feel the tangible power of God as it literally *flowed* through that crowd.

I was preaching that night on "Heaven's Light, Sin's Blight, and Redemption's Might." It was an account of the transfiguration of our Lord Jesus Christ on the mount. Scripture tells us that as He came down the mountain He met a man with a demon-possessed son. Jesus said, *"Bring him unto me."* He then commanded, in a militaristic manner, that the demon spirits depart. This was redemption's might.

As I began to recount this incident, you could feel the power of God suddenly falling over the audience. For the first time since I've been preaching, with that many people present, I felt a complete loss of control over the meeting. Tens of thousands were standing, shouting the praises of God. For a long moment it literally shook the stadium. Jesus was in our midst and His power was electric. When I gave the altar call, thousands upon thousands streamed down the aisles with tears wetting their cheeks.

Now this is what I'm talking about. This was a shield of gold. How, in rational analysis, could singers singing in English to a Spanish-speaking crowd with a preacher preaching in English (through an interpreter) draw such a crowd and produce such a reaction?

It was totally contrary to all theories of cross-cultural missions. According to the cross-cultural missions theory, this just *couldn't* produce results. But in practice it *does* work if you're willing to find and carry the cross of Jesus Christ. (Actually, the cross-cultural missions effort is usually a pride-of-life effort, an upward sin, and simply does not work — because it is man-centered instead of God-centered.)

WE ARE AT THE CROSSROADS

Many of our treasures are being lost. Shields of gold are being replaced with rock and roll music, psychological counseling, possibility thinking, inner healing, and — one might add — dead preachers preaching dead sermons to dead congregations.

God help us, we've become so accustomed to shields of brass that we wouldn't recognize the genuine article if we stumbled over it. We have no idea what we've lost. It isn't so much a matter of our being duped as it is our being *delighted* to be duped. We've become smug and self-satisfied with all our little seminars — when Holy Spirit revival is what we *really* need.

I have stated it before and I will state it again: The great Pentecostal fellowships are at the crossroads. We stand in mortal danger of losing our shields of gold; unless, that is, we haven't *already* lost them!

"YOUR OWN WILL TURN AGAINST YOU"

The other day, after a sleepless night, I was in deep travailing prayer, seeking the face of God. The day before, we had taped five television programs. I had said some things that I felt led by the Holy Spirit to say, but which disturbed me greatly to say. These were statements that would reverberate throughout the whole Pentecostal and Charismatic fellowship.

I had pulled no punches. I said it exactly the way I felt the Holy Spirit wanted me to, but it was so disturbing to do so that I hadn't slept all night.

The next morning, exhausted, I sobbed before the Lord. "Lord," I said, "I don't want to say these things. Do I have to go on antagonizing everyone throughout the Pentecostal world? Lord, is it *really* as bad as it sounds as I describe it over television and in print?"

Very gently, the Spirit of God began to speak to me. I don't think I will ever forget that moment. He said, *"The situation you are addressing in the Pentecostal and Charismatic fellowships is even* worse *than you realize."*

That was all the Spirit said and I started to sob more strongly. It was as if my heart would break. But at the same time a deep peace descended on me. For a little while it was as if the Spirit of God had lifted the burden from my heart.

One preacher asked me the other day (somewhat sarcastically), "Why don't you just preach 'Jesus saves' and ignore these other things?"

Well, in 1983 the Lord told me He had a message I was to deliver to the Pentecostal and Charismatic peoples. He said further that the opposition would be fierce, and even more ominously, that "my own" would turn against me.

I guess I've fought with myself to keep that from coming to pass. I've made every effort to build bridges and to plead for understanding in what I'm trying to do. But still I must obey God. I've resolved over and over again to say no more. But each time the Spirit of God brings me back as He says, *"Speak,"* and I have no choice.

The amazing thing about all this is that we are seeing more people saved than ever before. There is simply no comparison. Multiplied hundreds of thousands are coming to the Lord Jesus Christ. Tens of thousands are being baptized in the Holy Spirit. People are being healed. In fact, we are seeing more healings today than ever before. (And the Spirit of God has told me that this will become even more pronounced in the near future.)

I would, naturally, rather be liked as disliked. And, certainly, I'd rather be loved than hated. But despite this, I recognize that my sole mission is to act as the watchman on the wall (Ezek. 33:2-6). From there on, the reaction of the body of Christ is their responsibility as long as the trumpet's tone has been sounded.

THE GUARD WHICH KEPT THE DOOR

The Bible says that the shields of gold were entrusted to those who kept the door. Then when the shields of gold were taken by Shishak of Egypt, Rehoboam made shields of brass and gave them to those who guarded the king's house.

And what is happening to the body of Christ today? It's as one Methodist layman told me years ago. The great Methodist church didn't lose its way because of Methodist *laymen*, it was destroyed because its preachers were coming from seminaries where their faith had been destroyed. And *these preachers* were what led the once-great Methodist church down the garden path.

I am appalled to say that this is what is happening today within the Pentecostal and Charismatic churches. Where are the guards? Where are those who keep the doors?

If ever there was an hour when the Pentecostal message needed clarion voices, it is today. We need fearless men and women who refuse to be bought or sold, who do not concern themselves with whether or not they are popular, and whose only concern is to deliver *"thus saith the Lord."*

We desperately need evangelists who won't care whether the big churches will have them, who want only to deliver the message God has given them — if that means delivering it under a tree. I am equally persuaded that when God *finds* such young men and women, He will provide them with places to preach.

We need officials today in Pentecostal circles who don't care how many votes they win or lose, how popular they are or aren't, and who will, without fear or favor, take a position squarely against sin and the "spirit of the world."

For one can't help but feel that some of these preachers are walking around today with "For Sale" signs on their backs, while others wear "Sold to the Highest Bidder."

To be frank, many are selling out very cheaply. *Where are the guards who guard the door?* They may still be there but they are holding shields of brass handed to them by our latter-day Rehoboams.

I was preaching the Sunday service in one of our crusades in a great American city. Over ten thousand people were present as the Spirit of God began to speak to me:

"The Pentecostal church," He said, "be it Assemblies of God, Church of God, Foursquare, or what have you, cannot hope to compete with the denominational world in most areas." When it comes to education — even though we have made strides — we cannot compete with them. When it comes to acceptance by the world, no matter what type of label we try to place on the Pentecostal message, we'll still be looked on as "holy rollers." If the news media ever deigns to mention us, it is in a derogatory manner. So where is our strength?

Is it in the pretty buildings we've constructed? Is it in the few preachers who have earned their doctorates? Is it in the explosive growth we've experienced over the last few years? Is it because we have "finally arrived" and can boast that we now have "Christian psychologists" — just like all the more acceptable denominations?

No, it's none of these. Despite all the shields of brass we've accepted in our misbegotten desire to be "just like the world" (as represented by the hollow shells of the denominational churches) we do have something that draws the hungry to us. *And that's the power of the Holy Spirit.* Still, we're turning our backs on this, purely and simply.

WHAT HAPPENED TO
THE SPIRIT OF DISCERNMENT?

Why do I say that?

Turn on your Christian television programming. It may well be a Pentecostal or Charismatic production. And, with equal probability, it will be featuring "get-rich-quick" schemes, psychological philosophies, rock and roll entertainment, and all the way down to the exhibition of homosexual guests. Our sin, as the Spirit of God said to me, is great — greater than we even *begin* to realize.

Shields of gold and shields of brass: Why is it that our preachers can no longer differentiate between the world and God? Whatever happened to the spirit of *discernment*? Why is it that preachers, who are supposed to be the *leaders* in Pentecostal thinking, associate themselves with the humanist cause and with ministries that harbor, nurture, and promote the spirit of the world? The reason is obvious.

When guards carry shields of brass, they *know* their symbol of authority is of *base* materials. It is no different from all the worldly elements around them. Gold shields, on the other hand, are of *noble* material. They stand apart. You can see and feel the difference. And that's how it is with the things of God.

Many of our preachers today carry shields of brass, and the quality of their armaments affects their attitudes. Being *equipped* with the baser things, why shouldn't they *embrace* the baser things?

The other day I asked an official of a major Pentecostal fellowship, "Do you have any idea what you are *doing*?" Worldly entertainers with scant claim of knowing Jesus Christ are featured on the television programs of a particular organization of which he is a board member.

"Don't you realize," I asked, "that when these performers appear on these telecasts that you are in effect saying to a whole Pentecostal generation that the nightclub circuit is now an acceptable part of the Pentecostal and Charismatic scene?

"If they appear in honky-tonks and nightclubs, and then are welcomed on your program, what is wrong with our young people going to see them in the nightclubs and roadhouses?"

He just stared at me; he had no answer.

I then went on to say: "An organization that *purports* to be a ministry of God is helping, by example, to fill the nightclubs, honky-tonks, and places of worldly amusement with our Pentecostal young people."

God help us when church officials, pastors, and evangelists have sunk to the point where they can no longer discern right and wrong. *Nothing* is wrong anymore.

It seems that today everyone is for sale to the highest bidder.

"I AM SO GLAD," THE WOMAN SAID

Her husband lay dying. He had never accepted the Lord Jesus Christ. He had only hours to live.

His wife had prayed for him for year after agonizing year — and then it happened. He died the following day.

But on the day before he slipped into eternity, the television set was on in his hospital room.

The evangelist was, at that moment, preaching the great gospel of the Lord Jesus Christ. The preaching was buoyed by old-fashioned, Holy Spirit conviction. And for a few moments time, the convicting power of the Holy Spirit filled that room. It touched this man's heart, as only the Holy Spirit can.

Tears filled his eyes and rolled down his cheeks. He was very weak, but as the evangelist started to pray the sinner's prayer, the man's lips moved and he repeated it in a trembling voice.

It didn't take long — just a moment in time. But at that point his name was written down in the Lamb's book of life. Instantly he was transformed — by the miracle-working power of Almighty God. A few hours later he went home to be with Jesus.

His wife said, a few days later and with tears in her eyes, "Thank God, when that television set 'just happened' to be turned on that it was a man of God who was preaching. Thank God he wasn't wasting those few precious moments with appeals to worldly foolishness."

I leave it to you. What do we need today — shields of gold or shields of brass?

CHAPTER 3

THE GOSPEL OF SELF-ESTEEM

"But if thine eye be evil, thy whole body shall be full of darkness. If therefore the light that is in thee be darkness, how great is that darkness" (Matt. 6:23).

As the Apostle Paul said, the gospel of self-esteem is "another gospel." As such, it is man-made and man-oriented. It is totally unscriptural and contradictory to the true gospel of the Lord Jesus Christ.

WHAT DOES THE BIBLE SAY ABOUT MAN?

"For all have sinned, and come short of the glory of God" (Rom. 3:23).

"As it is written, There is none righteous, no, not one: There is none that understandeth, there is none that seeketh after God. They are all gone

> *out of the way, they are together become un-profitable; there is none that doeth good, no, not one. Their throat is an open sepulchre; with their tongues they have used deceit; the poison of asps is under their lips: Whose mouth is full of cursing and bitterness: Their feet are swift to shed blood: Destruction and misery are in their ways: And the way of peace have they not known: There is no fear of God before their eyes. Now we know that what things soever the law saith, it saith to them who are under the law: that every mouth may be stopped, and all the world may become guilty before God"* (Rom. 3:10-19).

In these passages we are reminded that the *whole world* is guilty before God — and that the purpose of the old law was to emphasize that all men *are* guilty before God. Then we are told:

> *"But now the righteousness of God without the law is manifested . . . Being justified freely by his grace through the redemption that is in Christ Jesus"* (Rom. 3:21, 24).

Man's only hope does *not* lie in works, but in the justification extended through His grace — which is all based on redemption through the cross.

In *Self-Esteem: The New Reformation,* Robert Schuller, one of the foremost proponents of the self-esteem gospel, has called for a "new reformation," stating that the sixteenth century movement (under Luther and Calvin) was a "reactionary movement" because it emphasized that men are sinners. Schuller tells us:

> Once a person believes he is an "unworthy sinner," it is doubtful if he can honestly accept the saving grace God offers in Jesus Christ.

Schuller offers the following as a blueprint for bringing sinners to salvation:

> If you want to know why Schuller smiles on television, if you want to know why I make people laugh once in a while, I'm giving them sounds and strokes, sounds and strokes (like you would a baby).
>
> It's a strategy. People who don't trust need to be stroked. People are born with a negative self-image. Because they do not trust, they cannot trust God.

If Schuller is right, accepted evangelistic practices are obviously wrong. We should then *stop* telling people they're sinners who need Jesus Christ as a Saviour. We must no longer convince them of their sin and rebellion against a holy God. We must never speak of hell, nor warn of the terrible, eternal consequences of rejecting the wonderful offer of salvation as an unmerited gift from God.

Instead we should begin to *stroke* men and women into faith, *smile* them into the kingdom of God, and *elevate* their self-esteem. I think you will agree that this is a major change in Christian perspective.

But Schuller has an even broader concept in mind. He goes on to say:

> A theology of self-esteem also produces a theology of social ethics and a theology of economics — and these produce a theology of government. It all rises from one foundation: the dignity of a person who was created in the image of God.

Basically, this self-esteem theology states that we need a new reformation and a new theology. What it also suggests — but does not openly state — is that we need a new Bible.

You see, the doctrine of self-esteem strikes at the very heart of the gospel of Jesus Christ. This, of course, states that man is a lost sinner who cannot save himself, and who thus desperately needs a Redeemer.

WHERE DID THIS "OTHER GOSPEL" COME FROM?

In order to place this new teaching into proper perspective, we should realize that so-called "Christian" psychologists and psychiatrists transplanted it from *outside* the church.

Bruce Narramore, a leading evangelical psychologist who vigorously promotes self-worth teaching, explains in *You're Someone Special*:

> Under the influence of humanistic psychologists like Carl Rogers and Abraham Maslow, many of us Christians have begun to see our need for self-love and self-esteem.

Satan's threefold, humanistic plan for taking over the world is basically simple, and you might be surprised at how well it correlates with this new theology.

- Darwinism (Darwin) — the concept of evolution as it affects the social man.
- Marxism (communism) — Satan's economic foundation.
- Freudianism (psychology) — a profound influence on the morals of man.

And there you have it: Satan's three-pronged assault — social, economic, and moral. The self-esteem philosophy comes directly from Freudian principles, and it *does* demand an entirely different theology.

"ALL TRUTH IS GOD'S TRUTH"

This is a standard statement, offered by "Christian" psychologists to justify the "self-help" philosophies and "new-speak" theologies. It is an "answer" in sloganized format.

"It doesn't matter," we are told, "if Adler and Maslow [psychologists] were humanists. If they stumbled upon truth, so be it. We must accept truth — no matter its source."

One "Christian" psychologist told me that Jesus used psychology in His ministry. In other words, Jesus was "a great psychologist." I wonder if he understands the blasphemy of such a statement.

What kind of psychology did Jesus use? Was it Freudian? That's somewhat difficult to imagine since Freud wasn't born until the 1800s. It should be noted also that Freud was a narcotics addict, a sexual pervert, and an unmitigated liar who falsified his medical results to make them conform to what he had already postulated as theory. These are well-known and accepted facts — admitted by even the most faithful of Freud's devotees.

Freud himself stated, in regard to his psychiatric method, "I would trash the whole business, but I don't know what else to turn to." How tragic that he never read John 14:6, which states:

"I am the way, the truth, and the life."

Jesus *is* truth. Without Him, there is no truth.

All that purports to be truth without Him is a lie. Psychotherapy — the wellspring of the self-esteem philosophy — is a lie. And, basically, what is being touted as truth today ("all truth is God's truth") is little more than disconnected facts *taken out of context.*

Pavlov's dogs were trained to respond by salivating at the ringing of a bell — and huge segments of the "science" of psychology are built on this minor point.

In keeping with this same policy of building great precepts on flimsy evidence, we are asked to accept this principle: "Even though it's not in the Bible, it can still be truth. And anything that *is* truth is God's truth, because all truth comes from God. We must, therefore, avail ourselves of any and all 'helps' that fall into our hands, whatever their sources."

How do you like that for a rationalization getting mixed up with all kinds of ungodly sources? (And we might mention here that *all* error is Satan's, and it always comes disguised as truth.)

Remember this: *Truth related by a liar becomes a lie.*

Self-esteem, psychology, and all the rest of these vain philosophies remind me of the little boy who was digging down into a huge, ten-foot pile of manure. When asked what he was doing he replied, "Well, with all this manure, there's got to be a pony down there somewhere."

IS MAN'S PROBLEM
ONE OF LOW SELF-ESTEEM?

To be completely objective, this much-touted philosophy is the precise *opposite* of reality.

Yes, there *are*, from time to time, people who have problems because of low self-esteem. But in the overwhelming number of cases, the almost universal problem of the human race — especially today — is one of *inflated* self-esteem, and this problem was evident in the Garden of Eden and even before that when Satan fell from grace.

> *"And the serpent said unto the woman, Ye shall not surely die: For God doth know that in*

*the day ye eat thereof, then your eyes shall be
opened, and ye shall be as gods, knowing good
and evil"* (Gen. 3:4, 5).

Ah, yes, ye shall be as gods . . .

And there's the problem. It is the ancient temptation
Satan used to beguile Eve, and he's still using the same,
tired ruse today. This is why we have so many dictators in
our present society. They all see themselves as gods. It is
the foundation for humanism. Man is the focal point,
replacing God. The whole world is now fascinated and
beguiled by the false god of man's importance.

Socialism and communism follow hard on the heels of
humanism. They are all man-centered concepts — and
Satan is the author of all such worldly systems.

This is the basic source of all the man-made philosophies that are permeating Pentecostal and Charismatic
circles today — philosophies such as "Christian" psychology, sociology, possibility thinking, positive thinking, the
fourth dimension, dream your own dream, inner healing,
self-esteem, etc. Man wants to play God.

In some Pentecostal and Charismatic circles, such
statements are being made as, "We *are* little gods. As
Adam was formerly god of this world and lost it, we have
now regained it. And we *are* now little gods under the Lord
Jesus Christ."

This is a dangerous, man-centered philosophy that will
undermine and grossly cheapen the magnificent gospel of
the Lord Jesus Christ.

*"Because thou sayest, I am rich, and
increased with goods, and have need of nothing;
and knowest not that thou art wretched, and
miserable, and poor, and blind, and naked: I
counsel thee . . . [that] As many as I love, I*

*rebuke and chasten: be zealous therefore, and
repent"* (Rev. 3:17-19).

In preaching over worldwide television, I have more
opportunity than most to address myself to unsaved people,
and we cover all stratas of society — from the intelligentsia
right down to the man on the street. So I can state with
some assurance that the biggest problem the preacher finds
in leading men to the Lord Jesus Christ is the "god syndrome" currently afflicting society.

"What do you mean, preacher, that *I* need a Saviour?
I'm not a sinner, I'm doing just fine."

Truly, the hardest thing in the world is to get a man to
admit that he is a sinner. And one *must* admit to himself
that he is lost before he can be saved.

One must admit he *needs* a Saviour before he can be
introduced to one. And the reason this matter of human
pride is such a successful tool of Satan's is that man's basic
problem is not one of low self-esteem, it is one of *inflated*
self-esteem. Ultimately, this single fact is causing *millions*
to perish.

THE DOMINION TEACHING
THEORY IS MAN-CENTERED

The other night I flicked the TV on to a particular
"Christian" network. A Pentecostal evangelist was ministering. The host of the Pentecostal network was seated with
his wife at his side. The evangelist was preaching on
dominion theology.

I listened for nearly half an hour and I was, frankly,
shocked. I had already known this was a misguided and
dangerous teaching, but until I saw it in action on this
telecast, I had no real understanding of just how destructive
it could really be.

"We are going to take over the world . . . *we* are going to solve the problems of mankind." It was *"we this"* and *"we that."* If Jesus Christ was mentioned, it was only in passing. I doubt very seriously that the proponents of this gospel even suspect what they're promoting. But at the core of it is the fact that Jesus Christ is relegated to an inferior position — *with man occupying the throne.*

Dominion teaching is doomed to failure, not only because it's unscriptural, *but because it's man-centered.* Whenever *any* philosophy ceases to be God-focused, it becomes unscriptural and heretical. It is easy to see the slimy trail of the serpent in this teaching as it parrots his original lie, *"Ye shall be as gods."*

A.W. Tozer said this:

> If self occupies any part of the throne, we cannot say that Jesus Christ is on the throne of our heart. Self is man's greatest enemy. He embodies selfishness, greed, and all that opposes God. If Jesus Christ is centered on the throne, self is eradicated. And until self is totally eradicated, there can be no Christ-centered throne in our lives.

Self-esteem caters to man's basest nature. This first became apparent at the fall in the Garden. It will lead no one to Christ. It will lead, rather, to the enshrinement of self. And the tragic fact is that thousands of Pentecostal and Charismatic preachers are falling all over each other to embrace this errant doctrine.

Jay E. Adams, in his book, *The Biblical View of Self-Esteem,* says:

> Any system that proposes to solve human problems, apart from the Bible and the power of the Holy Spirit (as all of these pagan systems, including the self-worth system, do) is automatically condemned by Scripture itself. Nor does this system in any way depend upon the message of

salvation. Love, joy, and peace are discussed as if they were not the fruits of the Spirit, but merely the fruits of right views of one's self, which anyone can attain without the Bible or the work of the Spirit in his heart.

For these reasons, the self-worth system with its claims of biblical correspondences must be rejected. It does not come from the Bible. Any resemblance between biblical teaching and the teaching of the self-worth originators is either contrived or coincidental.

Actually, the *only* thing the Bible says about self-esteem can be found in Philippians 2:3.

> *"Let nothing be done through strife or vainglory; but in lowliness of mind let each esteem other better than themselves."*

This teaches the precise opposite of puffed-up self opinions. It clearly tells us to have a humble view of ourselves, being ever aware of our own secret faults and shortcomings. This does *not* state that man's crying need is enhanced self-esteem. It says that man needs *less* emphasis on ego and self-gratification.

J.I. Packer said:

> Modern Christians spread a thin layer of Bible teaching over their mixture of popular psychology and common sense. But their overall approach clearly reflects the narcissism — the "selfism" or "meism" as it is sometimes called — that is the way of the world in the modern west.

The Apostle Paul plainly tells us that the person who fails to love others is "nothing":

> *"Though I speak with the tongues of men and of angels, and have not charity . . . I am nothing"* (I Cor. 13:1, 2).

Robert Schuller says that to glorify God, we must first love ourselves. Naturally, if one is to accept self-worth teaching, he or she must first be of worth to himself in order to love others and to glorify God. But on the other hand, the Lord said (through the Apostle Paul) that man is *nothing* — unless and until he loves others. It says nothing, incidentally, about loving one's self first.

In Psalm 8, the psalmist expresses amazement that God visits man. *"What is man?"* he asks. Then in Psalm 62 we have the answer to this question: Nothing. Man is *nothing*.

Obviously, God does not love man *because* of his moral traits, he loves him *despite* them. This is why the psalmist expressed amazement. It is a testimonial to God's greatness — not man's.

Our Lord said this:

> *"If any man will come after me, let him deny himself, and take up his cross, and follow me. For whosoever will save his life shall lose it: and whosoever will lose his life for my sake shall find it"* (Matt. 16:24, 25).

The Lord is here letting us know that we must put self to death — and we can only do this by forsaking ego and *"taking up the cross."* (Interestingly, Luke adds the word "daily," which certainly seems to indicate that this is a problem that must be constantly dredged up, analyzed, and subdued afresh.)

Taking up the cross has nothing to do with any specific sacrifice. In the Master's day, taking up the cross referred to the putting to death. It was then *the* method of execution. So the Lord is saying, "You must treat yourself — with your sinful ways, priorities, and desires — like a criminal.

Your sins must be condemned and utterly done away with."

This certainly says something about the self-image that Christ expects us to have — and it's a far cry from the elevated self-esteem being promoted today.

THE WORK OF THE HOLY SPIRIT

John 16:8 tells us that the work of the Holy Spirit is to *"reprove the world of sin, and of [self] righteousness, and of judgment."* This means, under the teaching of the gospel (as in I Cor. 1:21), that the Holy Spirit convicts men of sin — not of low self-esteem. It clearly states, furthermore, that man is a sinner.

When, according to the gospel, an individual is convicted (reproved) of sin, he is brought to a place of repentance. He suddenly sees himself as he is — which is "lost, undone, and without God."

In Peter's sermon on the Day of Pentecost (Acts 2), some three thousand were saved. Read this passage and you will search in vain for any reference to elevating the listeners' self-esteem. Instead, he said,

> *"Therefore let all the house of Israel know assuredly, that God hath made that same Jesus, whom ye have crucified, both Lord and Christ"* (Acts 2:36).

Peter didn't by any means appeal here to their vanities in an effort to raise their self-esteem.

And what happened?

> *"Now when they heard this, they were pricked in their heart, and said unto Peter and to the rest*

*of the apostles, Men and brethren, what shall we
do?"* (Acts 2:37).

This is Holy Spirit conviction in fact.

In Peter's second great sermon, as quoted in Acts 3, he
once more ignored the matter of the listeners' self-esteem.
Instead, he refocused on the darker sides of their natures.

> *"But ye denied the Holy One and the Just,
> and desired a murderer to be granted unto you;
> And killed the Prince of life, whom God hath
> raised from the dead; whereof we are witnesses"*
> (Acts 3:14, 15).

Again, what happened? This time, *five* thousand were
saved.

Now let's think about this. Clearly, this is the God-
approved principle of confronting men with the fact that
they are sinners and that they are lost without God. It then
becomes the responsibility of the Holy Spirit to *convict*
them and bring them to Jesus Christ. And where does all
this leave the gospel of self-esteem? The two are certainly
hard to reconcile. In truth, even though Jesus is *mentioned*
(and given lip service as Lord) the self-esteem gospel does
not bring biblical salvation. *It brings people to a man-
centered philosophy instead.*

As a result, individuals who respond to this siren song
of deceit are seldom (if ever) truly born again. They do not
turn to the Lord Jesus Christ as their Saviour. To be frank, it
is impossible for them to do so because the gospel has not
been preached to them; a vain philosophy has been ten-
dered in its place. They are confronted with the impossible
task of saving themselves.

> *"And if the blind lead the blind, both shall
> fall into the ditch"* (Matt. 15:14).

How many hundreds of thousands (or even millions) have listened to these philosophies and made an honest effort to come to the Lord Jesus Christ? Tragically, they end up instead on a road that leads nowhere. God have mercy on the souls of preachers who lead such astray.

THE FOOT-WASHING SPIRIT

The self-esteem spirit was the hardest spirit to purge out of the disciples. It was a battle that raged in their lives and ministries right up to the end.

> *"And there was also a strife among them, which of them should be accounted the greatest"* (Luke 22:24 — which is the account of the Last Supper).

Do you recall how the mother of James and John sought to have her sons seated at either side of Christ? You see, the self-esteem spirit is capable of invading *any* situation, no matter how holy in concept, and once there, can threaten the very future of that situation.

What it really amounts to is that man's standard of greatness lies in attaining the position where he will be served, while God's standard involves serving. Man's standard is to humble others, while God's is to humble oneself. Failure to observe these Godly principles led to the downfall of both Adam and Lucifer. It was the *"ye shall be gods"* principle in action, and this is again being promoted by way of the self-esteem gospel.

If this spirit of high self-esteem hadn't been purged from the disciples, the entire work of God might have been jeopardized. And the only way this could be accomplished was for the Master to demonstrate the foot-washing spirit — which He did at the Last Supper.

"After that he poureth water into a bason, and began to wash the disciples' feet, and to wipe them with the towel wherewith he was girded" (John 13:5).

(And we should note that Judas' feet were washed.) Jesus then asked them:

"Know ye what I have done to you?" (John 13:12).

No, the Lord was not instituting some new form of church ritual; He was instead demonstrating the principle of *humility* that He wanted them to adopt in their ministry.

MY EXPERIENCE WITH "EGO"

I've always prided myself on the fact that I had no difficulty with self-pride, ego, or self-esteem. I had always been very careful to give God all the glory. I never felt *I* had the answers. And I've always totally relied on God and His Holy Spirit for guidance.

Many times, newsmen asked me, "How does it feel to have all this power?"

Of course, they were referring to the telecast — aired as it is throughout most of the world — and with the tremendously large audience it draws.

But the funny thing is that their question seemed to have no relationship to my situation. I've never felt I had any particular power. In fact, it was far more of a case of responsibility — an ongoing state of "fear and trembling."

But then the Holy Spirit began to deal with me in depth on the problem of self. And as His spiritual omniscience began to cut through my all-too-human layers of self-deception, I began to see that my smugness in regard to a lack of ego was not legitimate. *The ego problem was there, I just had chosen not to recognize it.*

After the Holy Spirit revealed this to me, I realized that I had been the victim of an "inverted ego" (a term all my own, lest anyone think I've been dabbling in psychology on the side).

Now let me try to explain this. I had always looked at the problem of "self" as pertaining to the blessing of God, and of one becoming vain *because* he was receiving these blessings.

Actually, this wasn't my case at all. I had always been totally convinced that God was the author. I was well aware that He could remove His blessings at any moment, and that I had never been anything more than *His* instrument. I often boasted, "The blessings are His — the blunders are mine."

But the Lord showed me something. Frequently, services don't go as well as I'd like. Even though I've studied, worked, prayed, and believed God for a mighty Holy Spirit outpouring — nothing happens. The heavens seem to be as brass and nothing I can do will bring about audience response.

Of course, afterward, feeling like a complete personal failure, I will question my methods and want to give up — totally depressed. Naturally, this can be rationalized as "disappointment at failing in the work of God."

But is this the *real* reason?

Now this is where the Holy Spirit begins to shine His searchlight, and as you will admit if you've ever undergone such an experience, it's a humbling thing to have God begin to peel away the layers of self-deception.

In short, it was really nothing more than personal vanity, ego, or pride.

Now please understand, I am not irrational. I don't live in dream houses or build sand castles. I know that there are some sermons, services, and projects that just won't quite measure up to some theoretical ideal. We can't expect to *always* operate at the "superior" level — there will always be days when "okay" is the best we'll achieve. (And, of course, there are also those "I shouldn't have come to work today, period" days.)

But although I *know* this, I still will let my *zeal* for God tear me to pieces. During one period in the '60s, I nearly fell apart. I wanted revival so badly that I *knew* it would come about — if only I would keep doubling and redoubling my efforts.

But did it? No! Was I disappointed? I was almost destroyed!

And then I "happened" to pick up a book (written by a minister of the gospel). One line in that book suddenly shouted out to me. It said, *"The worker is more important than the work."*

The Holy Spirit used that phrase to get my attention. I had never realized that while the work of God is important, the person *performing* that work is even more important. I have found this concept to be a great comfort.

Regrettably, I still can't boast complete victory over my problem. But I'm striving mightily to hurl "self" into the garbage can and to create an *empty* vessel for the Lord to work with. I'm not there yet; there's still a lot of flesh and a lot of ego standing between me and the Lord. And whether it's "introverted" or "extroverted" ego, it must be rooted out and totally sublimated if we're to be what He wants us to be.

So I'm working at it. We *must* work, and be honest and open if we're ever to achieve optimal utility to the Lord — and thus victory. We've got to dredge out our fears of what others might think, or how they might judge us. *If we don't, it's only because we're basically trying to boost our own fragile little egos.*

And once we've done this, it becomes time to "let go and let God."

I recall the words of an old song my mother used to sing:

> Many years I've longed for rest,
> Perfect peace within my breast,
> I often sought the Lord alone in tears.
> I would not pay the price,
> Would not make the sacrifice,
> Just to lose myself and find it, Lord, in Thee.
>
> Let me lose myself and find it, Lord, in Thee.
> May all self be slain,
> My friends see only Thee.
> Though it cost me grief and pain,
> I will find my life again,
> Let me lose myself and find it, Lord, in thee.

CHAPTER 4

CHRISTIAN PSYCHOLOGY

 We should start out by stating that nothing contained herein should be misconstrued as questioning the Christian motivation or spiritual orientation of those who promote and support certain Christian alliances. And by "Christian alliances," I mean policies that seek to meld Christianity with those worldly disciplines that purport to deal expertly with — and solve — human problems.

I, as any regular reader will know, believe that Jesus Christ is able to, willing to, and capable of handling any problems His children might encounter — *if* they will *truly* turn them over to Him and stand steadfastly in "the shadow of His wing."

I feel led to bring this position *forcefully* before those Christians that I might be able to influence. But I do ask that my statements not be interpreted as attacks upon the Christian posture or spiritual stance of those who (in my opinion) are being lured out of Hamelin by a worldly Pied Piper.

The most devoted of individuals can be led astray. And I feel (because it has happened over and over again) that entire religious movements or fellowships can become misguided and misdirected. I conclude, with a heavy heart, that this is what is happening in the mainstream of religion today. And I speak particularly of the Pentecostal and Charismatic fellowships.

I am absolutely convinced that psychotherapy (psychological counseling) is rapidly replacing biblical counseling and that the whole Christian ministry is being, to a great extent, subverted by this "false religion."

I will make statements that might shock or annoy, but I will do so only because I am convinced they *must* be said. I hope I will be able to say them in a loving manner because it is Christian love and concern that motivate me. But I suspect, from long experience, that some will deny me this honest motivation. In any event, I will confess to a burning determination to see the truth — and then to preach this truth as I have come to see it.

IS PSYCHOTHERAPY (OR COUNSELING LACED WITH PSYCHOLOGY) REPLACING BIBLICAL COUNSELING AND PREACHING?

In a recent book review in the *Pentecostal Evangel* (the official voice of the Assemblies of God), a book entitled *The Holy Spirit in Counseling* was lauded. Here's what was said:

> Gilbert and Brock [the authors], both Assemblies of God ministers, examined the biblical foundations of the Holy Spirit's dynamics as Comforter in the counseling process.
>
> During the time of writing, both editors were professors in the Psychology Department at Evangel College, Springfield, Missouri. They attempt to show how a Godly synthesis can be made of biblical theology and psychological research. For instance:
>
> "It is impossible to separate psychology and theology

— as they relate to the counseling process. The object of counseling is a human being created in God's image. Wholeness is achieved only when life is lived in the manner in which He intended. Therefore, it is not a question of whether therapists rely upon the Holy Spirit or upon their counseling skills. We must equip ourselves with the best tools available, while being certain that the presence and power of the Holy Spirit permeate our personalities."

MANY DIFFERENT TYPES OF PSYCHOLOGY

To begin with, we should note that there are many different types of psychology.

- There is **educational psychology** which deals with learning disabilities, educational motivation, importance of organization, etc.
- There is **industrial psychology.** This delves into difficulties and problems associated with the work place.
- In addition, there are many **specialties** under the general umbrella of psychology that are purely scientific and provide valuable statistical data for better understanding of human reactions to a wide variety of situations.

However, these are *not* what we are discussing here. What we are talking about is psychotherapy as it relates to "cures for souls."

The primary Greek word *psycho* is the root from which we derive the English terms "psychology" or "psychologist." Interestingly, the word *psycho* is utilized in the New Testament for "soul." Hence, a psychologist is a "worker with souls."

A specific distinction should be made, however. The secular psychotherapist considers himself a worker with *minds,* while the (so-called) "Christian" psychologist considers himself a worker with *souls.*

Most of today's Bible colleges and seminaries offer at least *some* basic introduction to psychology for their would-be preachers of the gospel. Thus a foundation is laid for a subtle deflection *away* from the Bible and *toward* psychotherapy.

The courses offered to most of our future preachers only touch on the rudiments of their future association with the treatment of souls. However, the stage *is* set for a familiarity with (and affection for) things other than the Word of God.

I suspect that preachers — who earnestly desire to be of help to people — are particularly vulnerable during these formative years. Lacking in experience and self-confidence, they are delighted to discover something that is boldly placarded as a certifiable tool in delivering such help. "Christian" psychology supposedly offers an organized system for carrying out this weighty task, and formative minds are soon addicted to a method that seems to offer "a whole new way."

Bible colleges and seminaries of most denominations and fellowships now offer these courses. Naturally, a great legitimacy is thereby afforded them.

It is even suggested today that if a person has *only* Bible knowledge, he is ill-equipped to handle the pressing problems of humanity. He must (along with Bible training) be grounded in psychology to meet "human" needs. This is implanted early, with the unspoken implication that the Bible in itself is insufficient to solve human problems.

It is constantly being suggested that ministers are ill-prepared and ill-equipped to meet the needs of modern man. If the preacher is to be truly effective and proficient in his role, he should be referring a large percentage of those who seek his help to "professionals."

"Professionals," or "therapy," used within this context means, of course, psychologists or psychotherapy.

I recently received a letter from a Christian psychologist telling about his wife who had serious problems. He said, "We needed competent, Christian mental health care. We couldn't find it in the church; people didn't understand her emotional problems. We couldn't find it in the world; mental health professionals didn't understand our faith."

He went on to say that psychotherapy, combined with the Holy Spirit, gave her the victory.

Now I don't know exactly what he meant when he said, "We couldn't find it in the church." Perhaps he was speaking of the specific church they attended or a particular pastor — which is certainly understandable. But if he was speaking of "*the* church," meaning the body of Christ and the work of the Holy Spirit within that church, he was in effect saying that the Bible does not hold the answer to human problems and that we must look *outside* the Word of God for help. At the very least, it would seem that his statement suggests that we must *combine* the work of the Holy Spirit with secular psychotherapy. The end product of this growing dependence on "scientific" compromise is that:

- Psychotherapy has become widely accepted as "scientific" and, therefore, *must* be a useful tool. As a consequence, it has become accepted within many Pentecostal and Charismatic fellowships. (It has, of course, been *long* accepted within the denominational world.)
- Most Pentecostal Bible colleges and seminaries now promote psychotherapy as a legitimate tool for meeting "the human need."
- As a result, most of our younger preachers are now convinced that psychotherapy is "spiritually neutral." It is, therefore, a legitimate tool to be employed

with a clear conscience when trying to help humanity.

- The old-fashioned, tried-and-true Word of Almighty God (combined with the preaching of that Word) is given lesser place when considering methods for solving man's problems.

COUNSELING — THE EXPRESSWAY FOR HELP

The other day I spoke with a professor who has many years of experience in teaching in Pentecostal Bible colleges. I asked him why homiletics (the preparation of sermons) is seldom taught anymore in our Bible colleges.

His answer shocked me. He said, *"Most are no longer looking to preaching as a means of meeting humanity's needs. Counseling has now become the expressway for help in this area."*

Hence, there is no longer a need for sermon preparation. The colleges are gradually shifting over to a definite bias toward psychotherapy.

IS PSYCHOTHERAPY (COUNSELING PSYCHOLOGY) TRULY SCIENTIFIC AND THEREFORE "NEUTRAL"?

Proponents of psychotherapy call it scientific and camouflage its discrepancies with scientific jargon and medical argot. However, the questions must be asked: *Is psychotherapy a science or a superstition? Is it fact or fabrication?*

These questions must be asked, because we have come to venerate almost anything labeled as "science." If, indeed, psychology and psychotherapy are scientific, they *should* command our respect and be used within *every* community. However, if they are not, we have valid grounds for questioning the propriety of intruding them into the preacher's methodology.

In Martin and Deidre Bobgan's book, *The Psychological Way/The Spiritual Way,* they state:

> In attempting to evaluate the status of psychology, the American Psychological Association appointed Sigmund Koch to plan and direct a study which was subsidized by the National Science Foundation. This study involved eighty eminent scholars in assessing the facts, theories, and methods of psychology. The results of this extensive endeavor were then published in a seven-volume series entitled *Psychology: A Study of a Science.*
>
> After examining the results, Koch concludes, "I think it by this time utterly and finally clear that psychology cannot be a coherent science." He further declares that such activities as perception, motivation, social psychology, psychopathology, and creativity cannot be properly labeled "science."

E. Fuller Torrey, in *The Death of Psychiatry,* says:

> . . . the medical model of human behavior, when carried to its logical conclusions, is both nonsensical and non-functional. It doesn't answer the questions which are asked of it, it doesn't provide good service, and it leads to a stream of absurdities worthy of a Roman circus.

In a study (done some time ago) comparing modern-day psychology with witchcraft, the results came out a dead heat. The only discernible difference was that the witch doctors charged less and kept their patients a shorter period of time.

"For my people have committed two evils; they have forsaken me the fountain of living

waters, and hewed them out cisterns, broken
cisterns, that can hold no water" (Jer. 2:13).

In his book, *Psychological Seduction,* William Kirk
Kilpatrick says:

> True Christianity does not mix well with psychology.
> When you try to mix them, you end up with a watered-
> down Christianity instead of a Christianized psychology.
> But the process is subtle and is rarely noticed . . . It was
> not a frontal attack on Christianity . . . It was not a case of
> the wolf at the door: the wolf was already in the fold,
> dressed in sheep's clothing. And from the way it was petted
> and fed by some of the shepherds, one would think it was
> the prize sheep.

Jacob Needleman, writing in *Consciousness: Brain,*
States of Awareness, and Mysticism, says:

> Modern psychiatry arose out of the vision that man
> must change himself and not depend for help on an imagi-
> nary God. Over half a century ago, mainly through the
> insights of Freud and through the energies of those he
> influenced, the human psyche was wrested from the falter-
> ing hands of organized religion and was situated in the
> world of nature as a subject for scientific study.

Incidentally, Freud opened his office in Vienna, the
first devoted to psychotherapy, a little over one hundred
years ago.

Martin Gross, in his book, *The Psychological Society,*
says:

> When educated man lost faith in formal religion, he
> required a substitute belief that would be as reputable in
> the last half of the Twentieth Century as Christianity was in
> the first. Psychology and psychiatry have now assumed
> that special role.

Modern-day psychotherapy has its roots in atheism, evolution, and humanism. Psychology pretends to have a cure for troubled souls. It is taught in atheistic universities, oftentimes by atheistic professors. And this same subject, with the same foundations and influences, is accepted today as an integral part of the Christian curriculum in our Bible colleges and seminaries. There aren't two kinds of psychotherapy, there is only one. And as Paul Vitz says, "It is deeply anti-Christian."

Someone once said, "America's problem is not ignorance; America's problem is that she accepts a lie."

Now the problems with our preachers *may* once have been ignorance, but this is no longer the case. I am now concerned that what they accept (psychotherapy) is not truth — it is a lie.

I maintain that psychotherapy is not scientific, that it is not even an "art" as claimed. *It is a lie, purely and simply, and has no basis in scientific or biblical fact.* When Bible colleges offer it, they are offering a bald *fabrication.* When seminaries teach it, they are teaching a *lie.* When would-be preachers immerse themselves in it, they immerse themselves in *falsehood.* When individuals accept a doctorate in this nefarious *shamanism,* they are receiving a certificate without scientific validity.

I say that preachers of the gospel, attempting to meld psychotherapy with the Word of God, will help no one. They will deliver only confusion. People will be led away from the true help that is available through the Word of God.

The two are as immiscible and as antagonistic as oil and water.

WHAT IS THE BIBLICAL SYSTEM
FOR COUNSELING AND HELPING
THE "HUMAN CONDITION"?

I have been taken to task for stating that there is no such thing as a *Christian* psychologist. I have also been castigated for suggesting that one might as well say "Christian witch doctor" as "Christian psychologist."

Do we consider witchcraft a viable answer to the human condition? I think the answer is fairly obvious. So if psychotherapy (psychology) is not scientific or scriptural (and it isn't), if it is not what it claims to be, and if it can't do what it claims to do — then what is the difference in the terms "Christian psychology" and "Christian witch doctor"? Both are fundamental contradictions and should be recognized as such.

Martin Bobgan writes in *The Psychological Way/The Spiritual Way:*

> The psychological way — claiming to be scientific —
> is practiced as a profession. The spiritual way is a natural
> outflow of Christian love, as practiced in the body of
> Christ. The psychological way requires training in theories
> and techniques devised by men. Only designated, trained
> individuals may offer professional, psychological help.
>
> The spiritual way, on the other hand, may be practiced
> by any member of the body of Christ. Biblical counseling
> is not based on the theories or techniques of men, but
> rather is practiced by those who know the Bible, have
> applied God's Word in their own lives through the minis-
> tration of the Holy Spirit, and demonstrate love for others
> by the way they minister healing and life . . . The Bible is
> filled with information about the condition of humanity
> and with teachings that lead to emotional stability and
> power for living.

The Lord Jesus Christ, some 2,000 years ago, said:

"Come unto me, all ye that labour and are heavy laden, and I will give you rest. Take my yoke upon you, and learn of me; for I am meek and lowly in heart: and ye shall find rest unto your souls. For my yoke is easy, and my burden is light" (Matt. 11:28-30).

At the beginning of this chapter I quoted from a book by Gilbert and Brock. They state: "It is not a question of whether therapists rely upon the Holy Spirit or upon their counseling skills."

In other words, they are saying that it doesn't really matter where the help originates, whether it is from the Holy Spirit or from psychology. They then conclude that we *"must equip ourselves with the best tools available."*

Is psychology a tool?

When it was suggested that modern-day psychology is not found in the Bible, one preacher stated that neither is the automobile, the airplane, or the computer. We do not, he reasoned, resist utilization of these tools in our lives, so why should we resist the tool of psychology (or any other self-help method or technique)?

My answer is this:

Admittedly, the Bible has nothing to say about the automobile, computer, airplane, or a host of other crafts developed since it was written. The Bible does *not* claim to be a handbook on engineering, science, or whatever. These extraneous subjects are not man's *problems*. Man can be an expert scientist, a qualified engineer, or a host of other things — and still be a moral and spiritual wreck. *However, the Bible does claim to be a handbook on the "human condition" — and it does come right out and claim to hold all the answers to this particular human area.* Listen to this:

*"According as his divine power hath given
unto us all things that pertain unto life and
godliness, through the knowledge of him that
hath called us to glory and virtue: Whereby are
given unto us exceeding great and precious
promises: that by these ye might be partakers of
the divine nature, having escaped the corruption
that is in the world through lust"* (II Pet. 1:3, 4).

Now either the Bible *did* give us *all* things that pertain
unto life (verse 3) or it *didn't*. If it didn't, it lied, and we
then need to turn to the book, *The Holy Spirit in Counseling,* by Gilbert and Brock. We can then, forever after, rely
upon therapists who will combine their modern-day
"science" with the Word of God.

And if we can have Christian psychology, why not have
Christian medicine or Christian physics or Christian
biochemistry? Of course, the reason we *don't* have all these
things is that such things don't exist in real-life terms.
Medicine is the same for the Christian or for the non-
Christian. Chemistry is the same for the Christian or for the
non-Christian. However, our Christian educators have
attempted to take an ungodly, atheistic, anti-Christian,
immoral, unbiblical, worldly system called psychology
and integrate it into biblical counseling.

This just can't be done!

CAN A TRAINED COUNSELOR
HELP PEOPLE IF HE LOVES GOD AND
HAS A TRUE DESIRE TO BE OF SERVICE?

No! The counselor trained in psychology, even though
he has a strong desire to help people, can't be effective *until
he totally and completely renounces all psychological
training and turns to the Word of God as his sole source*

and guide. It is like mixing light with darkness. Scripture asks us this question:

> *"And what concord hath Christ with Belial?*
> *or what part hath he that believeth with an*
> *infidel?"* (II Cor. 6:15).

IS THE PREACHER QUALIFIED
TO DEAL WITH THE PROBLEMS OF MANKIND?

If the preacher of the gospel is thoroughly grounded in the Word of God, he is actually the *only* one who is capable of meeting these particular needs.

I realize it is being suggested today that the preacher of the gospel is not qualified to address the "human condition." He has not been specifically educated and trained in these areas. But the fact is, the so-called *professional* in the field of "the cure of the soul" is actually the one who is unqualified to help the individual in need.

Now this might seem ludicrous to some. Don't they have Masters or Doctorates in counseling or psychotherapy? Still, I am stating that they are not qualified to help the individual. They hold certificates in a system that is grounded in atheism and humanism. As such, the whole system has no basis in fact and has no inherent qualification for addressing itself to "the cure of the soul."

I want to say it again:

The Bible is the only casebook for the cure of souls. Only it *holds the answers.*

As a consequence, the preacher of the gospel (or, for that matter, anyone who is well-versed in the Word of God and committed to Christ) is eminently well-qualified to deal with human needs.

IS IT TRUE THAT OUR CHURCHES
ARE RESORTING TO COUNSELING
INSTEAD OF PREACHING THE GOSPEL?

Yes, it is, and the results are obviously catastrophic. I am going to make some statements that might seem harsh, but I feel they are true.

First, most marriage counselors or marriage seminars are ineffective at best and harmful at worst. There may be a few exceptions, but precious few.

I realize that marriage seminars (or workshops) are hailed as being the all-inclusive throughways to domestic health and happiness. But if this is so, why are so many marriages ending in divorce? (And only God knows how many others stay together *despite* all their problems.)

To be factual, the only answer for marriage problems is "fasting, prayer, and application of the Word." The Bible holds the answer. If only men and women would study it and seek God's face, their particular problems would evaporate.

"But marriage counseling and seminars *work,*" some insist.

No, they do *not* work. The truth of the matter is, if individuals would study the Word and seek God earnestly, they wouldn't need marriage seminars. And if they *did* learn something of value in a marriage seminar, you can rest assured it was already available in the Bible — if only they would have looked. In all these cases, they could have saved time and money by simply applying the Word of God *directly* to their problems.

Next, many people who attend marriage seminars do not *want* to live by the Bible.

And *finally,* most individuals who are *holding* marriage seminars are leaving the Word of God and trying to apply ineffective psychological principles to problems they aren't capable of solving.

HUNDREDS OF OUR PREACHERS ARE FALLING INTO IMMORALITY BECAUSE OF MARRIAGE COUNSELING

I might add that hundreds of individuals, be they preachers or otherwise, are falling into immorality because it is not God's way and it will not work.

I once heard A.N. Trotter say that it is not God's will or the Bible way for a preacher of the gospel to sit for hours listening to one sordid tale of woe after another. He went on to say that these endless stories of perversion, sin, and immorality come to permeate right down into the subconscious of the counselor, and will eventually take their deadly toll.

Brother Trotter was right. Hundreds (perhaps even thousands) of preachers (and others) are falling into immorality and sin — simply because they are trying to take the place of the Holy Spirit.

Ninety percent of all counseling in the church ought to be stopped. The preacher of the gospel should, instead, preach the Word with power and with the anointing of the Holy Spirit. The Word of God will then have its effect on people's lives. The Holy Spirit, utilizing the Word, will fly like an arrow — directly to the problem. He will not only point out the problem, He will supply the solution.

"For the word of God is quick, and powerful, and sharper than any twoedged sword, piercing even to the dividing asunder of soul and spirit, and of the joints and marrow, and is a discerner of the thoughts and intents of the heart. Neither is there any creature that is not

manifest in his sight: but all things are naked and opened unto the eyes of him with whom we have to do" (Heb. 4:12, 13).

The individual can kneel at an old-fashioned altar and let the Holy Spirit speak to his heart. And please understand, the reason we are having so many problems in our churches is that we are, to a great degree, ignoring this beautiful work of the Spirit, which is available at any time — for either the sinner or the Christian.

The Spirit of God should work in the services, the fallow ground should be broken, and people should be moved and touched. They should come before God broken and weeping. At these times the Holy Spirit touches their hearts and restores them to spiritual, emotional, and mental health. All the one-on-one counseling in the world cannot even *approach* what I suggest here.

And remember — this is not *one* of the answers, it is not *an* answer — it is the *only* answer.

BUT DOESN'T THE BIBLE
SUGGEST COUNSELING AS A PROPER HELP?

Yes, it does. But it is merely speaking of advice. It is not, by any trick of modern-day interpretation, recommending psychology or psychotherapy.

The Bible is full of advice specific to the human condition and doesn't need any help. To be completely frank, there is no help other than the Word of God.

If a person will apply the Bible to his problems, he will find *the* solution. If he goes to man for advice, he will only receive a man's solution — which will prove of little value.

Yes, I believe in biblical counseling. But I believe it should be of short duration, and with individuals being directed to specific areas of the Bible — and to their knees.

At *this* point, the Holy Spirit should be invited to perform His work of reconciliation. In this situation, the counselor is no longer a counselor in any sense; he is a minister.

However, something more should be added:

Counselors can develop an unwarranted sense of self-importance. People come to them for advice and counsel. All too often, their troubled wards become emotional addicts, totally dependent on a succession of counseling "fixes" to carry them through the short periods between visits.

Of course, this can become heady stuff for the therapist. With a steady parade of fawning clients at his feet, it is easy for the therapist to lose perspective and end up more confused than the patients.

As long as preachers accept psychology and depend on it as their main resource in ministering to individuals, they will continue to be saturated in perversion, adultery, and all the lowest types of immorality. And they will continue to fall by the hundreds and even thousands.

These poor individuals who go to Christian psychologists will be wasting their time and their money (if there is a charge for the services). They will be led down a path that offers no solutions.

The *help* offered may be sprinkled with words like "prayer" or "the Holy Spirit" and snatches of Scripture that *appear* to paper over the heavy doses of psychological jargon. But the mixture will not work and the individual will not be helped.

The greatest thing that could happen to the church (the body of Christ) would be if Christian psychologists, trained counselors, and the psychology departments of all our Bible colleges and seminaries would close up shop. Then the local churches could close down their counseling services, and before long we would be back to normal.

The congregations could then open their Bibles, start to read, and begin *living* what they read. They could find a church where the moving of the Spirit is evident, and they would there hear a preacher of the gospel expound the Word of God. This church would allow the Holy Spirit to apply the Word of God to their hearts and lives, and *they* would then allow the Spirit to deal with their hearts.

Now, wouldn't that be a day to look forward to?

Our problems, as far as this mortal vale is concerned, would be greatly helped. But they *will not* disappear as long as we put our faith in a false science instead of God.

Psychology and Christianity cannot be reconciled. Truth and lies cannot live together.

It might be said of psychology, as it was said of a particular sinister prison: *Abandon hope, all ye who enter here.*

> *"Beware lest any man spoil you through philosophy and vain deceit, after the tradition of men, after the rudiments of the world, and not after Christ. For in him dwelleth all the fulness of the Godhead bodily. And ye are complete in him, which is the head of all principality and power"* (Col. 2:8-10).

CHAPTER 5

THE PENTECOSTAL WAY

 I want to emphasize from the very outset that we are not promoting any particular church, denomination, movement, or fellowship. We *are* referring, rather, to the biblical manner of worship and service to God that (we believe) is clearly outlined in the New Testament.

We believe this "Pentecostal Way" started on the day of Pentecost and characterized the whole Early Church. We believe that the Early Church, as described in the book of Acts, is the foundation and basis for all subsequent *effective* church bodies. Any deviation from this pattern falls short of God's clearly defined pattern for His church.

THE WORD *PENTECOSTAL*

The term *Pentecostal* has come to describe specific groups, often referring to individual denominations or fellowships which reflect a common belief.

"And when the day of Pentecost was fully come, they were all with one accord in one

77

place. And suddenly there came a sound from
heaven as of a rushing mighty wind, and it filled
all the house where they were sitting. And there
appeared unto them cloven tongues like as of
fire, and it sat upon each of them. And they were
all filled with the Holy Ghost, and began to
speak with other tongues, as the Spirit gave them
utterance" (Acts 2:1-4).

The word *Pentecostal* is derived from the word *Pentecost* — taken from the Hebrew feast day known as "The Feast of Pentecost." This was the Greek word meaning "fifty." Actually, it was the fiftieth day after the Passover. Today, people who believe in this experience, as outlined in Acts 2 (the baptism in the Holy Spirit with the evidence of speaking with other tongues), are by and large referred to as "Pentecostal."

This message will, however, have little to do with the doctrine or the validity of speaking in tongues.

I think it is unfortunate that many believe that speaking in tongues defines whether or not one is "Pentecostal." It might, of course, *but the true Pentecostal way goes much deeper than just speaking in tongues.* This is what I'd like to address in this chapter.

I am particularly concerned today about the great Pentecostal message. I am concerned that in thousands of Pentecostal churches (by whatever denominational name), they are Pentecostal in name only. In truth, the Pentecostal way is all but lost to many who claim membership in these churches.

I am concerned that thousands of Pentecostal preachers now know little, if anything, about true Pentecost. The great Pentecostal way has faded more and more into the background until there is now little left but *glossolalia* — speaking in tongues.

But as we have just stated, the Pentecostal way is far more complex — and far more important than just speaking in tongues.

THE GREAT CHARISMATIC MOVEMENT

In the last two decades, we've seen an unprecedented outpouring of the Holy Spirit that has touched almost every denomination within Christendom. It is very difficult today to find any church, irrespective of denomination, that doesn't include at least some individuals who have been baptized in the Holy Spirit with the evidence of speaking in other tongues.

I would like to believe that we may have had some small part in this. Our radio program, "The Campmeeting Hour," went on the air January 1, 1969. Shortly thereafter we were broadcasting over six hundred radio stations daily. The Lord especially laid it on our hearts to deal specifically with the baptism in the Holy Spirit, the gifts of the Spirit, and other attributes of the Holy Spirit. And the mail literally flooded our offices. Our audience consisted not only of classical Pentecostals, but also multiplied thousands of denominational people who were hungry for a deeper walk with God. I thank the Lord that we had the opportunity to play at least a small part in this great outpouring of the Holy Spirit.

Today there are literal *thousands* of Charismatic churches dotting the land, and we thank God for them. And, perhaps surprisingly, some of these neo-Pentecostal and Charismatic churches are even more "Pentecostal" in orientation than some of the old-line Pentecostal churches.

(*Charismatic* is used to refer specifically to those who have been baptized in the Holy Spirit with the evidence of speaking with other tongues, but who have elected to remain within the framework of their traditional denominations. These do, however, maintain the Pentecostal evidence of worship, gifts of the Spirit, and speaking with other tongues.)

We thank God for the great outpouring of His Spirit, whatever the affiliation of those to whom it has been given. And I want to make it clear, as I develop this chapter, that I'm not singling out anyone for criticism. There have been times when I've cried to God in prayer, "Oh, Lord, I'm not at all certain if I personally know and understand the great Pentecostal way as it's *really* described in Your Word."

I strive day and night in earnest prayer — as well as by conduct, example, and method — to make Family Worship Center in Baton Rouge (in addition to our worldwide ministry) *truly* Pentecostal. I do so because I *know* it is the Bible way. Still, as I have often said to my church, "I am not sure that we really have a Pentecostal church."

So my statements are not to be interpreted as critical or accusatory. They are, hopefully, to be viewed instead as a heart-searching cry.

A FIRST STEP

I feel barely adequate to broach this subject. But perhaps some of what will follow might be food for thought. If that is the case, then at least a first step will have been taken.

Twenty-five years ago, I was preaching a camp meeting with one of the great Pentecostal pioneers — A.N. Trotter. I've known few men who I feel had the spiritual and biblical insights of this man who so greatly influenced my ministry. (He is now with the Lord.)

He made this statement:

"We have lost it. We have gone too far down the road of compromise. We have lost it."

I'll be frank with you, at the time, I didn't have the slightest idea what Brother Trotter was saying. Oh, I understood the subject and I understood his statement. But as we were walking across the road that day — after the morning service of the camp meeting — I pondered what he had said.

How could this be? What did he mean? The great Pentecostal message was (even then) beginning to explode around the world. It seemed to me — a young evangelist — that it was the message of the hour (and it truly was). Instead of weakness, there seemed to be tremendous strength, so I didn't understand what he was talking about.

"What do you mean?" I asked.

"Too much of the world, and too little of God," he said.

I pondered his statement but didn't question him further. In my heart I really didn't agree with him. But today, a quarter of a century later, I know exactly what he was saying. It alarms me and frightens me. Great moves of God are seldom destroyed from without. They are almost always destroyed from within.

THE PROPHECY AT AZUSA STREET

I'm going to mention a prophecy given in 1906. This occurred during the beginning of the great outpouring of the Holy Spirit that has subsequently revolutionized the world.

Today, the fastest growing churches in the world are Pentecostal. The Pentecostal message is truly the message of the hour. It has been stated that between fifty and one hundred million people in the last few decades have been baptized in the Holy Spirit with the evidence of speaking with other tongues. In our own crusades we routinely see from three hundred to two thousand people baptized in the Holy Spirit in a single service.

It has been further stated that by the turn of the century (if the Lord should tarry) over fifty percent of Christendom might well be Pentecostal — at least insofar as the baptism in the Holy Spirit and speaking with other tongues. Still, the prophecy that was given back in 1906 was, I believe, given for this time.

On Azusa Street, in the midst of a great outpouring of God, it must have seemed strange to hear such a prophecy being given. But, in essence, it said that three things would happen in the great Pentecostal movement:

• There will be an overemphasis on power, rather than on righteousness.

• There will be an overemphasis on praise, to a God they no longer pray to.

• There will be an overemphasis on the gifts of the Spirit — rather than on the lordship of Christ.

All this has come to pass before our very eyes.

I feel inadequate to address this, but I feel I must. Then, as I mentioned, at least a small first step shall have been taken toward the Pentecostal way.

THE PENTECOSTAL PURPOSE AND POSITION

The message of the hour in foreign lands (those outside the U.S. and Canada) is the Pentecostal message. As far as numbers are concerned, it has so far surpassed all other doctrines that there's little basis for comparison. I believe this is the reason for the great outpouring of the Holy Spirit, and to better understand this, let's look at the day on which the mighty outpouring of the Holy Spirit *first* fell — the Day of Pentecost.

As we've already said, this holy day was seven weeks (plus one day) after the Passover Feast. It was always on a Sunday. *It celebrated the harvest,* and this is significant.

When the Holy Spirit was poured out on this day,

designated by God centuries before, it was the prototype of the great outpouring of the Holy Spirit that would later come to the church.

Although Hebrew believers may not have understood what God was doing when He established this feast day, the types and shadows were, nonetheless, there. *It was established to celebrate the harvest.* But it had a much greater type in mind. The *greater* harvest would be the spread of the gospel throughout the world, made possible by the mighty power of the Holy Spirit.

> *"But ye shall receive power, after that the Holy Ghost is come upon you: and ye shall be witnesses unto me both in Jerusalem, and in all Judaea, and in Samaria, and unto the uttermost part of the earth"* (Acts 1:8).

Today, the promise of Pentecost has come to reality in amazing detail. It is truly a harvest. The harvest is abundant, and it is being gathered.

Please allow me to mention our own ministry. And understand, it is only a small part of the total move of God that is taking place all over the world.

Our telecast is aired in 145 countries. If everyone in these countries who owns a television set would tune in to our program, some three *billion* people could hear the old-fashioned, uncompromising gospel of the Lord Jesus Christ. We are told that well over five hundred million people do watch every week. I don't know really if that figure is accurate, but whatever the actual figure, it represents a *vast* audience.

God told us (in a prophecy in 1985) that He would turn the key in the lock and that we would be able to open the door. In country after country we have seen the door opened — even in communist and muslim countries — and we give God all the praise and the glory.

There was another tremendously important aspect of that original Feast of Pentecost. This feast came at the *completion* of the great barley harvest. I believe this tells us that Jesus Christ is soon to come, that we are nearing the end, and that the harvest we have seen is almost complete.

I believe the reason for the great Pentecostal way is to spread the gospel of the Lord Jesus Christ with power. Without the *power* given on the day of Pentecost, the dissemination of the gospel just wouldn't have taken place.

In **Acts 1:8**, we are told that *power* would be given to the church to take the gospel to the uttermost part of the earth. In **Acts 2**, the Holy Spirit was poured out, and a great message was preached by Peter, resulting in the conversion of thousands. In **Acts 3:25**, Peter said:

> *"And in thy seed shall all the kindreds of the earth be blessed."*

In **Acts 4**, thousands more were saved. In **Acts 5**, they were preaching and teaching in every house (verse 42). In **Acts 6**, they gave themselves continually to prayer and the ministry of the Word.

In **Acts 7**, Stephen gave his life for the cause of Christ. And in **Acts 8**, the work was taken to Samaria, resulting in a great revival there. In **Acts 9**, the great Apostle Paul was saved and, then, in **Acts 10**, the Holy Spirit fell on Cornelius and his household.

I think it is obvious from the examples noted, that by the end of the first one hundred years, much of the known civilized world of that day had been touched by the great gospel of Jesus Christ — and all this without any assistance from radio, television, the printing press, satellites, or any of the other modern technical tools we utilize in ministry today.

I think that from these examples we must admit that the Early Church was an evangelistic church. It was a Pentecostal church. It functioned in the Pentecostal way. And the moment our present Pentecostal churches cease to be evangelistic (or Pentecostal), they will wane and die.

This won't happen overnight, but it will happen. The Pentecostal way is always souls, souls, and souls. It is the altar call, it is the harvest. It is the flow and moving of the Holy Spirit touching hearts and lives. It is the convicting power of the Holy Spirit reaching out and touching men and bringing them to Jesus Christ.

Seminaries really can't train people for this. No amount of education can. Education might *aid* in some ways, but, in truth, it is a sovereign move of God that touches hearts and lives.

One missionary told me the other day, *"If you don't lose it on the home front, we won't lose it on the field."* But the sad fact is, we *are* losing it on the home front.

Today, missions giving in Pentecostal circles is, by and large, higher than it has ever been. And yet if we don't have revival in the Pentecostal way at home, missions giving will wane and die as well.

Missionaries aren't born in seminaries; neither are they born in academia. Beautiful buildings or costly structures have nothing to do with this great work of the Holy Spirit. Missionaries — as well as pastors and evangelists — are born in the white heat of Holy Spirit revival, which is encountered most commonly in the church.

The point is this: The Pentecostal way is the evangelistic way. It is the missionary thrust. It is taking the gospel of Jesus Christ to the entire world. However, we must have revival or the *roots* of this great missionary thrust will die. And once the roots die, it is only a question of time before the evangelistic branches die as well. Will this happen? The real concern is that the Pentecostal way has *already* begun to die.

PENTECOSTAL PRAYER AND PRAISE

The Pentecostal way is one of prayer and praise. This is the bulwark, the foundation, of any church, movement, or individual embracing the New Testament concept.

PRAYER

I thank the Lord that there are encouraging signs in that some churches are returning to prayer. Some pastors are encouraging their people to pray. Others are starting early morning prayer meetings. Only good can come from this, and we thank God for it. I pray that it's not too little, too late.

Our Pentecostal forefathers lived a life of prayer — it was their only resource, their source of supply.

They *had* to depend on God. They had nothing else. There was no money, and most had precious little education. They had no prestige or position. Their only alternative was a constant seeking of the face of God Almighty. Would it have been possible for the Pentecostal churches — by whatever name — to survive and prosper otherwise? It had to be of God or the Pentecostal way never would have succeeded.

I constantly tell our people in Family Worship Center in Baton Rouge that we thank God for the young people. We make every effort to bring them into our fellowship. "The youth are the strength of the church," is a common statement. However, this is not completely true.

Those few older people in the church who *really* know how to pray and touch God and reach Him (the people we refer to as "prayer warriors") are *really* the strength of the church. And even though there are some heartening signs, there are very few real prayer warriors left. I am concerned that they are a dying breed.

I remember a meeting I conducted many years ago which lasted for six glorious weeks. It was actually the first great move of God that I had seen in my ministry. And I later discovered at least *one* of the reasons for this great moving of the Spirit.

A particular brother who was a member of this church had been coming to church every morning at daybreak for several years. Regardless of the weather or personal interests, he never missed. He was seeking God for revival, groaning and praying in the Spirit. God answered those prayers.

As I've stated, I'm sure we have some like this left, but I can't help but wonder how many.

When Frances and I were first married, I would come home from my job (I was just starting to preach), clean up, and immediately go over to my grandmother's home.

My grandmother was one of those prayer warriors I've been discussing. She knew how to touch God and she taught me to pray. Actually, my "Bible School" was at her knees. She encouraged me in the faith and she taught me to seek God. It was she who taught me to believe "big."

I honestly believe that whatever success we've seen in this ministry has been built on her foundation. From that time on, everything we've ever known has come through soul-searching prayer — I mean importuning prayer at all hours of the day and night, sometimes spending entire days in God's Word and in prayer. This is the Pentecostal way.

PRAISE

Years ago, when I first started preaching revivals in Assemblies of God churches, waves of glory would sweep through the audience and hundreds of hands would be lifted spontaneously in praise to God. We don't see much of this anymore.

Most of the people in Family Worship Center in Baton Rouge are new converts, so they have very little knowledge of the Pentecostal way. I'm trying to introduce them to the true scriptural worship of God. Today, all too much of our worship consists of applause.

I mentioned A.N. Trotter earlier in this chapter (as I oftentimes do). I remember a camp meeting many years ago. I heard him say then (and it startled me) that when people sing or do something for the Lord in a church service, it is *wrong* to applaud them. Again I was confused by his statement. Even when he explained it, it left me confused. I hope (and believe) that I understand it better today.

He said that God will never glory in the flesh. He is no respecter of persons. No matter how beautifully someone might sing, or how well a preacher might speak, if we applaud the man, we are, in effect, applauding the *flesh*. This is displeasing to God. It is not the true Pentecostal way. The lifting up of holy hands in submission to God is a sign of surrender. It is a sign that we cannot ourselves accomplish the task and that our total dependence is on God. We must never depend on the flesh.

> *"I will therefore that men pray every where, lifting up holy hands, without wrath and doubting"* (I Tim. 2:8).

Yes, it is proper to applaud in church — *if* the applauding is for the moving and the work of the Holy Spirit. But it is never appropriate to applaud the flesh.

*"O clap your hands, all ye people; shout
unto God with the voice of triumph"* (Psa. 47:1).

I have to wonder today how much of our so-called
worship is anything more than entertainment, a display of
the flesh, and an atmosphere totally unsuitable for the
presence of the mighty Holy Spirit.

In how many of our Pentecostal churches today — be
they Assemblies of God, Foursquare, Church of God,
Pentecostal Church of God, Pentecostal Holiness, Independent, Full-Gospel, or Word of Faith — will one see
what we used to refer to as a *"Pentecostal Explosion"*?

No, I'm not speaking of a display of emotionalism or
any type of uncontrolled fanaticism. I'm speaking of a
demonstration of the power of God.

This is a sovereign move of the Holy Spirit and it can't
be generated artificially. It can't be created through feigned
enthusiasm or subterfuge. It is the result of a life of holiness, plus a deep and abiding consecration to God. It is
truly the Pentecostal way. No, the world doesn't, and never
will, understand it. It isn't *meant* to be understood by the
world. Anytime the world understands (and appreciates)
that which is purported to be of the Spirit, something must
be wrong. Even the majority of the *church* world will fail to
understand it.

But to be frank, this is what has made the Pentecostal
movement great.

YOUTH PASTORS CONFERENCE

In July 1986, Family Worship Center hosted its first
Youth Pastors Conference with over two thousand youth
pastors in attendance. On Tuesday night I preached a
simple little sermon, and I can testify that the message was
not responsible for what followed.

As I finished speaking, there was a wave of Holy Spirit anointing that swept across the audience. To be frank, I have seldom seen anything like it. It seemed to touch, in a sovereign, direct move of God, every individual in the auditorium.

Hundreds of youth pastors were on their faces on the floor, sobbing before God. It was a true Pentecostal wave of glory which, in a short time, would change lives for time and eternity.

There is nothing man can do that even remotely resembles it. Neither can it be explained. One can only say he was there — and how fortunate he was to *be* there.

The service started at seven o'clock that evening and we dismissed some time after eleven. (Actually, there was no dismissal as such. I left the church weeping and wept all the way home.) These were tears of joy. And yet there was a great hunger in my heart. I cried to God, *"Lord, this is what I want; this is what I've been pleading for; this is what our churches must have."*

Today, God help us, we seem to have replaced this Bible-based Pentecostal way with choreographed dancing, rock music, and rehearsed testimonies. It *used* to be that the power of God would fall and people would start to dance in the Spirit. Today, in all too many churches, pretty little girls and handsome little boys are selected, attractively costumed, and then rehearsed in routines that will supposedly enhance the mood that is *supposed* to be created.

Rock musicians are brought in. Strobe lights flicker and smoke pots erupt — with the spirit of the *world* permeating every visual and auditory assault.

The Holy Spirit has been bartered away and a new model called "the psychologist" adopted. God help us, we have traded shields of gold for shields of brass.

PENTECOSTAL POWER AND POSTURE

The Pentecostal way is a way of righteousness and holiness. But sometimes I wonder, do we actually know what righteousness and holiness *are* anymore? Both are *given* by the Holy Spirit and they are impossible to *earn*. They are *gifts* through grace. But how do we *maintain* these wondrous twins once we receive them?

I know all too well that the stock answer for holiness is, "It's a state of the heart."

Certainly this is true, and it probably says it better than anything else. But I heard a preacher make this statement years ago: *"Holiness is when we have arrived at a state with God where His every wish and desire is carried out within our lives."*

When we exist in a state of holiness, God's Spirit tells us what type of clothes to wear (and I'm speaking of decency here). He tells us where we should (and should not) go. Every facet of our life is controlled to please Him.

Once we reach the level where we can hear the Holy Spirit (and do His bidding in all areas) we have not only *attained* holiness, but our abiding *state* becomes holiness.

I heard another Pentecostal preacher say this: *"They do such things because they do not know or understand the holiness of God."*

He was speaking of some of the folly that is carried on in so many of our Pentecostal churches today. In fact, this very day I just heard of a heavy metal rock group that will be performing in one of our Pentecostal colleges. How can they allow this? *Because they know nothing of the holiness of God!*

The other day on a "Christian" television program, I watched girls in rehearsed routines, whirling with their skirts rising until their underclothing showed. And all this "in the name of God" and under the guise of "the Pentecostal message." Why would they allow something like this? *Because they know nothing of the holiness of God!*

Recently, in an advertisement for a minister's conference, a known humanist was listed as a principal speaker. How could a Spirit-filled brother extend such an invitation? *Because he does not understand the holiness of God!*

One Christian television show after another ballyhoos Hollywood characters as Christian examples. Rock groups blare their worldly music. It is called *contemporary* — meaning "in tune with the world." And for once they're right. How can they deviate so from propriety? *Because they understand nothing of the holiness of God!*

BIBLICAL EXAMPLES

In the Old Testament, when God's holiness was manifested (before the covering of the blood of Calvary) it presented itself in one of two ways:

If the people were generally following after the Lord, He manifested His displeasure and power by destroying those who had offended Him.

> *"And Nadab and Abihu, the sons of Aaron, took either of them his censer, and put fire therein, and put incense thereon, and offered strange fire before the Lord, which he commanded them not. And there went out fire from the Lord, and devoured them, and they died before the Lord"* (Lev. 10:1, 2).

However, when the people openly *defied* God, He would abandon them.

*"And the king of Babylon smote them, and
slew them at Riblah in the land of Hamath. So
Judah was carried away out of their land"* (II
Kings 25:21).

I have to wonder: Are we still sufficiently close to God
that we can experience chastisement and thus be restored to
Him through it? Or have we erred sufficiently that we are in
danger of total abandonment?

THE LORDSHIP OF CHRIST

At the beginning of this chapter, I mentioned the
prophecy given on Azusa Street in 1906. The third part of it
stated that there would be an overemphasis on the gifts of
the Spirit, rather than on the Lordship of Christ.

Turn on your television set to a Christian channel today
and I can guarantee that too often you will see bizarre
programming. Rock groups will perform, beer executives
will be guests, Hollywood personalities will be fawned
upon. And then, in the midst of all this, the host will turn to
the camera and give what he purports to be a word of
knowledge or some other one of the gifts. One might
consider this little more than mockery. Still, I'm convinced
that these poor hosts don't even know what they're doing. I
can't help wondering, though, if these were Old Testament
times, would they be in danger of being struck down before
their TV cameras?

I AM CONCERNED THAT MANY
OF OUR CHILDREN HAVE NEVER
SEEN THE TRUE PENTECOSTAL WAY

This has not been intended as an indictment, nor as an
accusation. Hard statements have been made, but it is

rather a cry, a plea, a weeping between the porch and the altar. I'm petitioning God for a revival and a restoration of the Pentecostal way.

> *"Thus saith the Lord, Stand ye in the ways, and see, and ask for the old paths, where is the good way, and walk therein, and ye shall find rest for your souls"* (Jer. 6:16).

A short time back, in Freeport, Bahamas, I was dedicating a beautiful new church just completed by Missionary Ernie DeLoach. The building was jammed. In a structure designed for two thousand people, as many as five thousand had gathered. The surrounding area was thronged and the halls were filled while the overflow rooms took up only *some* of the surplus.

I preached a simple message. And at the end of it, I began to sing without any accompaniment.

> I have found His grace is all complete,
> He supplieth ev'ry need.
> While I sit and learn at Jesus' feet,
> I am free, yes, free indeed.
> It is joy unspeakable and full of glory,
> Full of glory, full of glory,
> It is joy unspeakable and full of glory,
> Oh, the half has never yet been told.

About midway through the song, the organist hit a note in perfect harmony with the pitch of my voice and began to play. The congregation joined in and the anointing fell. For a few moments we were all caught up into that *"joy unspeakable and full of glory."* It was a little bit of heaven right here on earth.

Hundreds of faces were wet with tears. Individuals streamed down the aisles, under heavy conviction, coming to the Lord Jesus Christ.

Explain it? No.
Understand it? No.
Accept it? Yes!

It's the Pentecostal way and, praise God, it is the *only* way!

CHAPTER 6

THE MESSAGE OF THE CROSS

"For Christ sent me not to baptize, but to preach the gospel: not with wisdom of words, lest the cross of Christ should be made of none effect. For the preaching of the cross is to them that perish foolishness; but unto us which are saved it is the power of God . . . That no flesh should glory in his presence" (I Cor. 1:17, 18, 29).

"But God forbid that I should glory, save in the cross of our Lord Jesus Christ, by whom the world is crucified unto me, and I unto the world" (Gal. 6:14).

RELENTLESS ATTACKS

The history of Christianity is a relentless series of attacks upon the cross of Christ. And, lest any be confused, by the cross of Christ we mean a belief in the vicarious, atoning sacrifice of the shed blood of Jesus Christ at Calvary as the true and only antidote for man's fallen state.

Tragically, the majority of today's attacks upon the cross of Christ are being sponsored, supported, and promoted by the Pentecostal and Charismatic communities.

An incredible statement? Certainly. But one, nevertheless, that is true. And sadly, I believe that most (if not all) who are guilty of this blasphemy are totally unaware of what they are doing.

Motivation, of course, is at best a mitigating factor. Results are still results, and every year children are poisoned by drinking gasoline that has been stored in Pepsi bottles. Our theology today is riddled with an explosive mix of seemingly sweet theories disguised as "soft drinks."

When you hear such terms as the *power of positive thinking,* the *Kingdom Age, self-esteem, inner healing,* or *Christian psychology,* realize that you are being lured by a siren song that *seems* to be offering a panacea for the ills that beset mankind — but which is really an assault against the cross of Christ.

WE BELIEVE THE BIBLE TEACHES THIS

We believe, first of all, that **man is a sinner** — because the Bible says he is. That is not my opinion, it is God's. And man is not only lost, he is totally helpless — insofar as any capacity for saving himself. He has no solutions to his problems. We believe that the only answer lies in throwing oneself on the mercy of the Lord Jesus Christ and trusting solely in the provision for redemption made at Calvary.

We believe that **Calvary is the only source of salvation.** We further believe that **Calvary refutes every indictment that Satan brings against man:**

> ". . . *for the accuser of our brethren is cast down, which accused them before our God day and night"* (Rev. 12:10).

We believe that **nothing needs to be added to the price that our Lord paid at Calvary,** nor do we believe that anything *can* be added.

> *"For all have sinned, and come short of the glory of God"* (Rom. 3:23).

> *"Therefore we conclude that a man is justified by faith without the deeds of the law"* (Rom. 3:28).

> *"Forasmuch as ye know that ye were not redeemed with corruptible things, as silver and gold, from your vain conversation received by tradition from your fathers; But with the precious blood of Christ"* (I Pet. 1:18, 19).

We believe that **Scripture clearly establishes that the price paid at Calvary solves all problems of the "human condition."** Nothing needs to be added to it, and God forbid that anything should ever be taken away.

Still, when such excursions into worldliness as possibility thinking or Christian psychology are paraded before the church, they are in effect saying, "The blood of Jesus Christ does not meet the needs of mankind. For man to be 'well adjusted' or to 'realize his full potential,' he needs something in addition to the cross." Not surprisingly, it turns out that what he needs is one of these new-day, self-help philosophies.

This is, clearly and plainly, an attack upon the finished work of Christ at Calvary. And, tragically, as we said, much of it is emanating from the Pentecostal and Charismatic communities.

PREACHERS ARE TRYING
TO GO BEYOND THE CROSS

It tears my heart when I receive letters telling me that songs about the cross are no longer being sung in some of our churches. These are condemned as old-fashioned or too negative.

I have personally heard Pentecostal or Charismatic preachers on television or tape who belittle songs about the cross — even stating that it is improper to sing them.

A.N. Trotter made two statements that I shall never forget. *First,* he said, *"Every single blessing from heaven comes through the cross." Secondly,* he said, *"When we go beyond the cross, we backslide."*

At the time he said these, I was confused. When I first began preaching the gospel (sad to say) I did not know enough about the cross to understand his first statement. When he made the second statement, I did not really grasp the full import, but now I am beginning to see it fulfilled before my eyes.

Thousands of Pentecostal and Charismatic preachers are falling for these lies from hell — and yes, that is exactly what they are. They are trying to go beyond the cross. And, as they try to circumvent the cross (thinking that their little self-help philosophies are necessary to *augment* the cross of Christ), they are truly *losing* ground instead of advancing. If I have any grasp of the English language, that is a clear-cut case of backsliding.

I say it again and I say it plainly:

The finished work of Calvary needs no enhancement by man — or for man. Every price was paid at the cross. Man's full potential can only be realized through the cross of Christ, and it needs no slogan, formula, or incantation to bring it to fulfillment. Once a person has this, he has everything he needs to bring him to his full potential.

I repeat:

Any time you hear these terms bandied about over television (or anywhere else for that matter), realize that the individuals using them may not fully understand what they are saying. But at the same time, don't forget that they are actually suggesting that the cross is not enough, that it is necessary to augment Christ's finished work with some "scientific philosophy" in order to realize our full potential. In short, they are demeaning the work that was completed, once and for all, on the cross of Calvary.

Actually, this whole concept of "human potential" will be one of the church's greatest challenges in the days ahead.

MODERNISM

At the turn of the century, modernism began to rear its ugly head with a blatant attack upon the blood of Christ.

Liberal professors of theology openly ridiculed the shed blood of Jesus Christ. The ultimate blasphemous statement was probably made by Bishop James Pike. He said, *"The blood of Jesus Christ was of no more importance than the blood of a dead dog lying in the street."*

It took several years to complete the process, but this perverted philosophy has almost completely destroyed the denominational world. Major churches that were once evangelical bulwarks are now burned-out shells. Even the mighty Southern Baptists fight for their lives as adherents of the sick doctrine attempt to take command. And I want to make this statement:

It really does not matter how many gifts of the Spirit we may have in our Pentecostal and Charismatic circles. It makes no difference how often we speak in tongues. It makes no difference how many visions or dreams we might claim. We can boast of our power, but if these "mind-science" philosophies — which are a conscious or unconscious attack upon the cross of Christ — are allowed to hold sway, they will destroy the Pentecostal and Charismatic fellowships as surely as modernism destroyed the denominational world.

In many ways, I feel that this veiled effort by Satan is even more dangerous than the blatant frontal attack of modernism. At least we knew where the hypocritical proponents of modernism stood. But today millions of Christians accept those who appear to be spiritual giants — but who lure their listeners to apostasy through worldly diversions.

A MESSAGE OF PARDON

Now, let's look at the cross of Christ and what it truly represents.

Robert Schuller, who has an audience of millions, made this statement in a 1984 issue of *Christianity Today*:

> I don't think anything has been done in the name of Christ, and under the banner of Christianity, that has proved to be more destructive to human personality — and hence more counter-productive to the enterprise of evangelism — than the crude, uncouth, and unchristian strategy of attempting to make people aware of their lost and sinful condition.

This man then went on to say that the church has, for centuries, had a God-centered theology, while what it needs is a *man*-centered philosophy. He continued:

> Man is not basically bad, he is simply uninformed about how good he is. Guilt is a loss of self-esteem.

Then he went on to say that it is an insult to any human being to call him a sinner.

> Jesus would never do that!

If this good brother would bother to go to the Word of God and read the 23rd chapter of Matthew, he might perhaps change his mind. He might also profit by reading the 3rd chapter of Romans, starting with the 10th verse, down through the 18th. Then he could read, as Paul expands on this subject, in the 5th chapter of Romans.

> *"But God commendeth his love toward us, in that, while we were yet sinners, Christ died for us"* (verse 8).

It is blasphemy to say that we need some kind of man-centered theology to replace the traditional God-centered theology, that man's problems are simply a result of the lack of information on how good he is, or that guilt is no more than a loss of self-esteem. It is *catastrophic* blasphemy to suggest that man is not a sinner.

I wonder why Jesus had to come from heaven to pay such a terrible price at Calvary if man's condition is really little more than a problem of self-worth. But, of course, this good brother goes on to clarify this question:

> Jesus endured the cross to sanctify His self-esteem. He endured the cross to sanctify your self-esteem.

Have you ever heard such off-target reasoning? Scripture says:

> *"Looking unto Jesus the author and finisher of our faith; who for the joy that was set before*

> *him endured the cross, despising the shame, and*
> *is set down at the right hand of the throne of*
> *God"* (Heb. 12:2).

In this passage, if you set your mind to it, you might (perhaps) convince yourself that Jesus endured the cross to satisfy His self-esteem and our self-esteem. But it is more apparent that He endured the cross — with its accompanying agony and shame — *not* for some frivolous purpose, *but to satisfy the claims of heaven against mankind.*

Man is a terrible sinner, doomed to hell, and with no avenue to salvation. His lost condition is not just a matter of self-esteem — it is the far greater question of eternal salvation.

FIRE FROM THE ALTAR

A terrible rebellion is described in Numbers 16. This tells how the earth opened and swallowed up Korah and his fellow rebels as fire came down from heaven, even consuming others who were present.

Beginning with verse 41, we are told how the congregation — even after this terrible demonstration of God's wrath and judgment — continued to murmur against Moses and Aaron:

> *"But on the morrow all the congregation of*
> *the children of Israel murmured against Moses*
> *and against Aaron."*

Then, in verse 47, it says:

> *". . . and, behold, the plague was begun*
> *among the people."*

So Moses told Aaron to *"take a censer, and put fire therein from off the altar."* The altar represented Calvary. It represented judgment — the terrible judgment of God which would even fall upon His own Son, Jesus Christ, when He served as our substitute.

Aaron was told to go quickly into the congregation and make an atonement for the rebellious people. He was to stand between the dead and the living, and the Bible says that the plague was stayed (although 14,700 people died before this happened).

As we read this Old Testament account, we obtain some insight into just how deadly sin is — and the terrible price that was paid for it at Calvary.

THE LORD SPOKE THIS TO MY HEART

One night, a short time ago, I had been praying. I fell asleep on the sofa but was suddenly awakened. It must have been one or two o'clock in the morning. In any event, the rebellion of Korah began to fill my mind as the Spirit of God impressed upon me that I should preach this incident in a forthcoming crusade.

I remember it vividly. Lying there on the couch, I said, "But, Lord, people are not dying today of the plague."

Plain as day, the Lord spoke to my heart:

"What do you mean they are not dying? They are dying by the millions. They are dying in every conceivable way — because the same sin that killed these rebels is killing millions today."

He went on to say, "Their only hope lies in fire from the holy altar." In other words, our only hope rests in the cross of Calvary.

"Go everywhere and tell them. Remind them that Jesus Christ is the only answer. Instruct them that this deadly plague of sin upon their hearts and lives will damn them forever. The only alternative is the cross of Christ — the great Jesus Christ who died on that cross — paying the price for the sins of man. Tell them and tell them quickly."

I recall getting up and sobbing, bending under the weight of the great burden gripping my heart.

The cross of Christ is the only antidote for sin; there is no other. And when mere man shrugs off his terrible condition by calling it a loss of self-esteem, the utter blasphemy of such teaching is recognized.

The only way to convince people to come to Christ is to point out their lost and sinful condition. The Holy Spirit does this through the preaching of the Holy Word of God.

> *"And when he is come, he will reprove the world of sin, and of righteousness, and of judgment: Of sin, because they believe not on me; Of righteousness, because I go to my Father, and ye see me no more; Of judgment, because the prince of this world is judged"* (John 16:8-11).

> *"For after that in the wisdom of God the world by wisdom knew not God, it pleased God by the foolishness of preaching to save them that believe. For the Jews require a sign, and the Greeks seek after wisdom: But we preach Christ crucified, unto the Jews a stumblingblock, and unto the Greeks foolishness"* (I Cor. 1:21-23).

A MESSAGE OF PEACE

> *"But now in Christ Jesus ye who sometimes were far off are made nigh by the blood of Christ. For he is our peace, who hath made both one, and hath broken down the middle wall of partition between us"* (Eph. 2:13, 14).

The other day I listened with shock to a tape by a Pentecostal preacher who said that the Bible does not address itself to all of man's problems. He went on to state that the automobile, the computer, etc. are not specifically mentioned in the Bible, even though these technical developments are unquestionably given by God for the benefit of man. Then he went on to laud the self-help philosophies as further God-given "developments" for the furtherance of man's general well-being.

I am sure that the average listener would not recognize his subtle twisting of the Word of God.

It is true that the Bible gives little insight into chemistry, pharmacology, medicine, mathematics, etc. It is not a technical, self-help, know-how book about engineering or what have you. It is a book that deals with the creation, the fall, and the redemption of man. In other words, it deals only with the "human problem."

Jesus said:

> " . . . for a man's life consisteth not in the abundance of the things which he possesseth" (Luke 12:15).

In other words, a man can be an engineer, a scientist, a playwright, or any one of a thousand or more prestigious occupations and still be a mental, emotional, and spiritual disaster. (Conversely, a man can exist in the humblest of social and economic conditions and still be a spiritual giant.)

So, it was not God's intention to tell men how to be physicists or financial analysts. It was His desire to inform man of his lost condition and to point out to him his only source of salvation — Jesus Christ. In this, the Bible needs no assistance from any pitiful little self-help books.

Actually, this preacher was insinuating that the Bible does not contain all the answers to the human condition, that it needs the help of "possibility thinking," "the fourth dimension," or "Christian psychology."

It was amazing. I heard him say that Christian psychologists with whom he has dealt admitted that *ninety-five percent of what they had learned is garbage. But they take the other five percent and use it with the power of the Holy Spirit to help humanity.*

Can you conceive of going to college for six or eight years, knowing that ninety-five percent of your valuable time will be spent learning trash? I cannot imagine anyone spending years at a university if they *knew* that the bulk of the material they studied would end up useless. Still, this was being touted as the expressway to emotional well-being and success.

AN UNEQUAL YOKE

Sadly, Christians are turning in droves to these worldly cure-alls for personal and spiritual fulfillment and peace. Of course, there is no personal or spiritual fulfillment or peace to be found in any unequal yoke. It is all only an attempt by the world to join two incompatible religious systems and to impose an atheistic influence upon the church of Jesus Christ.

I maintain that "Christian" psychology is one of Satan's prime vehicles for the seduction of the church of Jesus Christ. Tragically, most Christians fail to realize this. In truth, there is no such thing as "Christian" psychology. We are dealing instead with two diametrically opposed religious beliefs and there is no way to reconcile them. It matters little what type of psychology one attempts to merge with Christianity. The fact is, oil and water will not mix.

Basically, "Christian" psychology is an unequal yoke that draws into the church the terrible influence of secularism.

Can one join righteousness with unrighteousness?

How can one wed God with Satan?

Norman Vincent Peale (if my memory serves me) was the first to try to join theology with psychology and psychiatry in his church in New York. I would hope that we would recognize in this the attempt at melding "mind science" with the Word of God. However, when I see scores of Pentecostal and Charismatic pastors flocking to seminars of the "possibility thinking" persuasion, I have to wonder if they would recognize any contradiction in the theology of Norman Vincent Peale.

No, this is not the answer. It is not the avenue through which man will find peace. The Word of God is more than sufficient to meet all of the needs of the average man — whether they be physical, emotional, or psychological. It holds every answer for the human condition. It leaves nothing wanting.

> *"According as his divine power hath given unto us all things that pertain unto life and godliness, through the knowledge of him that hath called us to glory and virtue:*
>
> *Whereby are given unto us exceeding great and precious promises: that by these ye might be partakers of the divine nature, having escaped the corruption that is in the world through lust"*
> (II Pet. 1:3, 4).

Once again I want to emphasize that I recognize that the proponents of these philosophies would be shocked if they were accused of impugning man's salvation and redemption through Christ's sacrifice. Still, this is exactly what these self-help philosophies do. They say, in effect, that the Bible does not sufficiently address itself to the human condition. It needs help. Consequently, possibility thinking, positive mental attitude, positive confession, visualization, inner healing, Christian psychology (and on and on) all attempt to "improve upon" what the Bible supposedly misses.

Ladies and gentlemen, *I maintain that the Bible, insofar as the human condition is concerned, answers every question and meets every need.*

Further, I suspect that the Holy Spirit will brook no interference with His moving and operation, according to the Word of God, in the hearts and lives of individuals.

Anything added to, or removed from, the Word of God amounts to heresy — irrespective of motives or intentions. And once again I wish to emphasize that we do not in any way question the motives of these individuals. We do question the results they are producing, which is the directing of people *away* from life and Godliness and, above all, the cross.

THE MESSAGE OF THE CROSS IS GOD-CENTERED, NOT MAN-CENTERED

"And they overcame him by the blood of the Lamb, and by the word of their testimony; and they loved not their lives unto the death" (Rev. 12:11).

- The answer to the sin problem is the blood of Jesus.
- The answer to the nicotine habit is the blood of Jesus.
- The answer to homosexuality is the blood of Jesus.
- The answer to a bad temper is the blood of Jesus.
- The answer to depression is the blood of Jesus.
- The answer to drug addiction is the blood of Jesus.
- The answer to malice and greed is the blood of Jesus.

- (And this list could go on and on, literally forever, so just insert here the problem that is causing upheaval in *your* life.)

Now I realize that some who are bothered by the cigarette habit might say, "But, Brother Swaggart, I can understand how it would take the mighty power of the blood of Jesus to set the homosexual free. But I do not appreciate being placed in the same category, when I only have the *small* problem of nicotine."

But this is the wonder of the cross. It meets *every* need. It is the answer to every question and the solution to every problem. You see, when we introduce another self-help effort, the product (irrespective of the labeling on the package) is the same old satanic ploy:

"The answer is within ourselves; we can do it if we will only learn the laws and principles that apply and then put them into operation by faith."

No matter how attractive this packaging, it is the same old lie. The goal is to always reward and glorify self. And then, buried somewhere deep beneath the frosting, we will unearth the thought, *"The blood of Jesus Christ is not enough. We need something more!"*

Again, this so-called "gospel" — just as the television preacher said — becomes "man-centered" instead of "God-centered." Man is somehow credited with being able to pull himself up by his own bootstraps. But it is the same old lie that Satan gave to Eve in the Garden of Eden:

"Ye shall be as gods" (Gen. 3:5).

It was at the very dawn of time that man *first* fell for this attractive lie, and he has been trying to play God ever since.

It is very difficult for man to realize, and to admit, that he is lost. It is even worse to face up to the fact that there is absolutely nothing he can do to save himself, that salvation is available only through Jesus Christ.

Jesus Christ alone paid the price for man's redemption. He alone has the answer. He needs no help. The word is finished and utterly complete. Any effort made by man on his own behalf is doomed to failure.

"BUT THEY WORK!"

No, they do not work. Irrespective of the constant parade of individuals who testify to miraculous results through the power of inner healing (or whatever current craze holds sway *this* week), they are all broken cisterns. They won't hold water.

Little by little, the church of Jesus Christ (yes — even the Pentecostal and Charismatic churches) is rejecting mankind's only help. We are bowing to dumb idols. We are discarding the tried and proven ways of the Word of God. Oh, all this is supposed to be based on the Word of God. In reality, however, Scriptures are taken and twisted and made to fit vain philosophies.

It used to be that in Pentecostal circles we looked only to "the Book." But now it is *any* book, as long as it is currently on the best-seller list. The fads change almost with the rising and setting of the sun. We run to and fro and there is no peace. Opportunists hang out their shingles and prosper — at least until the next fad comes along. When it does, multitudes will rush off to embrace *that*.

There was a day when preachers preached under the heavy anointing of the Holy Spirit. They opened up the Word of God. They expected the Spirit of God to move in hearts and lives. Heavy conviction would sweep over whole congregations. Man would be brought to a terrible awareness of his lost and sinful condition under the great convicting power of the Holy Spirit. Oftentimes, with tears streaming down his cheeks, the sinner would stumble down to the altar — where he would weep his way through to Calvary.

Christians with problems did the same thing. The answer was the same for the child of God as it was for the besotted drunkard. How many millions have knelt with a burden of sin — and have risen with their faces wreathed in smiles — changed by the power of Almighty God for all time and eternity?

It may be old-fashioned but it will never be out-of-date. And for anyone reading this who has a problem (whether it be a lost son or daughter, depression, or whatever), there is a solution as close as your Bible. Make your simple altar and just come clean with God. Let the Holy Spirit wash through your soul as you throw yourself into the open arms of Jesus. Let His blood wash away every stain of sin and you will rise a new man or new woman.

IT CAME IN THE MAIL

We received a letter the other day from a little ten-year-old boy.

Dear Brother Swaggart,

My mother and dad are alcoholics. For a long time I didn't know what to do. I dreaded coming home from school because I would often find Mom passed out on the floor. I dreaded the quarrels and fights while they were on drugs and alcohol.

But then I found Jesus. It's still not easy, but by His power and by the blood He shed on Calvary's cross, I can make it. I'm just trusting Him and believing Him from day to day. And He sees me through every time. If it weren't for Him, I don't think I could have made it.

Please continue to pray for me.

How is it that this ten-year-old child — who knew nothing about God, who was saved while watching our telecast, who has drunken parents, who actually lives in a hell on earth — can have the insight to totally trust the Lord Jesus Christ? At the same time, many preachers who should be experts in the Word of God are forsaking it and turning to vain philosophies.

An old song says:

> At the cross, at the cross,
> Where I first saw the light,
> And the burden of my heart rolled away,
> It was there by faith, I received my sight,
> And now I am happy all the day.

Those words are still true. And *that is* the message of the cross.

CHAPTER 7

THE COMING KINGDOM

 *"His dominion is an everlasting dominion, which shall not pass away, and his kingdom that which shall not be destroyed"* (Dan. 7:14).

The teaching of the Dominion Kingdom was presented during a "Satellite Network Seminar" held December 9-12, 1984, at Robert Tilton's Word of Faith World Outreach Center in Dallas, Texas. The four special speakers were Pat Robertson, Richard Roberts, Rex Humbard, and Robert Schuller.

Opening the series on the first night was founder and president of the Christian Broadcasting Network, Pat Robertson, who made the following astonishing predictions:

> What's coming next? . . . I want you to think of a world [with] . . . a school system . . . where humanism isn't taught anymore and people sincerely believe in the living God . . . a world in which there are no more abortions . . . juvenile delinquency is virtually unknown . . . the prisons are virtually empty . . . there's dignity

115

because people love the Lord Jesus Christ.

And I want you to imagine a society where the church members have taken dominion over the forces of the world, where Satan's power is bound by the people of God, and where there is no more disease and where there's no more demon possession. . . .

We're going to see a society where the people are living Godly, moral lives, and where the people of God . . . will have so much that they will lend to others but they will not have to borrow . . . and the people of God are going to be the most honored people in society . . . no drug addiction . . . pornographers no longer have any access to the public whatsoever . . . the people of God inherit the earth . . . there's a Spirit-filled President in the White House, the men in the Senate and the House of Representatives are Spirit-filled and worship Jesus, and the Judges do the same. . . .

You say, that's a description of the millennium when Jesus comes back . . . [but] these things . . . can take place now in this time . . . and they are going to, because I am persuaded that we are standing on the brink of the greatest spiritual revival the world has ever known! . . . hundreds of millions of people are coming into the kingdom . . . in the next several years.

. . . we've got to understand the nature of prosperity and prepare for what God's going to do . . . God is going to put us in positions of leadership and responsibility and we've . . . got to think that way . . . you mark my words, in the next year, two years . . . the next three or four, we're going to see things happen that will absolutely boggle our minds! Praise God!

Certainly every Christian should respond to the promise of such a world as enthusiastically as the audience did that evening. As much as we would all like to believe what Pat had to say, however, what are we to do with Bible prophecies concerning the Great Tribulation, the Antichrist, and Armageddon?

The belief that Christians are going to take over the world and present it as a flawless and polished jewel to the arriving Jesus Christ is widespread today. Now we must put this into proper perspective. You see, for those who accept the doctrine of the Kingdom Age, Positive Confession, or Possibility Thinking, anything is possible — if only you will unrelentingly *believe it!* And any suggestion that man (within himself) is doomed or that world conditions are going to get *worse,* not better, is a negative confession! The Kingdom Age/Possibility Thinking movement utterly rejects negative confession.

The doctrine that the Lord Jesus Christ will rapture the church away is considered an "escape theory." As such, it is considered to be unworthy of those who expect to take over the world and establish the kingdom of God on earth.

Earl Paulk, a pastor from Atlanta, Georgia, said this in his *Harvest Time* newsletter:

> When we first began to point out that the church was (foolishly) standing gazing into the heavens waiting for some dramatic escape from earth, some began to scream "heresy!"
>
> But . . . the Word proves that the earth is the Lord's and dominion over it is the church's premier obligation.
>
> Cast aside tradition and hear what the Spirit of God is trying to say to the church . . . Don't expect the "rapture" to rescue you! If you want to bring Christ back to earth, you can do it . . . *we* can do it.

Tragically, this idea that we Christians can overwhelm the world and transform it into a community of peace and prosperity is remarkably similar to the secular humanist philosophy. Basically, both paint the false picture of a utopia, or an Eden, constructed by *human hands* and *human minds.*

THIS IS WHAT SCRIPTURE SAYS

First — Even superficial reading of God's Holy Bible will reveal that Christians will *not* reform, and achieve domination over, the world — subsequently presenting it as a flawless jewel to the Lord Jesus Christ. Instead, Jesus Christ will take it over, flawed and unrepentant, in one cataclysmic moment.

> *"And I saw heaven opened, and behold a white horse; and he that sat upon him was called Faithful and True, and in righteousness he doth judge and make war. His eyes were as a flame of fire, and on his head were many crowns; and he had a name written, that no man knew, but he himself. And he was clothed with a vesture dipped in blood: and his name is called The Word of God. And the armies which were in heaven followed him upon white horses, clothed in fine linen, white and clean. And out of his mouth goeth a sharp sword, that with it he should smite the nations: and he shall rule them with a rod of iron: and he treadeth the winepress of the fierceness and wrath of Almighty God. And he hath on his vesture and on his thigh a name written, KING OF KINGS, AND LORD OF LORDS"* (Rev. 19:11-16).

Second — Before Jesus takes over the world, we will see a terrible apostasy — a falling away. In other words, the world will not suddenly reform. Regrettably (but scripturally), it will continue to deteriorate until that great and glorious moment when *He* suddenly appears in the sky.

> *"This know also, that in the last days perilous times shall come"* (II Tim. 3:1).

"For then shall be great tribulation, such as was not since the beginning of the world to this time, no, nor ever shall be" (Matt. 24:21).

"For when they shall say, Peace and safety; then sudden destruction cometh upon them, as travail upon a woman with child; and they shall not escape" (I Thes. 5:3).

Third — How many, even in the church of the living God, are today crying "peace and safety"? Many are rejecting the biblical doctrine of the rapture and are instead elevating themselves by stating that *we* (the Christians) will institute the kingdom.

We can take heart in the knowledge that this is the very time prophesied and that the rapture could take place at any moment.

"For the mystery of iniquity doth already work: only he who now letteth will let, until he be taken out of the way" (II Thes. 2:7).

"For the Lord himself shall descend from heaven with a shout, with the voice of the arch-angel, and with the trump of God: and the dead in Christ shall rise first: Then we which are alive and remain shall be caught up together with them in the clouds, to meet the Lord in the air: and so shall we ever be with the Lord. Wherefore comfort one another with these words" (I Thes. 4:16-18).

Fourth — *After* the rapture, the Great Tribulation (described by Jesus in Matt. 24:21) will take place.

Fifth — Then the great Second Coming will follow at the Battle of Armageddon, and this is described in Revelation 19:11-16.

Sixth — After this (and *only* after this) the millennial reign will begin.

> *"And they lived and reigned with Christ a thousand years . . . but they shall be priests of God and of Christ, and shall reign with him a thousand years"* (Rev. 20:4, 6).

> *"And the Lord shall be king over all the earth: in that day shall there be one Lord, and his name one"* (Zech. 14:9).

> *"That in the dispensation of the fulness of times he might gather together in one all things in Christ, both which are in heaven, and which are on earth"* (Eph. 1:10).

Seventh — After the thousand-year millennial reign is completed, the Bible states that Satan will be loosed from imprisonment for a short time and will go out to again deceive the nations.

> *"And when the thousand years are expired, Satan shall be loosed out of his prison, And shall go out to deceive the nations . . . and fire came down from God out of heaven, and devoured them"* (Rev. 20:7-9).

Eighth — Now, finally, the perfect age will arrive as the New Jerusalem comes down from God out of heaven.

"And I John saw the holy city, new Jerusalem, coming down from God out of heaven, prepared as a bride adorned for her husband . . . And the city lieth foursquare . . . And the nations of them which are saved shall walk in the light of it: and the kings of the earth do bring their glory and honour into it" (Rev. 21:2, 16, 24).

THE MAJOR DIFFERENCE

Let's look closer at the two divergent schools of thought competing today for Christian acceptance:

• One says, as we have stated, that the world will gradually improve through the prayerful attitudes and examples of the Christian population. As I heard one preacher say, "We [the Christians] will finally take over the world and present it to the Lord Jesus Christ."

• The other says that the world will gradually deteriorate and sink ever deeper into sin until a climax is reached: the awesome "Great Tribulation Period" forecast by our Lord in Matthew 24:21. Then Jesus will return, accompanied by the saints of God. He will defeat the armies of the antichrist and, finally, set up the great millennial reign.

WHICH IS RIGHT?

Let's put side by side the two teachings regarding the future that are most prevalent in Christianity today.

• **We believe in the fundamental truths of the Word of God.**

The Kingdom Age, or the New Kingdom teaching, refers to itself as Restoration, Restitution, Manifest Sons, Rebuilding the Tabernacle of David, Third Wave Theology,

New Wave Revival, Kingdom Now, Latter Rain, etc. However, not all of the people who use these particular terms are part of the Kingdom Age movement.

(We will hereafter refer to this philosophy as the Kingdom Age, or Kingdom Agers, teaching.)

• **We believe in the literal interpretation of Scripture.**

We believe that no Scripture is of private interpretation (II Pet. 1:20).

The Kingdom Agers have a nonliteral interpretation of the Word of God. The result is anarchy — *where every man becomes a law unto himself.*

• **We believe an open discussion on all subjects is possible.**

We plainly tell the people over our telecast and in our publications that no man's teaching should be accepted without question. All teaching (mine included) is subject to the Word of God.

The Kingdom Agers state that "God has spoken to us, and no man can evaluate what we say." Consequently, no discussion is possible.

Bishop Paulk, in his book, *The Wounded Body of Christ,* states:

> There is no judging by elders of the voice of the prophet if he or she is God's called-out man or woman who speaks as a prophet. If he is called as a prophet, there is no need for judging or proof because his ministry must prove itself.

Evidently, he completely ignores Paul's command to the church at Corinth:

> *"Let the prophets speak two or three, and let the other judge"* (I Cor. 14:29).

• **We believe the rapture of the church will take place at the end of this age** (I Thes. 4:16, 17).

We will receive our glorified bodies at the time of the rapture.

However, the Kingdom Agers say there will be no rapture. Some even say that "transformation is taking place now, before the coming of Christ." The Manifest Sons doctrine states that we will receive glorified and immortal bodies before the coming of Christ.

• **We believe the first resurrection of believers takes place at the rapture of the church** (I Cor. 15:51-57).

Some of the Kingdom Agers teach that the first resurrection takes place at the time of the believer's conversion.

• **We believe that the antichrist is a future literal person** (Dan. 7:11, 8:25; II Thes. 2:8-10; Rev. 19:11-21).

The Kingdom Agers teach that the antichrist is not a literal person. It (as they refer to him) is simply the principle of evil presently at work.

• **We believe that the Great Tribulation is a literal seven-year period in the future** (Dan. 9:27; Matt. 24:4-12, 29-31; Rev. 19:11-21).

We also teach that there can be a general tribulation that can befall the church at any time and has done so at periods of time down through the centuries. However, this is totally different from the Great Tribulation spoken of by the Lord Jesus Christ (Matt. 24:21).

The Kingdom Agers believe that there is really no such thing as a Great Tribulation, that the Tribulation is a present struggle. They also teach that the book of Revelation has little to do with the future. Some Kingdom Age preachers speak of a seven-month tribulation the church

124 *Spiritual High Treason*

will go through before the coming of Christ. (I have no idea where they derive this in Scripture.)

• **We believe that Armageddon is a future literal battle at the end of the seven-year Great Tribulation** (Ezek. 38 and 39; Joel 2 and 3; Zech. 9:12-17; Matt. 24:27-31; II Thes. 1:7-10, 2:8; Rev. 14:14-20, 16:13-16, 17:14, 19:11-21).

The Kingdom Agers believe there will be no literal Armageddon. They teach that Armageddon symbolizes the present struggles of the church against evil.

• **We believe that the millennium is a literal thousand-year reign of Christ on earth. It will follow the Great Tribulation Period. Satan will then be bound for a thousand years** (Isa. 2:1-4, 9:6-7; Dan. 2:44-45, 7:13-14; Zech. 14; Luke 1:32-33; Rev. 11:15, 20:4, 21:7).

The Kingdom Agers teach that the Kingdom is *now.* The thousand years, they say, is symbolic. And they say that Satan is bound now by the church.

• **We believe that Christ's coming will usher in the visible Kingdom. We believe the Kingdom is eternal but will have a thousand-year visible manifestation on earth** (Zech. 14; Rev. 19:11-21, 21:3).

The Kingdom Agers teach that the church establishes the Kingdom *before* Christ's return. Earl Paulk says that the church will establish the Kingdom and then, when it is finally established, will welcome the Lord back to take over an already-established Kingdom.

Pat Robertson says that God has called him to usher in the coming of the Lord Jesus Christ. He will — he says — provide worldwide television coverage of the Second Coming of Jesus Christ on the Mount of Olives. He made this statement in an address at Robert Tilton's church in Dallas:

I'm going to let you usher it in. Now where do you
usher in the coming? You usher in the coming where He's
going to come.

One Seattle pastor states:

In three years we're going to run this planet in the name
of Jesus. If we're not running it, we'll be on the way to
running it.

In Pat Robertson's book, *The Secret Kingdom,* he lays
out a scenario in which the church will exercise dominion
and take over the world for God during and in spite of the
Great Tribulation, which may not be so devastating after
all. I quote:

In the meantime [during the Tribulation], the Kingdom of God will move forward, its future never in doubt.
Those who choose to live under its rule will do so and be
continuously prepared for that time in history when Jesus
Christ will return to earth.

In another place in that book, he writes:

It is clear that God is saying, "I gave man dominion
over the earth, but he lost it. Now I desire mature sons and
daughters who will in My name exercise dominion over
the earth and will subdue Satan . . . take back my world
from those who would loot it and abuse it. Rule as I would
rule."

• **We believe that the rapture must be viewed as immi-
nent** (Matt. 24:36, 45-51; Luke 21:36; I Thes. 4:16-18,
5:6-11).

A major emphasis in the Kingdom Age doctrine is that
Jesus cannot come now. He will come only when the
church has "finished its task." This particular teaching

robs God of His sovereignty and foreknowledge. It makes the return of Christ subject to what man does.

• **We teach high evaluation of Scripture** (Matt. 4:4; Gal. 1:6-10; II Tim. 3:15-17, 4:1-4).

The teaching of the Kingdom Agers tends to produce low regard for the authority of the Bible. According to their teaching, *man's thoughts and personal revelations take precedence over the Word.* (And this is probably the most dangerous part of this teaching.)

• **We teach no compromise with modernism and cultism** (Matt. 4:4; Gal. 1:6-10; II Tim. 3:15-17, 4:1-4).

The biggest "message" today of the Kingdom Agers is the message of "unity." Basically anything is accepted. The occultists and modernists are accepted as long as there is no criticism of the "unity" or "Kingdom Age" message.

• **We believe that national Israel has a place in Bible prophecy** (Isa. 11:11, 14:1-2; Jer. 16:14-16, 23:5-8; Ezek. 11:17-20, 16:60-63, 20:33-44; Ezek. 37; Matt. 23:37-39; Luke 21:20-24).

The Kingdom Agers differ in their respective teaching concerning the Jews. Some have an anti-semitism slant, which is a doctrine of contempt for the Jews. Some of them also teach that the Jews are no different than we are, that actually the church today is the Jewish nation.

IS THE WORLD
GETTING BETTER AND BETTER?

The most optimistic TV viewer or newspaper reader will have to concede that the world is falling apart before our very eyes. I believe that the Bible predicts, in no uncertain terms, that this moral and spiritual dissolution will accelerate until it finally climaxes in the terrifying Great Tribulation.

Yes, a great and wonderful millennial reign is coming, but we Christians will not initiate it. Only the Lord Jesus Christ can.

As I sit writing this, our telecast is aired in 145 countries. If every set in these countries were tuned to our program, three billion people would be exposed to the gospel as we preach it — according to the written Word of God.

I am an evangelist. God has called me to carry His Word to the world. I am doing my best to comply.

> *"And he said unto them, Go ye into all the world, and preach the gospel to every creature"* (Mark 16:15).

However, we must understand that all evangelists in the world, plus all the pastors, will never by themselves establish the kingdom of God on earth. *This can only be done by Jesus Christ.*

The Great Commission was given two thousand years ago, and it was meant for every succeeding generation. Just as I am doing my best to take the gospel to the entire world, generations that preceded me should have done *their* best to accomplish the same end. Because of contemporary technical advancements, we are naturally able to reach far more individuals today.

But it must be realized that I am only doing what thousands of preachers and Christian workers have themselves done over the ages.

And what have the results been?

Despite this, the world has little improved, nor will it improve very much until the Lord returns to personally accomplish its conversion.

Has all this then been to no avail?

No, it has been *tremendously* productive. *However, you see, it hasn't been our responsibility to reform the world, but to win souls to Him.* What I (and every other preacher of the gospel) am doing *will* make the world better — but *only* for those individuals who give their hearts and lives to the Lord Jesus Christ and by so doing become *"the salt of the earth."*

This is the way it has been since the Lord's first appearance, and this is the way it will remain until He returns. As far as our "transforming the world," there is nothing in Scripture to even *suggest* that this will take place.

To be sure, the child of God *will* eventually prevail. We *will* inherit the earth (Matt. 5:5). But this will only take place when Jesus Christ returns. *He alone has the power.*

If we could gradually influence and improve the earth, and eventually resurrect or restore it, why would we have to look forward to Jesus' return? But to do what must be done, He must personally be present to subdue the powers of darkness at His Second Coming. We know, scripturally, that this *will* come to pass.

The teaching of the Kingdom Age is false. It is an erroneous doctrine that will weaken the body of Christ instead of strengthen it. It will cause many to deviate from the faith, rather than bring them to the faith. It will cause — and promote — loose living, false teaching, and erratic thinking.

This is why "Kingdom Age" teaching is harmful. Let us look at it in a little closer detail.

THE GREAT FALLING AWAY

"Let no man deceive you by any means: for that day shall not come, except there come a

falling away first, and that man of sin be revealed, the son of perdition" (II Thes. 2:3).

"For the time will come when they will not endure sound doctrine; but after their own lusts shall they heap to themselves teachers, having itching ears; And they shall turn away their ears from the truth, and shall be turned unto fables" (II Tim. 4:3, 4).

The Kingdom Agers and the Positive Confession crowd tell us we are going to see a steady improvement in the world. However, this optimistic projection would seem to fly in the face of Paul's prophecy of apostasy, set forth in his letters to the church at Thessalonica and to Timothy (which we have just quoted).

Still, many Christian leaders are preaching success, prosperity, and Christian transformation of the world. Unfortunately, this is rapidly becoming an integral part of a general philosophy that is pervading the Christian community.

Oh, yes, the Kingdom Age message is a stirring message. It is a particularly attractive concept in that it promises *success!* Naturally, everyone wants to be successful. And it features prosperity, and most would like to be wealthy. Christians taking over the world? What a beautiful thought. Everyone wants to be on top of the heap. So this is an easy philosophy to sell to those who base their beliefs on their *personal human dreams* — rather than on careful Bible study.

Tragically, most of our television evangelists are pandering to these normal, human aspirations. Notice, the next time you tune to your favorite Christian programming, how many are promoting the theory that if you follow *their* teaching, you will suddenly find yourself successful — and wealthy. The word "success" is constantly intruded into their sermons. If you are not a success, you are not attaining God's intended pattern for your life.

Their definition of success (if you will notice and read carefully between the lines) is usually associated with such concepts as "money," "top of the ladder," or "worldly goods."

This list goes on and on.

Have you noticed how materialistic this is? Where's the spiritual element? Time and again, Christian programs proclaim these goals and it is all made to fit hand in glove with Christian renewal of the world.

Of course, I — and some few others — preach about the coming holocaust and the perilous times that are just around the corner. We preach about hell, about judgment, about repentance, and about the terrible need mankind has for a Saviour. Not surprisingly, we're labeled as "gloom and doomers" and as negative.

GLOOM AND DOOM

Let's look at the Pentecostal and Charismatic communities as they exist today. If a preacher preaches repentance, he is labeled a "gloom and doomer." If he talks about the coming holocaust or preaches against sin, he is castigated for preaching a negative gospel. After all, "good Christians" will avoid like the plague anything that isn't "positive" in orientation.

Just the other day, Dave Roever was telling me of a meeting that he was preaching. Dave is a walking miracle, having been horribly wounded in Vietnam and, by the grace of God, brought back almost from the dead.

On this particular occasion he was to give his testimony on how he had come so close to dying, with some sixty pounds of flesh blown away from his body by a phosphorous grenade. And would you believe, a number of people got up and walked out.

Would you like to know why?

"If he would have had faith," they said, "he never would have been wounded in the first place." So they walked out!

Can you believe the incredible narrowness of this attitude? But that's the point we have come to. In many Pentecostal circles (and in *most* Charismatic circles), John the Baptist would have been booed out of the pulpit. His message would not have meshed with the "Kingdom Age" and "Positive Gospel" crowds of today. Come to think of it, just about every Old and New Testament prophet would have been rejected today. Picture gloomy old Jeremiah trying to get his message across to today's Pollyannas.

ELIMINATING HELL

Sometime ago I preached a television message on hell (and I'm going to start doing a lot more preaching on this subject because it is desperately needed in the 145 countries in which our program is aired). In an Assemblies of God church, this was derided by several members of the congregation.

Why?

Their position was, "This is a doctrine we don't preach anymore. It is not positive."

No, not all Assemblies of God churches see it this way, but every day more are jumping on the bandwagon.

The message today for all too many Pentecostal and Charismatic congregations is Possibility Thinking, Dream Your Own Dreams, Name It and Claim It, Success and Prosperity, and the Power of Positive Thinking. These are the messages of most television evangelists, and these are the root philosophies of more and more Pentecostal and Charismatic churches every day.

BUT WHAT ABOUT THE MESSAGE OF THE BIBLE?

"Now after that John was put in prison, Jesus came into Galilee, preaching the gospel of the kingdom of God, And saying, The time is fulfilled, and the kingdom of God is at hand: repent ye, and believe the gospel" (Mark 1:14, 15).

"From that time Jesus began to preach, and to say, Repent: for the kingdom of heaven is at hand" (Matt. 4:17).

"Testifying both to the Jews, and also to the Greeks, repentance toward God, and faith toward our Lord Jesus Christ" (Acts 20:21).

"Not willing that any should perish, but that all should come to repentance" (II Pet.3:9).

So it would seem, from the Word of God, that the New Testament message is not so much a "positive gospel" as it is a message of *repentance!*

CHRISTIAN TELEVISION PROGRAMMING

I cannot speak for all Pentecostal and Charismatic churches, and I am sure there are many exceptions, but in looking at so-called "Christian" television, about all we see is promotion of what *appears* to be God's gospel but which is actually *another* gospel.

Is this what people want?

*". . . shall they heap to themselves teachers,
having itching ears"* (II Tim. 4:3).

Many people ask what I see for the future — great apostasy or worldwide revival? My answer has always been in this vein:

We can expect to see both tremendous apostasy and revival. Scripture clearly states this. Paul said (as noted) that *"in the last days perilous times shall come"* (II Tim. 3:1).

The Bible also says:

"And it shall come to pass in the last days, saith God, I will pour out of my Spirit upon all flesh: and your sons and your daughters shall prophesy, and your young men shall see visions, and your old men shall dream dreams: And on my servants and on my handmaidens I will pour out in those days of my Spirit; and they shall prophesy" (Acts 2:17, 18).

So the Bible indicates that in the last days there will be tremendous apostasy, a tremendous falling away, and a great deviation from the truth. But, simultaneously, there will be a great revival. There will be a tremendous outpouring of the Holy Spirit. And at the selfsame time there will be enormous religious *deception,* and — God help us — that is precisely what we are seeing today.

LITTLE GODS

In Kingdom Age teaching there is the integral element of "the little gods." Many television preachers make such references as *"in God's class."*

Others say, *"God made man a god — a god under God"* (whatever this is meant to imply).

Still another TV evangelist says, *"You don't have a God living in you, you are one!"*

Earl Paulk, in *Satan Unmasked,* said:

> Just as dogs have puppies and cats have kittens, God has little gods . . .
> Until we comprehend that we are little gods, and begin to act like little gods, we cannot manifest the Kingdom of God.

Now are you starting to understand the thinking of these who are preaching that we as Christians are going to bring in the new Kingdom Age? That we are going to take over the world and present it as a completed work to the Lord Jesus Christ? The "little god" teaching fits the Kingdom Age philosophy perfectly.

WHAT DOES THE BIBLE SAY ABOUT THIS "LITTLE GOD" SCENARIO?

The same spirit that is infecting our age is what caused the fall of Adam and Eve in the Garden.

> *"And the serpent said unto the woman, Ye shall not surely die: For God doth know that in the day ye eat thereof, then your eyes shall be opened, and ye shall be as gods, knowing good and evil"* (Gen. 3:4, 5).

Satan fell of this same spirit:

> *"How art thou fallen from heaven, O Lucifer, son of the morning! . . . For thou hast*

*said in thine heart, I will ascend into heaven, I
will exalt my throne above the stars of God: I
will sit also upon the mount of the congregation,
in the sides of the north: I will ascend above the
heights of the clouds; I will be like the most
High"* (Isa. 14:12-14).

Satan fell because he lusted to be God. He introduced
this idea into the heads of Adam and Eve. And in a way,
they did become gods, but it was not at all what they
thought it would be.

They lost their capacity to do good and gained the
power to do evil. *They traded God-consciousness for
self-consciousness.* Satan is called the god of this world
(II Cor. 4:4), and he is still promoting this destructive spirit
to (and through) people who *should* know better.

And let us look at something here: It was this same
spirit that intruded into and caused dissension among
Christ's very disciples.

> *"And there was also a strife among them, which
> of them should be accounted the greatest . . .
> But ye shall not be so: but he that is greatest among
> you, let him be as the younger; and he that is chief,
> as he that doth serve . . . but I am among you as
> he that serveth"* (Luke 22:24, 26, 27).

> *"And he came to Capernaum: and being in
> the house he asked them, What was it that ye
> disputed among yourselves by the way? But they
> held their peace: for by the way they had dis-
> puted among themselves, who should be the
> greatest"* (Mark 9:33, 34).

Sadly enough, even at the Last Supper, this strife generated by the little-god spirit was in evidence, as you can read

in Luke 22:24. If it had continued, it would have destroyed the work of God and His church. But, praise God, He was able to teach them what true greatness involved as He washed their feet.

> *"After that he poureth water into a bason, and began to wash the disciples' feet, and to wipe them with the towel wherewith he was girded"* (John 13:5).

Jesus then said:

> *"If I then, your Lord and Master, have washed your feet; ye also ought to wash one another's feet"* (John 13:14).

No, Jesus was not instituting foot washing as an ordinance or a ceremony. He was actually saying, to His disciples and to all of us, that we are to develop a *foot-washing spirit*.

This is the true spirit of humility. Jesus dropped to His knees, removed their sandals, and washed their dirty feet. (There were no paved roads then and everyone wore open sandals. Dirty feet were universal and just "a sign of the times.") He thus taught them the spirit of humility (or the servant principle), rather than the little-god principle being promoted today.

I think if you will look closely at many Pentecostal and Charismatic churches and "Christian" television programming, you will see this little-god syndrome in operation: success and prosperity teaching, possibility thinking, the power of positive thinking, and the positive confession principle. It all fits.

In order to take over the world, we must be some type of superhuman. To do this, we also have to be successful, powerful, strong, and dominating. There must always be a positive approach. And, naturally, we must never be accused of negativism because this would not be appropriate for a Kingdom Ager or a superhuman "little god."

IS THERE A KINGDOM AGE COMING?

Yes, there definitely is. But as we have already stated, it will come about only after a tremendous falling away, with the "man of sin" revealed. It will be only after the great apostasy and the Apocalypse — as recorded in the book of Revelation.

To be brutally frank (but scriptural), *dark days are coming*. Instead of the scenario being painted by the Kingdom Agers, the Bible tells us the very opposite. It speaks of millions dying of hunger. It speaks of unimaginable conflicts and excruciating suffering.

Is this gloom and doom? I'm sure it is, *but it is the truth*. The Bible then tells us of the terrible Battle of Armageddon, closely followed by the great Second Coming of the Lord (Rev. 19). *Only then will the Kingdom Age be instituted*. It will be ushered in by the great power of the Lord Jesus Christ, *not* by Christians making the world better and better and better. His coming will be sudden. It will be cataclysmic. He will literally smite the nations (Rev. 19:15).

The Bible also says:

> *"And I [John] saw an angel come down from heaven, having the key of the bottomless pit and a great chain in his hand. And he laid hold on the dragon, that old serpent, which is the Devil, and Satan, and bound him a thousand years, And cast him into the bottomless pit, and shut him up, and set a seal upon him, that he should*

deceive the nations no more, till the thousand years should be fulfilled: and after that he must be loosed a little season" (Rev. 20:1-3).

Then Jesus Christ will set up a *true* Kingdom Age. You must remember this — *you cannot have a kingdom until you have a king.* That king is Jesus Christ.

"And it shall come to pass in the last days, that the mountain of the Lord's house shall be established in the top of the mountains, and shall be exalted above the hills; and all nations shall flow unto it. And many people shall go and say, Come ye, and let us go up to the mountain of the Lord, to the house of the God of Jacob; and he will teach us of his ways, and we will walk in his paths: for out of Zion shall go forth the law, and the word of the Lord from Jerusalem. And he shall judge among the nations, and shall rebuke many people: and they shall beat their swords into plowshares, and their spears into pruninghooks: nation shall not lift up sword against nation, neither shall they learn war any more" (Isa. 2:2-4).

CHAPTER 8

THE UNITY OF THE BODY . . . AT ANY COST?

"Beloved, when I gave all diligence to write unto you of the common salvation, it was needful for me to write unto you, and exhort you that ye should earnestly contend for the faith which was once delivered unto the saints" (Jude 3).

A STRONG DEMAND FOR UNITY

Some time ago I received a unique distinction. A representative of the National Council of Churches cited me as the individual most responsible for disrupting the Ecumenical movement in Louisiana. While he considered this an insult, I truly felt it was an honor.

Today, the strident plea for unity among the body of Christ permeates the entire Pentecostal and Charismatic fellowships.

Are today's efforts toward spiritual unity a complement to the Holy Spirit's program, or are they divisive?

I believe it is the compelling desire of the Holy Spirit to see unity within the body. But I think there is the preliminary problem of first defining "the body," and then the further questions of *discipline, correction,* and *sound doctrine.*

OUR LORD'S LONGEST PRAYER

John, chapter 17, supplies a transcription of the longest prayer by Jesus reported verbatim within the Word of God. Of course, He prayed "all night" on a number of occasions, but there is no record of the actual words used during these incidents. Here the specific prayer *is* reported, however, for our examination, and the very foundation of this prayer is unity within the body. He specifically mentions unity in five separate statements:

- *"that they may be one, as we are"* (11).
- *"that they all may be one"* (21).
- *"that they also may be one in us"* (21).
- *"that they may be one, even as we are one"* (22).
- *"I in them, and thou in me, that they may be made perfect in one"* (23).

So five times He mentioned unity within the body.

And this unity within the body is the single biggest problem within the church today.

Now, we should interject this thought:

The body of Christ is not a human organization arranged and supported by worldly powers. It is not sustained and nourished by secular influences.

The true church of the Lord Jesus Christ is the total company of true Christians of all churches and of all times.

The Lord Jesus Christ (*head* of the church) said:

*"For where two or three are gathered to-
gether in my name, there am I in the midst of
them"* (Matt. 18:20).

So, obviously, there are thousands, perhaps even millions, of churches without any national or international
affiliation. The true church of the Lord Jesus Christ bears
the stamp of the Holy Spirit — supplying His singular
influence to produce faith, courage, and confidence in its
faithful martyrs over the centuries.

The true church has carried a variety of names over the
years. In God's view, it is made up of the sons of God.
These sons can claim only one merit, and this is that they
have obeyed their hearts — rejecting the doctrines of men
and accepting instead those God has revealed through His
Holy Word. Even though the true body of Christ is the most
powerful force on the face of the earth, it has been horribly
weakened because of splintering within the body. That's
the reason Jesus said (five times as recorded in John 17) that
we must seek unity among the brethren.

So I think we can conclude that this unity within the
true body of Christ is tremendously important.

IS IT POSSIBLE TO CREATE
UNITY WITHIN THE BODY OF CHRIST?

One of the main reasons for the effectiveness of the
Early Church was its cohesion. There was only one church.
Yes, it was called the *catholic* church (which meant universal) but not the *Roman* Catholic church. It had one basic
belief supporting this foundational principle, and it reaped
the rewards Jesus Christ had promised in Acts 1:8.

In its first one hundred years — without the aid of the
printing press, television, radio, airplane, or any of the
communication devices now available — they evangelized

most of the known civilized world. Even *with* the aid of all of our modern "miracles," we have today (sad to say) fallen far short of the goal of world evangelization.

Why?

I believe it is clear that the answer is today's lack of unity within the body of Christ. This is the single most disruptive element within the myriad organizations that claim to be the true branch springing forth from Christ's roots.

Sad to say, unity will not come about until Jesus Christ returns. The schisms are deep; the differences are great. We should certainly endeavor (with certain reservations) to work toward unity in the body. This is important. *But we must also realize that it is never to be "unity at any cost."*

IS UNITY *THE* MOST IMPORTANT FACTOR IN CHRISTIANITY TODAY?

I would say that it is *a* most important factor. But the elements involved in reaching this unity can be even more important. You see, it must be a unity based on the Word of God, and one approved by the Holy Spirit. (And, of course, if it is based faithfully on the Word of God, it *will* be approved by the Holy Spirit.)

In light of the statement just made, *truth* becomes the single most important factor. We want unity; we should (and will) strive for unity. But unity must be based on truth — and truth is the Word of God.

If we do not have unity based upon truth, we have no unity at all. We have an unacceptable compromise instead. We have diluted the Word. We have made a mockery of all for which Jesus died, and for which the apostles spilled their blood.

The bulk of the New Testament is *not* written to bring about unity, it is written to bring about truth. God, in His omniscience, knows that when truth is followed it must bring about unity. So, when you get down to fundamentals, the issue is not unity — it is truth!

Truth is the touchstone upon which we will sink or swim, live or die. And God help us, it is on this issue that we are sinking, and dying. Tragically, it seems that even in Pentecostal circles, truth is being sacrificed for unity. Actually, no preacher is called to preach unity. He is called to *"Preach the word"* (II Tim. 4:2).

IS THE GOSPEL OF JESUS CHRIST ALWAYS "POSITIVE" AND ALWAYS A GOSPEL OF "LOVE"?

H.S. Ironside, longtime pastor of Moody Memorial Church in Chicago, said that it's impossible to be positive while contending for truth. To contend for all of God's truth, he continued, necessitates some negative teaching. ". . . any error, or any truth-and-error mixture, calls for definite exposure and repudiation. To condone such is to be unfaithful to God and His Word, and treacherous to imperiled souls for whom Christ died."

God help us.

Who could say it better? It is on this statement, along with the Word of God (written by Jude some two thousand years ago), that I want to base this message.

I fear that today we don't really know what love is. Does true love condone error? Does it embrace heresy? Does it approve sin?

No.

But this "unity gospel" (as it is being promoted today) forbids us to speak out against the evils specifically pointed out in God's Word. If one speaks out against sin, he is indicted for lacking love.

In a message delivered at Unity Headquarters in Lee's Summit, Missouri, Robert Schuller stated:

> I talk a great deal to groups that are not positive . . . even to what we would call fundamentalists . . . who deal constantly with words like sin, salvation, repentance, guilt, and that sort of thing. So, when I'm dealing with these people . . . what we have to do is positivize the words that have classically only had negative interpretations.

He also stated in *Christianity Today:*

> I don't think anything has been done in the name of Christ and under the banner of Christianity that has proven more destructive to human personality and, hence, counterproductive to the evangelism enterprise than the often crude, uncouth, and un-Christian strategy of attempting to make people aware of their lost and sinful condition.

There are, sad to say, some Christian television programs, stations, and even whole networks where guests are specifically cautioned against speaking negatively of Mormonism, Christian Science, etc. Everything must be "positive." By extension, anything that is positive is love.

Have you ever considered that there can't *be* a positive without a negative?

Do you realize that true love does *not* condone sin and does not embrace heresy? True love *must* also discipline and correct. If it doesn't, it isn't true love.

God is love. Still, there is a positive and a negative in all of God's dealings with men. Along with tenderness, gentleness, and compassion, there is also discipline and correction. There is always the potential for mercy, but inevitably there is the confrontation with *justice* (Heb. 10:26-31).

Does the preacher fail to demonstrate love when he preaches against sin? Isn't he exhibiting love when he sternly rebukes the sinner?

> *"All scripture is given by inspiration of God, and is profitable for doctrine, for reproof, for correction, for instruction in righteousness: That the man of God may be perfect, throughly furnished unto all good works"* (II Tim. 3:16, 17).

THE LORD HAD THREE APPROACHES TO HIS MINISTRY

Basically, the Lord Jesus Christ approached the public in three distinct ways: to the sinner, to the worldling, and to the religious leaders.

To those who were lost in sin (even the worst types of bondage), He had nothing but compassion and love.

> *"For God sent not his Son into the world to condemn the world; but that the world through him might be saved"* (John 3:17).

But for the worldling he had nothing but sarcasm.

> *"And he said unto them, Go ye, and tell that fox, Behold, I cast out devils, and I do cures to day and to morrow, and the third day I shall be perfected"* (Luke 13:32).

For the "religious" crowd (that had denied God) He had nothing but scathing denunciation.

> *"Woe unto you, scribes and Pharisees, hypocrites! . . . Ye serpents, ye generation of vipers, how can ye escape the damnation of hell?"* (Matt. 23:29, 33).

While the Lord Jesus Christ was unquestionably positive, He was also negative — as I think we have demonstrated by Scripture.

Who would deny that He was the epitome of love? But He also disciplined and corrected.

I must say it again:

True love will not condone sin. It will not accept erroneous doctrine. It will be tender, compassionate, gentle, and longsuffering. But at the same time, it will discipline and correct.

DIVIDING THE BODY

The cry today is that nothing must be done that will bring division to the body of Christ. Is this correct? Is divisiveness always bad? If it is, then we immediately have a problem with the Lord's teaching and ministry. He too caused a great deal of "division."

> *"Think not that I am come to send peace on earth: I came not to send peace, but a sword. For I am come to set a man at variance against his father, and the daughter against her mother, and the daughter in law against her mother in law. And a man's foes shall be they of his own household"* (Matt. 10:34-36).

> *"Suppose ye that I am come to give peace on earth? I tell you, Nay; but rather division: For from henceforth there shall be five in one house*

divided, three against two, and two against three" (Luke 12:51, 52).

"And there was much murmuring among the people concerning him: for some said, He is a good man: others said, Nay; but he deceiveth the people" (John 7:12).

"Therefore said some of the Pharisees, This man is not of God, because he keepeth not the sabbath day. Others said, How can a man that is a sinner do such miracles? And there was a division among them" (John 9:16).

Christ's teaching rightly divides truth from error, right from wrong.

Since it is impossible to have contradictory claims which are both true, there must be a "division" (a disagreement) between conflicting viewpoints. So, how do we know when division is good?

Quite simple, really.

It is good when truth has been distinguished from error.

We are commanded to admonish and correct. Without admonishment and correction we might have unity (absence of disagreement) but we would be a far cry from what Christ expects for (and demands of) His followers.

"For the time will come when they will not endure sound doctrine; but after their own lusts shall they heap to themselves teachers, having itching ears; And they shall turn away their ears from the truth, and shall be turned unto fables" (II Tim. 4:3, 4).

IDEA EXCHANGE

Sometime back, about four hundred ministers met in Charlotte, North Carolina, for what was referred to as an "Idea Exchange." Most of the ministers were either Pentecostal or Charismatic. Among them were the pastors of some of America's largest churches.

This group consisted primarily of Assemblies of God, a few Churches of God, and quite a number of Charismatics. There were also a small number of Catholic Charismatics present.

I was sent the audio tapes of part of this meeting, where almost the entire discussion was on "the unity of the body."

What I heard broke my heart. It was so shocking and startling that I could hardly believe my ears.

Up until then, I hadn't realized that the Pentecostal message had been compromised to the point where "anything goes."

The bulk of the meeting (at least the part I heard) seemed to be devoted to appeasing the few Catholics present. Discussion was held at length as to how communion could be taken with both the Catholics and the "Protestants" participating.

Never mind that the Catholic church believes in the doctrine of transubstantiation — which claims that the bread actually turns into the body of the Lord Jesus Christ and the wine into His blood — and the claim that under Catholic doctrine Jesus is sacrificed anew each time Catholics participate in the mass.

The Roman Catholic church teaches that its "holy mass" is an expiatory (sin-removing) sacrifice in which the Son of God is actually resacrificed on the cross. Jesus literally descends into the priest's hands during the act of transubstantiation, wherein the elements of "the host" (the wafer) are physically transformed into the body, blood, soul, and divinity of our Lord Jesus Christ. This was defined as such by the Council of Trent — although inconsequential alterations were made in wording during the Second Vatican Council.

Further, the Catholic church teaches that this repeated sacrifice of Christ can be specifically applied to the benefit of deceased souls. This is arranged by the living who buy "mass cards" which subsidize the "expense" of the masses said for the deceased for this purpose.

Canon One, on "the most Holy Sacrament of the Eucharist," reads:

> If anyone deny it, that in the sacrament of the most Holy Eucharist are contained truly, really, and substantially, the body and blood, together with the soul and divinity of our Lord Jesus Christ, and consequently the whole Christ, but saith that He is only therein as in a sign, or in figure, or virtue, let him be anathema.

In other words, any person who fails to accept the Catholic doctrine of transubstantiation is eternally lost.

In the Roman Catholic mind the mass is a sacrament, which implies a sacrifice. This belief lies at the very heart of Catholicism.

Paul said:

> *"Wherefore whosoever shall eat this bread, and drink this cup of the Lord, unworthily, shall be guilty of the body and blood of the Lord. But let a man examine himself, and so let him eat of that bread, and drink of that cup. For he that eateth and drinketh unworthily, eateth and drinketh damnation to himself, not discerning the Lord's body"* (I Cor. 11:27-29).

"Whosoever transgresseth, and abideth not in the doctrine of Christ, hath not God. He that abideth in the doctrine of Christ, he hath both the Father and the Son. If there come any unto you, and bring not this doctrine, receive him not into your house, neither bid him God speed: For he that biddeth him God speed is partaker of his evil deeds" (II John 9-11).

Shall I mention purgatory, confession to the priest, praying to saints?

Yes, many Catholics have been saved and many have been baptized in the Holy Spirit. I thank God a thousand times over for them. But when we tell these Catholic Charismatics that it is perfectly proper for them to remain under false doctrine, we not only do them a terrible disservice — we may well be working toward damning their souls to hell.

We should love the Catholics. We should pray for them. We should treat them with kindness and compassion. But we should also preach the truth to them. If we don't reveal the truth to them, how will they ever know the depths of their error?

The false doctrine now dominating the Charismatic movement insists that nothing must cause dissension. "Let the Holy Spirit take care of the problems."

But how does the Holy Spirit take care of these problems? He can do so only through honest preaching and teaching of the Word of God. And what does Scripture say?

"How then shall they call on him in whom they have not believed? and how shall they believe in him of whom they have not heard? and how shall they hear without a preacher? And how shall they preach, except they be sent? as it

is written, How beautiful are the feet of them
that preach the gospel of peace, and bring glad
tidings of good things! . . . So then faith cometh
by hearing, and hearing by the word of God"
(Rom. 10:14, 15, 17).

The Holy Spirit can only act through the infallible
Word of God. He can only function through truth. He
expects the man of God to deliver the truth. He expects him
to deliver it with compassion, with love, and with understanding. But at the same time *he must deliver it!*

According to the tapes of this Idea Exchange, they
were, without exception, telling the Catholic Charismatics, "Your doctrine is satisfactory; we can accept it."

Actually, the only condemnation was for those who
dare to speak out against the compendium of errors that
make up the foundation of the Catholic faith.

THERE *WAS* SOME OPPOSITION

Among the hundreds there, I'm sure that some were in
opposition to the ideas presented. But they were either
forbidden to speak or were afraid to stand up and voice
their reservations.

Actually, one gentleman *did* stand and voice his reser-
vation. He was evidently a Catholic priest, and he said,
"Gentlemen, I am sorry but we cannot participate in any
type of joint communion service. The 'discipline' of our
church does not allow it."

I thought it was somewhat ironic that the only voice of
objection was from the Catholics themselves and *not* the
Protestants.

The simple fact is, Catholicism is a mixture of Christianity and paganism. It has led untold millions down the
path to hell — and millions more are on the way. As I've

repeatedly mentioned, I thank God for the Catholics who have come to God and been born again; many have.

I thank God for those who have been baptized in the Holy Spirit. However, I maintain that the Spirit of God always adheres to truth and sound doctrine — which is the Word of God. If Catholic Charismatics do not forsake their pagan doctrines, they are destined for spiritual dissolution and eventual loss of the tremendous spiritual gift they have received. Yes, they *must* come out. And it is our responsibility to point this out to them.

And then the question begs to be asked: Are we demonstrating love if we shelter them from this truth?

> *"Am I therefore become your enemy, because
> I tell you the truth?"* (Gal. 4:16)

On this tape I heard reference after reference to the Vatican — what the Vatican wanted and what the Vatican didn't want — and this from Pentecostal and Charismatic preachers.

The statement was emphatically made that "the Vatican has moved much closer to our position."

Brethren, the Vatican has not moved at all. It is *we* who have moved closer to *their* position.

No, I am not "picking on Catholics." I would say the same things to the Protestant brethren. When a false doctrine of any stripe is transplanted into the kingdom, it must be stripped of its camouflage.

However, there is something we must remember:

We may disagree on the nonessentials (such as sanctification, the pretribulational rapture, evidence of the infilling of the Holy Spirit, and a host of other matters), but we must never disagree on the essentials. By this I mean the universal biblical basis for salvation.

Basically, even though most Protestant denominations disagree on the peripheral interpretations of Scripture, there is almost universal acceptance of the *fact* of salvation, which is faith and trust alone in the *atoning sacrifice of Christ*. On the other hand, within Catholicism, the basis of salvation is not faith, but works. There is no way these can be reconciled.

IS "SPEAKING IN TONGUES" A CONFIRMATION THAT EVERYTHING IS SATISFACTORY — THAT GOD CONDONES ERRANT DOCTRINES?

We believe that speaking in tongues is the initial, physical evidence that one has received the baptism in the Holy Spirit (Acts 2:4).

However, the fact that God has baptized an individual in the Holy Spirit in no way implies that this individual has suddenly become a repository of infinite knowledge and that he is no longer capable of error. It simply means that an individual has been saved by the blood of Jesus and has evidenced faith to receive the infilling of the baptism in the Holy Spirit.

The Corinthian church could hardly be held up as an example of doctrinal infallibility. The Apostle Paul wrote two books (I and II Corinthians) correcting the many errors within this church. Yet, they had been baptized in the Holy Spirit with the evidence of speaking in other tongues. The mere fact that they had been baptized in the Holy Spirit, however, in no way led Paul to approve their erroneous doctrines.

He strongly admonished them:

> *"Now I beseech you, brethren, by the name*
> *of our Lord Jesus Christ, that ye all speak the*

*same thing, and that there be no divisions
among you; but that ye be perfectly joined
together in the same mind and in the same judgment"* (I Cor. 1:10).

WE MUST PREACH TRUTH

He did not hesitate to preach the truth to them.

Paul had no alternative. Yet, to gain the "acceptance"
of the Catholic hierarchy, we will abandon every standard
and mute our voices.

I will say it again.

*We should love them. We should pray for them. We
should treat them with all kindness and consideration. But
we must tell them the truth!*

I'm sorry but I can't, in good conscience, sit on any
board or committee in company with Catholics who are
still praying to Mary, who are still confessing to priests,
and who are still attending mass — thinking it delivers
salvation to them. Even though they may speak in tongues
and talk about some form of "world evangelization," God
cannot bless activities based on such false premises. In all
honesty, there will be no world evangelization if it is to
be delivered on a scaffolding of false doctrine.

God cannot bless error. He cannot bless teachings that
are clearly contrary to His Word, especially when they
oppose the most basic of Christian tenets.

How can we join hands with those who believe in
baptizing infants, thinking this act is responsible for their
salvation? Brethren, these doctrines are of the devil. For
there to be any type of Holy Spirit unity based on the Word
of God, these evil, erroneous, wicked doctrines — born in
hell for the express purpose of the loss of souls — must be
abandoned and denounced.

Yes, we have disagreements in regard to peripheral doctrines. But we *must* hold the line when it comes to the basic fact of salvation. If we don't, there can never be any ground for agreement.

What are we doing?

We are trying to build unity from difference and harmony from discord, and we're trying to mix darkness with light.

I doubt if there are many preachers of the gospel who can speak with more authority on this subject than I. In the some 145 countries throughout the world where our telecast is aired, many are predominately Catholic. I believe I can state without fear of contradiction that we've seen more Catholics brought to the Lord Jesus Christ than any other ministry in the world. I think that the number must be well into the hundreds of thousands.

And how did we do this?

Not by compromising the Word of God. We did it by loving them, by being kind and compassionate toward them, but at the same time (and in no uncertain terms) *telling them the truth.*

What kind of doctor would place a Band-Aid over a cancer? What kind of an engineer would accept an improper mix of concrete for the bridge he was building? And what kind of preacher would hide the gospel of Jesus Christ from those who walk in darkness?

Unity of the body? No, we don't want unity at any cost. We *do* want truth at any cost. Unfortunately, the two may well be mutually incompatible. *"Can two walk together, except they be agreed?"* (Amos 3:3)

CHAPTER 9

THAT I MAY THRUST OUT YOUR RIGHT EYE

 *"Then Nahash the Ammonite came up, and encamped against Jabesh-gilead: and all the men of Jabesh said unto Nahash, Make a covenant with us, and we will serve thee. And Nahash the Ammonite answered them, On this condition will I make a covenant with you, that I may thrust out all your right eyes, and lay it for a reproach upon all Israel"* (I Sam. 11:1, 2).

The incident described here occurred more than three thousand years ago. God had just anointed — through the prophet Samuel — Saul as king of Israel. Saul's new throne was in jeopardy. Israel was confronted by the mighty (and evil) forces of Nahash the Ammonite who had encamped before Jabesh-gilead. Nahash's forces were much greater than those within the city of Jabesh-gilead.

The Scriptures quoted describe how the men of Jabesh-gilead sued for peace with Nahash. *"Make a covenant with us,"* they pleaded, *"and we will serve thee."* Nahash's answer? *"On this condition will I make a covenant with you, that I may thrust out all your right eyes, and lay it for a reproach upon all Israel."*

THIS AGE-OLD CONFLICT CONTINUES

The name Jabesh-gilead meant *"hill of witnessing."*

"But ye shall receive power, after that the Holy Ghost is come upon you: and ye shall be witnesses unto me" (Acts 1:8).

The word Nahash meant *"bright, shining serpent."* So the analogy is obvious. Israel was God's witness in the world then, as *we* are God's witnesses today. Satan, through Nahash (the bright and shining serpent), opposed them. Satan, the serpent, opposes us today.

This conflict has existed since the beginning of time and will continue until the day the Lord Jesus returns. Satan not only desires to destroy us, but he also desires that we compromise our message and our mission by conceding his power over us. Although his price is high, millions are paying it today.

"THRUST OUT ALL YOUR RIGHT EYES"

Why this strange request to *"thrust out all your right eyes"*?

In addition to its symbolic and demeaning aspects, there was a practical reason for this request as well. Warriors of that day fought with swords in their right hands and shields in their left. The shields almost totally covered them from attack and were designed to be held over their faces, leaving only the right eyes available for vision. This is why Nahash demanded that all the fighting men of Jabesh-gilead (the hill of witnessing) have their right eyes put out. In effect, he was seeking to remove their potential for attack — or for defense — by making them blind.

MILLIONS TODAY HAVE ALLOWED SATAN TO PUT OUT THEIR RIGHT EYES

A Pentecostal preacher told me the other day, "I don't see anything wrong with today's movies." He couldn't "see" the filth and moral decay promoted by such pictures. Why? Because his "right" eye — the one that discerns the good and decent from the sordid and immoral — had been put out a long time ago. As such, what kind of witness can he be for God? Spiritually, he is effectively blind. And what does Scripture say?

> ". . . they [preachers] be blind leaders of
> the blind. And if the blind lead the blind, both
> shall fall into the ditch" (Matt. 15:14).

SHEPHERDS, SHEEPHERDERS, AND HIRELINGS

Sad to say, there are precious few shepherds today, and perhaps they have always been in too short supply. But there are scores upon scores of sheepherders.

What is the difference? *Sheepherders have no convictions;* they stand for nothing. They are more than content to let the sheep pick the easiest route while they just tag along, doing little more than whipping the stragglers into line. Sheep, of course, fall easily into the trap of accepting sheepherders for shepherds. Is it possible that many of today's pastors in the Pentecostal realm are little more than sheepherders?

Then there are the hirelings. *Hirelings are wolves in sheep's clothing.* They are individuals who exploit the body and have little concern for spiritual development and growth. They are there only for the personal gain they can derive from association with the flock.

With hirelings, everything comes down to money. One could label the so-called "Christian" rock and roll singers as hirelings. They call themselves the new prophets of the youth, but behind all of them the major motivation is money. Their inspiration comes from the demigods of the rock culture — and they have the audacity to link this with the Holy Spirit. These are hirelings in the grossest inter-pretation of the word.

Still other hirelings are the purveyors of today's so-called "prosperity gospel." Many of these know in their hearts that it is wrong, but they have gone so far down this path that they fear making a clean break. If they did, would they not lose their audiences? But the gullible devotedly seek to find a quick and easy way to become rich — and so much the better if it can all be cloaked in spirituality. These too are hirelings.

And so we have shepherds, sheepherders, and hire-lings intermixed within our Pentecostal community.

EVANGELISTS

The early churches were started by evangelists. When the Apostle Paul founded the individual churches at Thessalonica, Philippi, Corinth, etc., he was an evangelist. (He also served as pastor, teacher, apostle, and prophet as well.) Most of the apostles served as evangelists at one time or another. In fact, the four gospels are called the "Evangelists."

Just about every major church in Protestantism was founded by evangelists. John Wesley was an evangelist when the great Methodist church began. The Holiness movements basically were started the same way. Bud Robinson was the evangelist used in the Nazarene movement. The same thing took place during the beginnings of the great Baptist movement.

Oh, yes, many of the men who functioned during those early stages were pastors, but they were serving as evangelists as they planted the seeds that would soon bloom into great movements.

When we look at the Pentecostal movement, I think it becomes clear that evangelists started just about every Pentecostal fellowship in existence today. Are we demeaning the role of the pastor, teacher, etc. when we point this out? No! But I would like to stress this in light of the fact that the evangelist is under fire today. How many evangelists do we have in Pentecostal circles today? When one looks to the denominational world, there are almost none, and, unfortunately, the situation within Pentecostalism is little better.

When Frances and I began this ministry in 1958, there were a number of good evangelists in the field. Today, there aren't a handful. The role of the evangelist has been diminished almost to the point of extinction. As a general rule, college professors make fun of them. Teaching is now exalted as the backbone of the Pentecostal movement. Pastors are still looked up to and respected (which is the way it ought to be), while evangelists are ridiculed (which is the way it ought *not* to be).

I cannot answer for all Pentecostal fellowships, but within the Assemblies of God (wherein I am ordained), if there ever has been an evangelist asked to sit on a decision-making committee, I am not aware of it. The few that are left are totally ignored, and, as far as I know, they always *have* been ignored.

"When the evangelist dies, everything dies." Does this demean the role of the teacher, the pastor, the prophet, and the apostle? Certainly not. But God gave the *fivefold* ministry (as delineated in Ephesians 4) for a specific reason. When any one of these members weakens (or dies), all the others are rendered that much less effective. If there are no teachers, there is no growth. If there are no pastors, there are no shepherds. If there are no apostles, there are no "sent ones." If there are no prophets, there is no "thus saith the Lord." And if there are no evangelists, there is no evangelism.

Today we have tried to replace the evangelist with door-to-door visitation, soul-winning teams, street ministries, cell groups — and a hundred and one additional plans and projects. Now, all these methods may be good (or sometimes not so good), but *nothing* will ever replace the well-balanced, Holy Spirit-anointed, and God-designed ministry.

WHY ARE THERE
SO FEW EVANGELISTS TODAY?

Now this is where we get to the root of the problem. Evangelists are born in Holy Spirit revival, in churches where the Spirit of God is moving and souls are being saved — and by saved we do not mean indoctrination or membership drives, we mean born again. When believers are filled with the Holy Spirit, a Pentecostal atmosphere prevails. It is in this atmosphere that evangelists are born and called.

I predict that out of our Family Worship Center and the Jimmy Swaggart Bible College there will come *scores* of evangelists and missionaries. If this does not happen, I pray

God will raise up a *different* ministry that *will* produce evangelists. If we do not have evangelists, the Pentecostal movements will surely die.

Who do you have today who describe themselves as "evangelists"? We have television talk show hosts. We have counselors (who come under every persuasion and stripe). We have seminar directors. We have prosperity promoters. But we have precious few evangelists. The system may be large and growing, but is this a healthy growth? Cancerous tumors grow, but no one would ever claim they are healthy. Eventually they will kill you. And despite the "growth" we are seeing today, the Pentecostal churches are dying.

At a recent NRB (National Religious Broadcasters) convention, reporters were asking broadcasting owners and general managers what type of ministry would be forthcoming in the near future. The answer, by and large, was this: "The old fire-and-brimstone days are over. This is the age of family counseling — the seminar."

I thought, when I heard this, "God, help us."

Are seminars important? Can they be productive? Certainly. They often perform a valuable service. But once again, God's order is never displaced.

> *"There was a man sent from God, whose name was John"* (John 1:6).

Individuals who teach seminars are almost inevitably trained by other *men*. They are seldom called by God. They see an opportunity and respond to it. Now there is nothing wrong with this. However, the calling of the evangelist (just like that of the pastor, teacher, apostle, and prophet) comes straight from God. These other ministries would fall into the classification of "helps."

There are few evangelists today, because the seedbed of evangelism has been misplaced. The shouts of praise and the hallelujahs are sadly missing. Weeping at the altar is rarely heard anymore. Our young people are encouraged to obtain degrees in everything from A to Z.

On the other hand, evangelists are born before the altar; they are formed in the crucible of the fire of God, as the Spirit of God touches their hearts and lives. But such a climate too little prevails in our modern-day Pentecostal churches — and, as a result, we are seeing fewer and fewer evangelists.

This is the call (among other things) that God placed on my life. I would not step down to be President of the United States.

A lot of people have asked me, "Why do you preach as you do? Why do you say the things you say?"

They look a little confused when I tell them, "This is what God called me to do."

"Preach the word; be instant in season, out of season; reprove, rebuke, exhort with all long-suffering and doctrine . . . do the work of an evangelist" (II Tim. 4:2, 5).

These *specific* tasks, among others, are the literal work of the evangelist.

ARE WE DIVIDING THE BODY?

Today, if anyone preaches the unadulterated Word and reproves and rebukes, he is accused of "dividing the body." As a consequence, we now have puppets instead of prophets.

Today we wallow in conformity. No one is supposed to be *against* anything. We must never disagree. We are, instead, to approve all winds of doctrine. We are living in an age of *compromise*.

The other day a lady wrote that her church was having a Catholic priest in to minister. An Assemblies of God school had a Catholic priest lecturing to its students.

Now we should love our Catholic friends and do everything we can to help them; however, Catholic doctrine is unscriptural. It is literally leading millions to hell. And to place a Catholic priest in a position of spiritual leadership before our people is appalling.

Today our teenagers have little idea of what is right and what is wrong. Where does the problem lie? The problem, in all too many cases, is occupying the *pulpit*. Our preachers are not preaching anymore. (And to be perfectly frank, we are not even *developing* preachers. We are producing talk show hosts and individuals with conformist degrees.) As a result, within Pentecost, preaching is becoming a lost art — and this will prove to be our downfall.

Why do two million teenagers attempt suicide every year — and a number of them succeed? Why are so many of our teenage girls pregnant before they are married? Why do so many young people contract syphilis or gonorrhea? Now we can blame the kids, but that would be a mistake. The problem lies in the pulpit.

If the preachers of the gospel were men enough to stand and say, "Thus saith the Lord . . ." and tell their parishioners that social drinking is wrong and that premarital sex is wrong (and not stumble or equivocate in saying it); if they would condemn movies for what they are — purveyors of filth — and tell the people that dancing, gambling, nightclubbing, and partying are wrong; if pastors would caution young people and parents about the filth coming into their homes via television — we could prevent much of today's moral degeneration. But if anything *is* said nowadays, the preacher is accused of "dividing the body" or of "being controversial."

Of course, the body *needs* to be called to repentance — and desperately so. But today we are afraid we will hurt someone's feelings. Brothers and sisters, we *need* to hurt feelings!

Our preachers need to preach about hell again. They need to preach about heaven, and they need to preach repentance. We should be hearing about the Holy Spirit, and until the fallow ground is broken — with men and women coming down the aisles, tears streaming down their faces — there is no hope. But what are we doing?

We are holding seminars instructing people on how to become rich. We are telling our seekers to confess bank accounts or automobiles — when what they need are new hearts. We are referring the troubled to "Christian psychologists" when they need an old-fashioned bout with the Holy Spirit. We are coming up with this new thing called "inner healing" — when we should be preaching sanctification and justification. Today the role of the pulpit has become more and more *minor* while the counselor's office has become the very center of the church. As a result, we are dying.

We are going to have to come back to the pulpit. Men of God must again be empowered by the Holy Spirit to stand up and preach the Word — irrespective of who does or does not like it. That is the reason God calls preachers.

No, this may not be a pleasant message, and maybe it never was pleasant. But just because it *is not* pleasant does not mean we can turn our backs on it and preach only love and understanding for *everyone*.

We *should* love everyone. But to truly love someone ultimately demands that we tell them the truth. The self-serving, ear-tickling pap that passes for love today is not love at all — it is hypocrisy. Love everyone. Don't disagree.

Accept anything. Never reprove or rebuke. Is this scriptural? I maintain that it is not at all scriptural, it is satanic!

I wonder what caused Cain to murder Abel? I wonder why the world thought Enoch and Noah were crazy?

Jeremiah was buried in mud up to his armpits. Tradition says Isaiah was sawed in half.

Tradition tells us that every single apostle except John died a martyr's death. The Apostle Paul was beheaded.

Is it possible that most of our preachers have lost their convictions? Why do they think nothing is *wrong* anymore? Why is any wind of doctrine acceptable? One Pentecostal preacher said the other day that God is not interested in our doctrines or what we believe. What must be the source of *that* statement?

BUT WHAT DID PAUL SAY? AND JOHN?

"All scripture is given by inspiration of God, and is profitable for doctrine, for reproof, for correction, for instruction in righteousness: That the man of God may be perfect, throughly furnished unto all good works" (II Tim. 3:16, 17).

"Whosoever transgresseth, and abideth not in the doctrine of Christ, hath not God . . . If there come any unto you, and bring not this doctrine, receive him not into your house, neither bid him God speed: For he that biddeth him God speed is partaker of his evil deeds" (II John 9-11).

Obviously, some are *not* using the Word of God but are seeking more "acceptable" doctrines.

Paul told Timothy:

" . . . do the work of an evangelist" (II Tim. 4:5).

Now I always thought Paul was saying that Timothy was an evangelist — but I now realize I was wrong. Going to the Greek root word we find what Paul was *really* saying. He started out in that chapter by saying:

> *"I charge thee therefore before God."*

This is, therefore, God's charge to the young pastor, Timothy — the one upon whose shoulders he is now placing responsibility for care of the churches, and for leadership and maintenance of the faith once delivered unto the saints. It is given in view of the spiritual dissolution and departure from true doctrine which had even then begun — and which is seeing its culmination in our day.

In verse two, where he told Timothy to *"preach the word,"* it was in the verb form of a summary command, to be obeyed at once as if given in a military situation. The words would be characterized by the note of authority which would command the attention and reaction of the listener. In short, there is no place for hesitation or deviation in the pulpit of Jesus Christ.

The preacher, as a herald, cannot choose his message. He is *given* the message to proclaim by his Sovereign. If he chooses not to proclaim it, he should immediately abdicate his position as a messenger.

He is to proclaim the Word not only when the time is opportune and favorable — but also when circumstances seem completely *un*favorable.

The Greek word for "reprove," in II Timothy 4:2, speaks of a rebuke, which would result in the guilty party's admission of guilt (or, if not in his confession, at least in his conviction of sin). Thus the preacher is to deal with sin, either in the lives of his unsaved hearers or in the lives of the saints to whom he ministers. He is to do so with no compromises.

The word "sin" does not seem to be in our preaching vocabulary anymore. However, a preacher has to be specific and deal directly with the sin confronting him as he preaches. He is to expect results — the salvation of the lost and the sanctification of the saints.

The word "rebuke," in the Greek, implies a sharp, severe reprimand, with perhaps a suggestion of impending penalty. Even where the preacher has experienced a failure (or a *series* of failures), he is to persist in attacking sin.

Not only is he to speak out strongly against sin, he is to *exhort*. And this word carries the idea of support and encouragement.

In the third verse, Paul speaks about individuals heaping to themselves teachers having itching ears. Such teachers give people only what they want — not what they *need*.

In verse five, Timothy is warned to watch and to endure afflictions. The word "endure" means to undergo with military stoicism.

How sorely the ministry needs that injunction today.

We are so afraid to come out clearly in support of the truth. We tremble at the idea of taking a stand against false doctrine, fearing the rejection, and even ostracism, of our fellow ministers and the ecclesiastical displeasure of our superiors — or the cutting off of our means of livelihood.

And then, in the fifth verse, when Paul tells Timothy to *"do the work of an evangelist,"* he really means that the local pastor should be evangelistic in his message and his methods. Along with his teaching, he must also stand boldly against sin.

THEIR RIGHT EYES ARE BLINDED BY NAHASH

Pentecostal preachers are calling out people for "psychological rehabilitation." Sin is not called sin anymore; it is "psychological." Thus man does not need repentance, but "rehabilitation."

But sin is still sin, and sin calls for repentance. Why do preachers miss the mark so widely today? Is it possible they have compromised with Nahash and had their right eyes blinded?

One pastor told a friend the other day that he would never think of calling people down the aisle to publicly pray before the Lord. He considered this "uncouth." Has Nahash put out his right eye?

After the Sunday service in one Pentecostal church recently, the pastor stepped to the pulpit (after the guest speaker had finished) and invited the congregation to come back to the church recreation room and watch the Super Bowl on television. *He is blind; his right eye has been put out by Nahash.*

A rock singer came to the Lord. He cut his hair, took the earring out of his ear, and cleaned himself up because Jesus had come into his heart. But his pastor told him to let his hair grow back and to replace the earring in his ear. If he would *continue* to sing rock and roll, perhaps he could attract young people to the church. Is this pastor blind? Has his eye been put out? Has he made a covenant with the bright and shining serpent?

Oh, yes, that young rock artist might draw people to the *church,* but he won't be drawing them to Jesus Christ!

"And if the blind lead the blind, both shall fall into the ditch" (Matt. 15:14).

Anything goes anymore. Drinking is fine — if it's "social" drinking. Gambling is all right — as long as you don't get hooked. There's nothing wrong with "good, clean, wholesome" dancing. Nightclubbing is perfectly okay — as long as the entertainer is a professed Christian. (There's nothing wrong anymore with *professed* Christians entertaining in nightclubs!) Going to a concert to hear a country and western star isn't wrong.

These things *are* wrong. They are destroying our young people, just as surely as if a gun were being placed to their heads and the trigger pulled. We are killing them because the preachers' lips are sealed. If we say anything, we might "divide the body of Christ."

I KNOW THERE ARE STILL SOME GODLY MEN OUT THERE

I know there are preachers out there who haven't made a covenant with Nahash and who still believe in the old-fashioned power of God and winning souls. I know there are still those who stand up *against* sin and *for* righteousness. I know there are preachers who spend their time studying the Word of God and who have heard from heaven. But there just aren't enough of them.

I cry before God, "Raise up pastors who will be shepherds. Raise up, O Lord, evangelists who will cry, 'Thus saith the Lord.' Raise up men and women who will hold true to their convictions, who will stand for something, who will believe in something.

"Send us preachers who will abhor the itching-ear gospel, men who will take a stand regardless of what it costs and preach without fear or favor, men who will preach repentance, men who will call sin by its name.

"Deliver unto us men who will reprove and rebuke — as well as show tenderness, sympathy, and love. Deliver unto us preachers who, in thundering tones, will preach the Word, mincing no words, pulling no punches, blowing the trumpet with no uncertain sound.

"Send us men who will not compromise their message, even if their churches won't accept it — men who, if the money doesn't come in, still won't compromise their principles. Give us leaders who will lead — instead of bowing down to political expediency."

The Pentecostal ministry is standing today at Jabesh-gilead, the hall of witnessing. They are faced by Nahash, the bright and shining serpent. There is going to be a battle. Blood is going to be spilled. The men of Jabesh-gilead say, *"Make a covenant with us, and we will serve thee."*

The price is stiff. Nahash the Ammonite says, in effect, "Then I must thrust out your right eyes."

WHAT IS THE ANSWER?

> *"And the spirit of God came upon Saul when he heard those tidings, and his anger was kindled greatly"* (I Sam. 11:6).

The *only* answer is the Spirit of God. Our degrees won't do it, our great church buildings won't do it, our counseling sessions won't do it, rock concerts won't do it, and "inner healing" won't do it. But the Spirit of God *can* come, just as He came to Saul.

When this happens, we will get angry with a good Christian anger. We will be enraged at sin. We will hate the destructive powers of Satan. It will be a holy anger, but the anger *will* be there.

Which will it be — *"And the spirit of God came . . ."* or *"Make a covenant with us, and we will serve thee"?*

We are at the devil's bargaining table — and only we can make the choice.

CHAPTER 10

CHRISTIAN ENTERTAINMENT

 "For ye were sometimes darkness, but now are ye light in the Lord: walk as children of light: (For the fruit of the Spirit is in all goodness and righteousness and truth;) Proving what is acceptable unto the Lord. And have no fellowship with the unfruitful works of darkness, but rather reprove them" (Eph. 5:8-11).

I was speaking the other day with the publisher of a popular music magazine. He said, "Brother Swaggart, I'll admit that a lot of contemporary Christian music has no spiritual foundation. But it is good clean Christian entertainment."

After he left, I thought about his words. And even though it may seem shocking, I have to say that there is no such thing as Christian "entertainment."

A. W. Tozer once said that the church had for centuries stood against worldly entertainment, recognizing it as a device for wasting time, a refuge from conscience, and a scheme to divert attention from accountability. Now, he added, it seems the church has decided to embrace the god Entertainment.

173

ENTERTAINMENT: THE
GREATEST GROWTH-INDUSTRY

I think it is obvious that one of the greatest growth-industries in this nation (and throughout the world) is the entertainment industry:

- Hollywood is putting out the most expensive movies ever. They're individually grossing hundreds of millions of dollars.
- The record business is booming.
- The rock concert industry has always been big, and it still is.
- Theme parks have become monstrous — and they've just announced that a huge Disney World complex is to be built in Paris.

It could probably be said that this is the largest growth-industry in this country — and in the world.

This same spirit of *play now, pay later* has permeated the church. It is subtle and has been accepted by most Christians — and this is what makes it so dangerous. It's called "good clean Christian entertainment" (among other things) and has become widespread throughout the church of the living God. Just as it is now one of the largest growth-industries in the secular world, it has also become widespread within the religious world.

But a question must be asked. Is there actually such an entity as *"Christian* entertainment"? To be honest, as well as realistic, the answer must be a resounding *no!*

While I realize this will not please a large segment of the so-called Christian population, it is, nevertheless, the truth. Christian entertainment, as far as the Word of God is concerned, has never existed in the past, *and it does not exist today!*

There *are* Christians who are in the entertainment business. There are Christians who either themselves entertain, or who participate in some aspect of the entertainment business. Of course, some of this is harmless and innocent, and some *isn't*. Nevertheless, "Christian" entertainment is a misnomer.

The theory is that the Christian community should provide optional entertainment so Christians will have a wholesome alternative. However, this whole concept is un-Christian and unscriptural. And further, it holds no basis in fact.

THE HOLY SPIRIT IS NOT IN THE ENTERTAINMENT BUSINESS

One can search in vain throughout the New Testament for any type of approval (or even suggestion) of what we refer to today as entertainment. It just doesn't exist. To be brutally frank, any time entertainment *is* mentioned, it is in a negative sense.

In Exodus 32, we read of Israel's sin in constructing the golden calf. In the sixth verse, it says:

> *"And they rose up early on the morrow, and offered burnt offerings, and brought peace offerings; and the people sat down to eat and to drink, and rose up to play."*

Just the other day, I turned on my television and saw what was purported to be a Christian play. I watched as girls danced lasciviously. Nothing reflected the things of God, but portrayed, instead, demonic activity. I was repulsed, and I sensed that the Holy Spirit was displeased, immensely so.

I once heard A. N. Trotter say, *"The reason people do such things is that they do not understand the holiness of God."*

During His three and one-half years of public ministry, the Lord Jesus Christ touched the very heart of Israel. And there isn't a single instance recorded where the Holy Spirit (who anointed Him to do what He did) led Jesus to "entertain" the people. Jesus said:

> *"I must be about my Father's business"*
> (Luke 2:49).

That business obviously did not include pandering to the carnal, the sensual, or the frivolous nature of man.

We are told in John 16, verses 8-11, what the Holy Spirit represents:

> *"And when he is come, he will reprove the world of sin, and of righteousness, and of judgment: Of sin, because they believe not on me; Of righteousness, because I go to my Father, and ye see me no more; Of judgment, because the prince of this world is judged."*

I don't find entertainment included anywhere where the works of the Holy Spirit are described.

THE WORK OF GOD
IS A DEADLY SERIOUS BUSINESS

> *"Thou therefore, my son, be strong in the grace that is in Christ Jesus. And the things that thou hast heard of me among many witnesses, the same commit thou to faithful men, who shall be able to teach others also. Thou therefore*

endure hardness, as a good soldier of Jesus Christ. No man that warreth entangleth himself with the affairs of this life; that he may please him who hath chosen him to be a soldier" (II Tim. 2:1-4).

The salvation of souls is the most compelling business on the face of the earth. The spiritual warfare in which we are engaged is a warfare unto the death; no quarter is asked and none is given. Satan is not in sympathy with anything we're doing, and *it's going to take more than "clean Christian entertainment" to set the captives free.*
Our God-given business is:

• The salvation of souls;
• Victorious Christian living by the power of the Holy Spirit;
• Healing of sick bodies; and
• Preaching the soon and eminent return of Jesus Christ.

Every ounce of strength we can muster is required to see these aims advanced from concept to accomplishment. It isn't fun and games; it is the greatest, most powerful, and most deadly serious work on the face of the earth.

TOTAL FULFILLMENT CAN BE ACCOMPLISHED ONLY IN JESUS CHRIST

Many will no doubt feel that we are trying to promote some type of spiritual asceticism — which is to deprive oneself of any form of pleasure or enjoyment. Actually, nothing could be further from the truth. We're trying to promote the very opposite. The truth is, anything that is of this world will never bring any true sense of fulfillment.

Only total commitment to the Lord Jesus Christ can do that. We are to be *in* the world, but not *of* the world.

> *"Love not the world, neither the things that are in the world. If any man love the world, the love of the Father is not in him. For all that is in the world, the lust of the flesh, and the lust of the eyes, and the pride of life, is not of the Father, but is of the world"* (I John 2:15, 16).

This, of course, is where many Christians have a problem. They are in the world, and also, to a lesser or greater degree, *of* the world. As a result, they live in a spiritual twilight zone. They can't immerse themselves completely in the world's pleasures because of conscience, but at the same time they deprive themselves of a fulfilling relationship with God for a lack of consecration.

Oh, yes, they're saved, but they really never come to know the satisfaction that depends on total abandonment to Jesus. By the same token, they can't truly embrace mammon because they *have* been delivered from darkness. So they end up sitting on the fence. There's little fulfillment and no real joy. They're holding onto the world with one hand and grasping for God with the other. And it simply cannot be done.

Absolute commitment to Jesus Christ is the only totally satisfying involvement for man. And to be completely frank and honest, most of the entertainments of this world — even those we might rate as harmless or innocent — are not appropriate diversions for the child of God.

I think it is fair to say that today's entertainment is largely devoid of any wholesomeness. It caters to, and stirs, man's basest nature. It excites man.

Even those we accept as normal (such as baseball and football) have been almost completely perverted by the powers of darkness. Oh, the games themselves are innocent enough, but everything surrounding them seems to have been preempted by Satan. I'll explain.

Years ago, I was invited to attend my first professional football game. I sat there for half an hour before leaving. Why did I leave? Because all around me individuals were drinking heavily. Many were, frankly, drunk, and those who weren't seemed to be working diligently to get there. Profanity and foul language dominated the scene.

I'd never been to a game of this type before. I had been to high school football games as a youngster, and even played a little. But I'd never encountered anything like this. I have no idea what takes place at high school games today, but I hope it isn't like what I saw at that professional game. I pray that high school sports still retain some of the innocence of former days.

Then add to this the drugs endemic to the sporting scene, the gambling, and the complete disregard for the pledged word (as represented in signed contracts). What type of influence does this have on young people who are inclined to make examples of sports heroes?

I can't understand how the child of God can choose to place himself in the position of supporting and associating with anyone this sordid. Why would anyone choose to expose himself to such a cesspool of profanity, filth, and drunkenness? Any Christian who would knowingly do so has to be in serious spiritual trouble.

As a matter of fact, fan behavior at most public sporting events has become so degenerate that rules are being formulated to reduce alcoholic sales in the hope of eliminating brawls and near-riots. I think we can assume that the situation has become quite serious when even the world recognizes that it's getting out of hand.

And should a Christian feel at home in such a setting? I think not.

THE WAYS OF THE WORLD

You must understand that even though we speak of "wholesome Christian entertainment," it is still entertainment, and as such it is borrowed from the world. In other words, it is *"the way of the world."* The very *type* of entertainment that is being intruded into our Christian environment is basically mimicking mammon. Clean it up a little bit and put a more decent face on it, but basically its roots are still the same.

Professional choreographers are being hired to teach dance steps — for the so-called interpretive dancing within some of our churches. Christian music is aping secular music to the point where smoke pots are employed to reflect dancing strobe lights, giving the appearance of a rock concert.

Someone said, "But this draws the unsaved young people — and without it we couldn't interest them." Let me say something about this, and I hope I can state it convincingly:

Sacred music is *not meant* to draw unsaved young people or the unsaved in general. If it is sacred and holy, it will little *appeal* to them. Sacred (gospel) music is for one purpose only — and that is to worship God. If sacred music is drawing hordes of unsaved people, it just might be that our standards have been lowered — not that the world has elevated theirs.

In other words, without the Holy Spirit, music is a worldly work. We're simply running rock and roll shows.

We're bringing theme parks into our environment under the guise of "good clean Christian entertainment." I can't help but wonder how long it will be before we succumb to the methods of the other churches and start promoting bingo games and bars in the church basement.

Now you might throw your hands up in horror, but I fear we're much closer to this than anyone might realize.

I SUPPOSE I AM ABOUT THE MOST DISLIKED PREACHER IN THE WORLD BY OTHER PREACHERS

That's not a very pleasant thought. Oh, to be sure, I realize there are a lot of preachers who are praying for us and who love us. These stand behind us, and I thank God for them. At the same time, however, I'm afraid I have more *preachers* who dislike me than any other preacher in the world.

Admittedly, I am a highly visible preacher and that makes me an easy target. But I think I've learned the reason for much of this animosity.

Naturally when we point out what we believe to be incorrect doctrine, or doctrinal error, we inevitably incur resentment. This is understandable. That's not the real problem, however. Basically we're discussing preachers who have very little disagreement with what we're saying doctrinally. Still, they dislike us, and I think I know the reason they do.

Not long ago, one of the men who works with our overseas offices happened to be thrown in with several preachers of our affiliation. One of these was very critical of this ministry. The problem, it turned out, was that he didn't want to be deprived of the country and western music that he loved. Now let's think about this.

The people who *depend* on this ministry and this preacher are looking for spiritual guidance. So let's consider this: *Would you rather sit at the feet of a preacher who has prayed up on "Amazing Grace" — or with "Your Cheating Heart"?*

This is what we're discussing. Too many preachers — even Pentecostals — are offended when they're told it's harmful to attend movies. But how can a preacher sit in a theater and absorb the nudity, the profanity, and the filth pervading today's movies and come out with something edifying for the people in his charge? How can a preacher spend his time in a bowling alley and keep his mind on the things that will feed his sheep?

Can a true preacher listen to the rock that passes for gospel music today? Can he watch the smoke bombs as they go off and see the jarring motion of the strobe lights and deny that it's demonic? *Even the world understands its source.*

How can such a preacher weep for the lost and shout with the redeemed? How can he listen to country and western music, with all of its sexual overtones, infidelity, and outright filth? Even some of the country and western stars have admitted that *"our music has done more to drag down the morals of this nation than anything else."* Still, a preacher can support such garbage — and think he's preaching the gospel of Jesus Christ!

How can a preacher put a country and western singer, a Hollywood actor, or some so-called Christian entertainer in his pulpit, knowing he or she supports a life-style that *degrades* the Christian image? Oh, they might well be *philosophically Christian,* but what of their example? Can such a pastor truly expect his church to be grounded and anchored in the faith?

How many young people have been "turned on" to nightclubs because their pastor placed an entertainer in his pulpit — or a televangelist placed one on his program — who purports to be a Christian? If they appear in the church or on a Christian television program, while at the same time appearing in nightclubs, the nightclubs then do not look so bad.

I wonder when Christians are going to stop supporting with their money this heresy?

As A. W. Tozer said, *"We could not conquer the great god Entertainment — so we embraced him instead."*

ROCK AND ROLL CHURCHES

A strange contradiction, to be sure, but they do exist today.

We now have churches, and sad to say they're almost all in the Charismatic ranks, that could well be labeled "Rock and Roll" churches. What do we mean by this?

These churches have become a haven for "religious" rock and roll stars. The rock and roll mentality, which is a symptom of our sick world system, is brought directly into the church of the living God. These individuals are made to feel welcome and a part of the so-called body of Christ.

Not surprisingly, these churches draw their adherents mainly from the young people and the younger married couples. There is great deference paid to the "teaching ability" of the pastor. Tragically, it's not the Word of God that's being taught, however. Precious little attention is paid to sin. Instead, a so-called "positive gospel" is preached.

Unfortunately, in the majority of such churches, there is little foundation in the Word of God or in standards. Social drinking and partying are accepted, and movies and dancing are commonplace. And we wonder why such churches produce as many divorces as the world!

A little "dancing before the Lord," tongues and interpretations, some so-called demonstrations of the gifts of the Holy Spirit, and all is made to seem spiritual. Obviously, this is "the way to go."

To be frank, we're discussing the rock and roll mentality; it's the philosophy of the world. It is borrowed from the world and then cloaked with a thin veneer of Christianity to make it palatable to poor misguided Christians.

The individuals attending these churches discover (too late) that this unholy alliance is incompatible with true Christianity. When the crunch comes — and it will come — Satan will laugh because he has once again been allowed to intrude into an area where he has no place.

WHAT HAVE I DONE TO THEM?

I've often wondered at the terrible animosity directed toward this ministry. I've asked myself, "What have I *done* to them? What have I said that offended them?"

And almost without exception I find they want to speak in tongues and call themselves full-gospel — while attending their parties, movies, and rock and roll concerts.

They want to seem spiritual while, at the same time, they are drinking and dancing. They want to wallow in the mire of country and western music without being reminded of its evil influence. But, ladies and gentlemen, they're *wrong*. The world is our enemy, and we must as Christians be extremely careful in how we deal with it.

"BOOGIE"

"But we have this treasure in earthen vessels, that the excellency of the power may be of God, and not of us" (II Cor. 4:7).

I want to draw your attention particularly to the latter portion of this Scripture where it says *"and not of us."*

I believe in dancing before the Lord. I feel that the exuberance and joy manifested within a church service is a God-send to those who strive to worship the Lord in *"the beauty of holiness."*

I remember, some years ago in a revival we were conducting, a man who would run during every service. He didn't make a disturbance, he didn't bother anyone, he would just run.

On some nights the service would be buoyant and joyous, and he would run. Then on other nights, when the service was somber and serious, he would run.

I found out later why he did this. (And please understand, he didn't make a spectacle of himself, and he was not giving vent to fanaticism. This was a genuine "delight" in his heart before the Lord.)

This man had been sent home by the Mayo Clinic to die. He had a crippling disease that had twisted his body to a degree that beggared description. The Veterans Administration had even sent his family a check for $300 to help pay funeral expenses.

The doctors said it was impossible for him to live. Because of the pain, it would take him up to thirty minutes to put on a shirt. To make the story short, one Sunday morning he was gloriously healed. It was an undeniable miracle. It stirred the hearts of the entire city.

In talking with him one day at his place of work, he said (with tears in his eyes), "Brother Swaggart, you may wonder why I run during services. But there was a day when I couldn't run. I couldn't even walk. My body was bowed together, the bones were twisted and out of joint. And then the Lord Jesus Christ gloriously set me free. Now I feel that I *have* to run before the Lord as I worship Him."

Praise God, he *did* have to run, and he should have.

So anyone who says that I don't believe in dancing in the Spirit, or dancing before the Lord, doesn't know what he's talking about.

However, I'm concerned that little by little we've turned church services into nothing more than dance marathons. It's getting to where people have become convinced that if the services don't feature dancing prominently, they've been deprived of their chance to dance before the Lord. Their conclusion? Obviously that such a church is not spiritual and they've been deprived of a proper service.

Soon they find themselves attending church specifically for the dancing. The Word becomes secondary. Elements of true importance take a back seat. Dancing before the Lord becomes paramount. I hate to be this blunt, but, in other words, they're going to church to "boogie."

THE SPIRIT OF THE WORLD

Paul said:

> *"Now we have received, not the spirit of the world, but the spirit which is of God"* (I Cor. 2:12).

Unfortunately we *have* received the spirit of the world. Oh, it doesn't come from God. Everything from God is freely given, it is spiritual — and naturally uplifting and fulfilling. The spirit of the world is none of these; it is that which Satan gives.

Of course it comes in many ways, but it is always of Satan. The spirit which characterizes his efforts and the whole field of entertainment certainly characterizes this *"spirit of the world."*

We have traded anointing for entertainment, and I am concerned that, as Dave Wilkerson said, *"Corrupt sheep will draw to themselves corrupt shepherds."*

WHAT IS GOING TO HAPPEN?

The great Pentecostal and Charismatic movement is even now in spirit accepting the same errors that have rent the non-Pentecostal denominations in the past. This has resulted in denominational splitting over the years, and if we Pentecostals and Charismatics don't tighten our ranks and *"look unto the rock whence [we] are hewn"* (Isa. 51:1), we can expect to see the Pentecostal community shattered as well.

Two rivers are flowing in the Pentecostal realm. They're side by side, but they're flowing in *opposite* directions. Satan is applying pressure at the same time the Holy Spirit is trying to influence. *Sadder still, the majority of today's preachers sit on the sidelines and take no stand.* But, in reality, by shirking their responsibilities, they *have* taken a stand, and it is on the side of the spirit of the world — as represented by the false god, Christian Entertainment.

Is there such a thing as "Christian entertainment"? No, there isn't. There are Christians (as we have stated) who are amused by worldly entertainment, and there are Christians who are professional entertainers. But when it comes to the entertainment industry — even though it has invaded the church wholesale — it is a devious ploy of Satan. Tragically, millions of Christians are being deceived, and so are many preachers.

A long time ago a great statesman-prophet by the name of Daniel, who was in the world but never a part of it, made this statement:

> *"And they that be wise shall shine as the brightness of the firmament; and they that turn many to righteousness as the stars for ever and ever"* (Dan. 12:3).

And then he said:

> *"Many shall be purified, and made white, and tried; but the wicked shall do wickedly: and none of the wicked shall understand; but the wise shall understand"* (Dan. 12:10).

CHAPTER | 11

THE WOMAN AND THE LEAVEN

"Another parable spake he unto them; The kingdom of heaven is like unto leaven, which a woman took, and hid in three measures of meal, till the whole was leavened" (Matt. 13:33).

This parable is one of if not *the* shortest ever given by the Lord Jesus Christ. (It contains only twenty-four words.) Because it is so short, it's easy to read past it quickly and completely miss its import. But, for all its brevity, it contains one of the most important messages to ever fall from the lips of our Lord. It is a warning so graphic and startling that it literally staggers the imagination.

Jesus was speaking specifically to the nation of Israel for that time, but His message has equal application to the Christian church today.

THE PARABLE OF THE LEAVEN

This parable warns that the kingdom of God, with its teachings and spiritual direction, would be infiltrated and subverted by false doctrines and counterproductive programs until the plan of God is totally perverted (Luke 18:8; I Tim. 4:1-8; II Tim. 3:5; II Pet. 3:3, 4). Considering this warning from God, it isn't surprising to see this precise scenario unfolding today.

Now for clarification let's dissect our Lord's words so we can better understand their application to our present situation.

THE WOMAN

In Scripture, the figure of a woman can be used to illustrate two diametrically opposed forces — good or evil. When used to represent evil, woman always suggests ultimate wickedness, lack of integrity, uncleanness, and infidelity.

"Jerusalem is as a menstruous woman among them" (Lam. 1:17).

"But thou didst trust in thine own beauty, and playedst the harlot" (Ezek. 16:15).

"And, behold, there was lifted up a talent of lead: and this is a woman that sitteth in the midst of the ephah. And he said, This is wickedness" (Zech. 5:7, 8).

Of course, woman can also be used as a type of Godliness and virtue, as in Revelation 12. But in the parable discussed here, Jesus uses her as a representation of evil.

WICKEDNESS IN THE CHURCH

Here, where the word "woman" is used by Jesus, it does not refer to the church itself. It refers instead to wickedness *within* the church. Now that may sound harsh, but I fear we are much closer to fulfillment of this parable than any of us might suspect. So let's look at both the Catholic and the Protestant churches as they exist today.

I have had — due to the call of God on my life — a great deal of contact with both priests and preachers. As a result, I suspect I might have a better insight into the clerical mind than most. And, of course, generalizations are always suspect.

Some priests do genuinely love the Lord and endeavor to please Him and do their best for the kingdom of God. Similarly, there are Protestant pastors within the various denominations who are truly spiritual individuals, striving to promote the kingdom of God. However, when taken in the broad view, the situation is bleak indeed. And while I know this sounds negative, the truth must be told.

A PARTICULAR PASTOR

The other day I was talking to a young man who is a former Catholic. He now pastors an Assemblies of God church in a major southern city. I asked him how he came to the Lord, and he recounted the events resulting in his salvation and baptism in the Holy Spirit — this being after a lifetime in which he and his whole family had known only Catholic doctrine.

I asked him how he came to make the break from the Catholic church. He laughed and said he didn't have to break away from the Catholic church, it broke away from him. Then he went on to describe how, standing before a Catholic congregation, he delivered the account of his conversion.

There wasn't one derogatory comment against the Catholic church in this testimony. But how did the church's priest react? In front of all the people, the priest publicly rebuked him — and called him a terrible name.

I asked him, "Do you mean that the priest actually addressed you by this profanity — and before the people?"

He laughed again and said, "It was nothing out of the ordinary; he did it all the time. And he also tended a bar across the street."

I have been criticized sternly — even by my Protestant brothers — for trying to bring truth to the Catholic people. But I have found that millions of Catholics are hungry for God. I know this to be a fact; I receive their letters and I talk to them. By and large, if they hope to receive any spiritual nourishment or instruction (according to the Word of God) from their priests, they will be disappointed. So if someone like myself doesn't step forward and bring them the truth, based on the Word of God, they will be eternally lost.

If there are hungry hearts out there, I believe the Holy Spirit will deliver the Word to them, slake their thirst, and satisfy their hunger. I thank God if I've had some small part in bringing this to pass.

Now I want to make something abundantly clear: When it comes to wickedness (as represented by the woman Jesus spoke of in Matt. 13:33), *there is just as much leaven infecting the Protestant churches as there is the Catholic.*

READ THIS!

The minister of a United Methodist church says a counseling program conducted by his church included nude therapy sessions.

"We were trying to find some way for our children to withstand the onslaught of sexuality that is stressed in advertising, television programs, and in other ways," he said.

The pastor went on to say that the sessions lasted about two months, with twenty to twenty-five men and women participating. He said there were about six experiments, some involving physical contact but none involving sexual intercourse.

At least one session — which a woman participant said was the first one and began spontaneously — was held in the church.

The account of the nude therapy sessions first surfaced during two child custody cases in which the husbands charged that their wives were unfit mothers because they had participated in the sessions, according to a particular newspaper.

The minister did not deny reports that the nude sessions included a weekend at a motel in Kenosha, Wisconsin. The pastor also would not deny a report that he and church leaders led therapy sessions in which men, women, and children breast-fed on women who had stripped to the waist. The pastor said that the United Methodist District Superintendent "was kept informed about what we were doing and said that we had his full support." This particular District Superintendent was not available for comment.

By and large, almost all denominational churches have turned their backs on God. Naturally, there are *exceptions,* and we thank God for them. There are Godly pastors in the denominational fold, but as a general rule the system is almost totally corrupt.

ONE CAN NO LONGER
LOOK TO HIS DENOMINATION

There was a time when a person could say, "I'm a Baptist" (or Methodist, or Presbyterian, or whatever) and a clear perception of his spiritual orientation would follow. But today this no longer applies.

I believe that God has emphatically directed me in recent months to say this:

The time has come when we must remove our eyes from denominations. We must completely ignore denominational affiliations. Instead, we must totally direct our eyes toward Jesus Christ and the Word of God.

Millions will be led astray and end up in hell because they aren't doing this. The vast majority of Christians know little or nothing about the Word of God. What little they do believe merely parrots the views of their pastors or their denominational hierarchy. They accept all denominational doctrines and, like sheep, follow serenely to the slaughter.

On the day they stand before God and He says, *"Depart from me, I've never known you,"* the shouts of protest will be deafening. They will point their fingers at their pastors and priests, but the pastors and priests won't be blamed. God will hold every individual responsible for his own salvation.

Every Christian must see what the Word of God says and personally look toward Jesus Christ. If your church doesn't teach this, *leave it and find one that does.*

THE LEAVEN

> *"Your glorying is not good. Know ye not that a little leaven leaveneth the whole lump? Purge out therefore the old leaven, that ye may be a new lump, as ye are unleavened. For even Christ our passover is sacrificed for us: Therefore let us keep the feast, not with old leaven, neither with the leaven of malice and wickedness; but with the unleavened bread of sincerity and truth"* (I Cor. 5:6-8).

Here the Apostle Paul is telling us (as the Master previously told us), *"A little leaven leaveneth the whole lump."* And this is the major problem in the Christian church today.

When Jesus mentioned leaven in Matthew 13:33, it represented sin, false doctrines, and hypocrisy. And what I'm about to say is at the heart of what He was talking about.

CHRISTIAN TELEVISION

I walked into our bedroom one morning before leaving for the office and the television was on. A Christian program was playing and a Nashville country and western star was featured.

I paused to watch as they went through their routine of telling jokes and putting on their "show." This has, of course, become quite common on "Christian" television. A Hollywood performer, a movie actor, a Nashville star, a television personality — they're all featured on Christian programs in the hope that they will attract a larger audience.

It used to be that disclaimers were used. These stated, "We don't agree with everything they do, but . . . ." Today, even this has apparently gone by the boards.

They rationalize that these people have a wide appeal and so the Christian programming will gain a wider audience, and thus do more good. Of course, the churches and television ministries that do this completely fail to understand the move, or plan, of God for the world today.

To begin with, God will accept no strange fire. Secondly, *a little leaven leaveneth the whole lump.* In other words, when you insert a small amount of leaven (yeast) into flour, the leaven will soon permeate the whole batch. And it only takes a minute amount to begin this process.

If you will recall, at the Passover Supper they ate only unleavened bread — because leaven was a type of sin. (And let's not forget, it is this same ingredient in leaven that is added to beer, which causes it to rot and ferment — thus giving it its alcoholic "kick.")

As we previously mentioned, the Apostle Paul used leaven as a symbol for sin, and we are facing the same problem today!

In Paul's day they were trying to insert "just a little" Hebrew law into grace. Of course, this couldn't work. *All* Hebrew law had to be totally eliminated as the "new vessel" of salvation-through-grace took its place.

The principle is the same today. We are endeavoring to use the ways of the world to further the work of God. And we do so because we really don't understand the holiness of God, or His ways.

"All the potential good," they say, "will surely outweigh the little bad."

However, this should be noted: *The small amount of leaven (evil) that is placed in a lump will gradually corrupt the whole lump.* The deceptive reasoning that is so prevalent in Pentecostal circles today will destroy the whole message as surely as I write these words on this paper.

There are quite a number of ministries today that people write us about. They say, "Yes, I'll admit there are a lot of things that aren't right in them, but they're doing so much good."

I beg to differ. *No good is being accomplished.* Some things are being done that might *appear* to be good, but this is only an illusion. I know that sounds strong, but what I'm saying is the truth, and I'll say it again.

Using these methods, no good is being accomplished!

God will simply refuse to operate under such conditions. Such an effort immediately becomes "religious" and is totally dependent on man's earthly ingenuity.

It may look good to the crowd and it may sound good to the masses, but inside it is rotten and corrupt — because leaven has been introduced.

FALSE DOCTRINES

Any false doctrine promulgated in a church, fellowship, movement, or denomination will eventually take its deadly toll. It will eventually corrupt the whole. Let's look, for instance, at the doctrine of "unconditional eternal security."

This unscriptural doctrine has so saturated the Baptist denomination (plus other fellowships) that millions today make little or no effort to live Godly lives. Still, they claim their "eternal security" as a result of this false doctrine.

What was once a *part* of Baptist doctrine has now become the whole. This rejection of the Holy Spirit and denial of the power of God was, in the beginning, only a small lump of leaven within the Baptist camp. Today it permeates the whole lump.

Or we can look at the Catholic church and its doctrine of "Mariolatry." This was, at one time, just a part of Catholic philosophy. But today the worship of Mary permeates the whole spectrum of Catholic thought.

"A little leaven leaveneth the whole lump."

THE MEAL

"The meal," as Jesus uses it here, represents the Word of God.

> *"Verily, verily, I say unto you, He that believeth on me hath everlasting life. I am that bread of life. Your fathers did eat manna in the*

*wilderness, and are dead. This is the bread
which cometh down from heaven . . . if any man
eat of this bread, he shall live for ever: and the
bread that I will give is my flesh, which I will give
for the life of the world"* (John 6:47-51).

Now I'm going to make a shocking statement: The
single most used instrument for promoting false doctrines
is the Word of God. All false teachings, false religious
programs, and professed "Christian lives" seek to hide
behind the Word of God. This gives them an air of surface
respectability and legitimacy, and it deceives so many,
many people.

False doctrines inevitably claim to be based on the
Word of God. All religious programs claim to be Bible-
based. All professed Christian teachings (which in reality
aren't Christian at all) claim a foundation in the Word.

This is why I stated at the beginning of this chapter
that individuals will have to be very judicious in evaluating
what is presented to them. Millions will be led astray. They
will see something over television — individuals will go
through all the spiritual motions, the right words will be
uttered, and it will "look good," "sound good," and
"appear to be right." But in reality it will be false teaching,
representing only *professed* Christianity — *and the leaven
will eventually corrupt the whole. The same can be said of
many churches across our land.*

Use of the meal (the Word of God) makes almost
anything appear legitimate. *Jesus said the leaven was
hidden in three measures of meal and the whole was
leavened.* Millions will be led astray and eternally lost
because they've been persuaded that "all is well."

YOU WILL HAVE TO UNDERSTAND

As a child of God, you will have to be *personally* knowledgeable in the Word. You will have to know and understand the moving of the Holy Spirit *in your life!* You will have to be able to look at what's being taught from your pulpit or on your television set in the name of Christianity, and be able to discern whether or not it's from God. You will have to be able to look through the thin veneer of religiosity and recognize the leaven.

And if the leaven is there, you will have to understand something else.

You will have to understand that many actions may be presented as being in the name of the Lord. It will even be pointed out that much good is being accomplished. But if this is based on leaven, great harm will result.

As a matter of fact, the whole effort will eventually be totally corrupted. It may take some time to recognize this, but that will be its ultimate end.

The only answer is to root out the leaven. That's what Paul said, as quoted from I Corinthians 5: *"Purge out therefore the old leaven"* (verse 7). This *must* be removed in the effort to be Godlike and Christ-centered — and to bring forth Christlike results.

God has a way of doing things that is not man's way.

"There is a way which seemeth right unto a man, but the end thereof are the ways of death" (Prov. 14:12).

God will not deviate from *His* way. He will not shift or veer the slightest degree. *It must be His way — or no way at all.*

CLOSER TO HOME

I've discussed the Catholic church and denominational Protestantism. Now I must state, as I've been suggesting for the past few paragraphs, that the Pentecostal movement is, as a whole, shot through with worldly leaven.

I still believe that the message being delivered by the Pentecostal churches is the message delivered within the Word of God. But this too appears to be changing. If the leaven is not purged out of our worship, our services, our thinking, and our music, we will go the way of all the others.

As mentioned elsewhere, the idea that the end justifies the means (despite the error of the means) might well be the *most dangerous* leaven of all.

The sad fact is that we are blind. We look at the meal. It's shot through with leaven and we don't recognize it. I have a letter on my desk right now from a pastor of a Foursquare church. He said this to me:

> Brother Swaggart, my heart is broken. I find myself weeping uncontrollably for what is happening in the name of Christ.

He went on to describe a so-called "Christian" concert he attended with his six-year-old.

> The music reeked with the ungodly spirit of rock. It had the audience dancing, but not before God. The sensual gyrations of the dancers were not those inspired by the Holy Spirit. The shouts and applause did not honor Christ — they honored the fleshly entertainers on the stage . . . Some say people can be reached in this manner for the Lord Jesus Christ, but this is debatable, especially in light of II Peter 2:19-21:

> *"While they promise them liberty, they them-*
> *selves are the servants of corruption: for of*
> *whom a man is overcome, of the same is he*
> *brought in bondage. For if after they have*
> *escaped the pollutions of the world through the*
> *knowledge of the Lord and Saviour Jesus Christ,*
> *they are again entangled therein, and overcome,*
> *the latter end is worse with them than the begin-*
> *ning. For it had been better for them not to have*
> *known the way of righteousness, than, after they*
> *have known it, to turn from the holy command-*
> *ment delivered unto them."*

I can only say "amen" to our good brother's observations. It is enough to make you weep for what is happening
in the name of Christ.

I PREDICT

If there isn't a reversal among our Pentecostal brethren,
I fear the following will take place very soon:

- "Christian" television programs will have dancing to
  worldly music — and all in the name of the Lord.
- They will soon be advocating social drinking — on
  "Christian" television.
- On "Christian" television, they will be openly promoting movies — and I mean those that are coming
  out of Hollywood, with all of its filth, degradation,
  and defilement of biblical standards.
- On Christian Pentecostal programming, they will be
  openly ridiculing the moving of the Holy Spirit and
  the power of God — in favor of secular humanism
  (or Pentecostal humanism?) and psychological gim-
  micks to solve the problems of man.

I predict these will spread to the churches — simply because millions (particularly young people) will view such on so-called Christian television and will be influenced. The sad fact is, most pastors won't even *recognize* the wrong. They will be swept along with the tide — and I predict that we will see all of this much sooner than anyone even suspects.

Tragically, Spirit-filled, tongues-speaking Christians will give their dollars to support it — even though the programming is shot through with leaven that it should be completely obvious. But it won't be recognized by a lot of Christians because *anyone* can sell them a bill of goods as long as the label on the sack is "meal" (the Word of God).

AN EXAMPLE

Some time ago my sister-in-law told her teenage daughter she couldn't watch "Solid Gold." But then her authority in the matter was eroded when a Pentecostal, Christian television show presented the host of Solid Gold on its program — and lauded the "consecrated and dedicated" life of this alleged Christian entertainer.

I hasten to add — to the good Christians who have never seen it — that the program in question is one of the most vulgar, ribald, and filthy offerings of musical pornography that's ever been aired over television.

By the one simple act of "showcasing" this host on Christian television, the program was "legitimized" in the eyes and minds of hundreds of thousands of Christian young people — making it extremely difficult for their parents to guide them in the path of righteousness.

My niece's words were these: "This is a Christian program. They're putting her on as their guest. They think it's all right. Why do you object?"

IN CONCLUSION

As I close this chapter, I realize that many will read it and conclude that there's only a mite of leaven in the meal. Unfortunately it is far beyond that.

Today the work of God, even in Pentecostal circles, is so filled with leaven that we are very close to seeing the whole meal corrupted. Tragically, many churches will follow the trend of so-called Christian television, powerless to do otherwise.

Two thousand years ago, when Jesus uttered these words, Judaism (the meal) was totally corrupted. They were only a short way from complete destruction.

Today, the church of the living God is close to the state that Judah was in two thousand years ago.

Is this meant to be negative? Do we mean to say that there will be no Christians ready when the rapture takes place? No, not at all.

I believe that many — perhaps millions — will recognize the leaven in the meal. I believe there is a tremendous move, fostered and nurtured by the Holy Spirit, that is driving people to their knees and causing them to search the Scriptures. And, little by little, they're beginning to look with skepticism at their denominations.

This will not necessarily mean that they will stop attending some specific church. What it does mean is that they are getting their eyes off preachers, denominations, and religion — and onto Jesus Christ.

It means they're blessed by certain preachers and blessed by certain fellowships — but they no longer follow anyone or anything blindly down the road just because the label is "meal."

But still I fear for millions who could be lost. The wickedness represented by the leaven is boiling and bubbling in the meal today. The Lord is winnowing. It's going to be more and more important to put your trust only in the Lord Jesus Christ.

Beyond Him, there is no hope.

CHAPTER 12

PENTECOSTAL HUMANISM

STRANGE FIRE

"And Nadab and Abihu, the sons of Aaron, took either of them his censer, and put fire therein, and put incense thereon, and offered strange fire before the Lord, which he commanded them not. And there went out fire from the Lord, and devoured them, and they died before the Lord" (Lev. 10:1, 2).

"And Nadab and Abihu died before the Lord, when they offered strange fire before the Lord, in the wilderness of Sinai, and they had no children" (Num. 3:4).

Nadab and Abihu were priests, ordained of God. They were sons of the Great High Priest, Aaron — Moses' brother.

Few men on earth have seen the positive manifestations of God that these two saw. God had invited them by name to accompany Moses as he had gone up Mt. Sinai to confer with God (Exo. 24:1-11). They had been set apart for the ministry (Lev. 8:13-36). Despite all this, they allowed egotism, self-pride, and drunkenness (Lev. 10:9) to confuse their spiritual direction and they died in God's fire. This was God's punishment to them for violation of their sacred office.

NADAB AND ABIHU'S SINS

- In the process of divine services, Nadab and Abihu deviated from God's prescribed plans.
- They offered strange fire — that of their own making and not of the altar — before Jehovah (Num. 3:4).
- They offered incense when not directed by God to do so.
- They failed to sanctify themselves before Jehovah and the congregation, which was in a state of religious ecstasy at the time (Lev. 9:24).
- They became drunk, and they conducted religious services while in this drunken condition (Lev. 10:9).

GOD GAVE THESE COMMANDS
TO AARON WHEN HIS SONS DIED

"Uncover not your heads, neither rend your clothes; lest ye die, and lest wrath come upon all the people: but let your brethren, the whole house of Israel, bewail the burning which the Lord hath kindled. And ye shall not go out from the door of the tabernacle of the congregation, lest ye die" (Lev. 10:6, 7).

He also told them, in effect, "You are not to mourn for the dead or show any sign of their death, even though these are your sons. Jehovah has judged these men correctly and nothing is to be done by the Great High Priest to make it look otherwise."

WHAT WAS THE STRANGE FIRE?

Nadab and Abihu took flames from their own cooking fire, and from a fire kindled near the tabernacle, and offered this to God. It was not fire from the altar, and God considered it "strange fire" because it had not been consecrated.

Nadab and Abihu knew they were to use only fire from the brazen altar for worship because it was a type of Calvary, always speaking of the innocent blood shed there. They were to offer this fire up on the altar of incense. The incense was to be poured over the fire, creating a beautiful fragrance and the smoke that would fill the holy place.

According to Hebrew tradition, the fire of the brazen altar was originally kindled by the Lord, and was thereafter maintained as a "perpetual flame" until the dedication of the temple of Solomon (II Chr. 7:1). Here the fire was *re*kindled by God (although it still burned) to show His approval of the ceremony.

> *"And there came a fire out from before the Lord, and consumed upon the altar the burnt offering and the fat: which when all the people saw, they shouted, and fell on their faces"* (Lev. 9:24).

The altar of incense was a worship altar and not an altar to be used for sacrifice. The only connection it had with sacrifice was that its fire came from the brazen altar where sacrifices were offered. There's an important lesson in this for us today:

God will accept no worship unless it is based on the fire of Calvary and the shed blood of the Lord Jesus Christ. Anything else is "strange fire."

Nadab and Abihu died for the act they committed — and rightly so. They knew the meaning of the brazen altar and what it represented. They also knew that only the fire from the brazen altar could be used for the incense offering. But drink addled their minds and they ignored God's injunctions. As a result, they died.

It must always be understood that departure from God's prescribed ways will result in spiritual death.

PENTECOSTAL FIRE

The great Pentecostal message, with its attendant worship, is a continuation of the old Levitical law. But that which was then done physically is now done spiritually.

We now offer holy worship to God from the altar of incense in our hearts. But it must still be understood that God will accept no worship from the altar of incense (spiritually speaking) unless it comes first from Calvary and the shed blood of Christ.

"But the hour cometh, and now is, when the true worshippers shall worship the Father in spirit and in truth: for the Father seeketh such to worship him. God is a Spirit: and they that worship Him must worship him in spirit and in truth" (John 4:23, 24).

If our worship doesn't follow God's prescribed way (coming from the fire derived from the holy altar of Jesus' sacrifice), it will bring death — just as surely as it brought death to Nadab and Abihu.

We have a real problem today in the second generation of Pentecostals who know little of the great Pentecostal experience.

The miraculous move of God, touching hearts and lives and gloriously changing them, has never really been experienced by many of the younger people in our churches. They have never really lived through their Pentecost.

The Holy Spirit baptism is a revolutionary experience. There is nothing in the worldly realm that can describe it. It truly mirrors John's great statement of two thousand years ago when he said:

> *"I indeed baptize you with water; but one mightier than I cometh . . . he shall baptize you with the Holy Ghost and with fire"* (Luke 3:16).

PENTECOSTAL TERMINOLOGY

Terminology common in the great days of the Pentecostal outpouring (such as "praying through," "the glory fell," "Pentecostal explosion," and "a mighty moving of the power of God") is still being used to some extent in Pentecostal circles today. But it is becoming less and less common because the phenomenon connected with the terminology is absent from many Pentecostal fellowships.

As a result, our young people have little personal experience with the moving of the Holy Spirit or the power of God. The Pentecostal experience has unfortunately degenerated into "getting saved and speaking in tongues." Of course, the experience should be infinitely more than this.

SECULAR *AND* CHRISTIAN HUMANISM

Most Christians are familiar with the term *secular humanism.* This basically means that man is the center of the universe — and there is no God. Consequently, seeking after God is unnecessary. Man can solve his own problems and bring about a utopian paradise — hence, the term *secular,* which means "earthly" or "worldly." *Humanism,* of course, refers to the human race.

In the denominational Christian world, Christian humanism has become the dominant philosophy.

Dave Hunt and T. A. McMahon, in their book *The Seduction of Christianity,* said the seduction of Christianity will not appear as a frontal assault or overt suppression of our religious beliefs. Instead, it will come as the latest fashionable philosophy, promising to make us happier, healthier, better educated — and even more spiritual.

The denominational world has almost totally abandoned the moving and the operation of the Holy Spirit as their *source* for solving the problems of mankind. Instead they look toward the "fashionable philosophies" (such as positive thinking, the healing of the memories, possibility thinking, self-help philosophies, and psychology). The total rejection of the force of the Holy Spirit has almost overwhelmed our religious institutions.

However, most Pentecostal fellowships are in no position to look with pious self-righteousness on their denominational brethren. We Pentecostals are, in fact, so riddled with a *"departure from the faith"* that we should only point the finger at ourselves.

WORSHIP AND MUSIC

Once again I want us to turn our attention to music as it affects worship. I hope to show that powerful music is an adjunct to worship, and that Satan is working diligently to neutralize that worship by stifling the anointing that descends from God's Holy Spirit when music is a *proper* element in our services.

I remember a time years ago when Frances and I were conducting a particular crusade in a midwestern city. This was long before anyone had heard of contemporary gospel music.

God gave us a great meeting. It lasted some four or five weeks, with great numbers coming to the Lord Jesus Christ and many being filled with the baptism in the Holy Spirit.

The music of those days was completely opposite to the rock offerings of today. In fact, the cold, staid, formalistic type of music was the only kind that was considered "proper" in many of our Pentecostal churches. Unfortunately there was no worship that accompanied this music, because no worship *could* accompany it.

To be honest, it was an effort to be like the rest of the denominations, so there was little joy and little or no praise. This was a cold, dead stereotype.

At the time I was attempting, with what ability and talent God had given me and the leading of His Holy Spirit within my soul, to change this because I felt that music was a tremendous instrument to be used by God in worship. I felt it should promote the flow of the Holy Spirit and should elicit praise and bring joy.

Now there were a couple of Christian Bible schools in this particular city, and I don't think I've ever received so much opposition in my life. It was as if the powers of darkness made every effort to hinder the progress God was helping us to effect.

They told me my method wouldn't work. But, of course, time has proven that it will work. And to be honest, it isn't "my" method at all; it's the Holy Spirit's method, and I only try to go where the Holy Spirit leads.

This cold, religious formality almost destroyed many of our Pentecostal churches before they began to wake up. But, thank God, some have awakened and started to live. Still, Satan is launching another terrible attack as many lurch to the other extreme and embrace an even more insidious concept — "contemporary gospel 'Rock' music." This demonic music is the vehicle for carrying the brethren away from Pentecostal fire and into the great morass of Pentecostal humanism!

ANOINTED MUSIC AND SINGING ARE GOD'S VEHICLES FOR THE FLOW AND THE MOVING OF THE HOLY SPIRIT

This is so important that I want to emphasize it:

In our worship services today, music is the single most important element in producing an environment conducive to the anointing and flow of the Holy Spirit.

Satan knows that if he can tamper with the music in the church — hinder it, or pervert it (through the introduction of contemporary gospel music) — he can divert the congregation's attention from the leading of the Holy Spirit. This will disorient the entire service and jeopardize the most important part of all — the preaching of the Word of God.

The book of Psalms is earth's first songbook, and one can't help but note its tremendous spiritual flow. The last two Psalms sum up the great moving of the Holy Spirit through music and its relationship to worship of the Lord.

In the Old Testament there are seven Hebrew words describing worship. They are as follows:

• **YADAH** — This is a verb with a root meaning "the extended hand, to throw out the hand"; therefore, "to worship with extended hand." And the opposite meaning is to bemoan, or the wringing of the hands. In other words, if you refuse to lift your hands in victorious worship, you might be wringing them in whimpering defeat. This word means to act with your will and to throw your hands upward in power and praise. II Chronicles 20:19-21 is an example of the *yadah* (extended hands in worship) type of praise.

• **TOWDAH** — This word comes from the same principal Hebrew root that we've just discussed. Both *yadah* and *towdah* involve the extension of the hand, but *towdah* includes a little more. It is the modern Hebrew word for thanksgiving. Properly, it is an extension of the hand in adoration, avowal, or acceptance. It means "to worship the Lord and to thank Him for things not yet received as well as for things already at hand." An example is found in Psalm 50:23.

• **HALAL** — From this primary root comes our word "Hallelujah." It means "to clear, to shine, to boast, to show, to rave, to celebrate, or to clamor foolishly." This is perhaps the most commonly practiced expression of praise. Christians boast of the exploits of the Lord Jesus Christ and extol His greatness. And we should do it until we are clamorously foolish. Examples of this are found in Psalms 113 and 114.

• **SHABACH** — This means "to address with a loud tone, to command, to triumph, to glory, to shout." Examples of this are found in Psalm 117:1 and Psalm 63:1-3.

• **BARAK** — This means "to kneel and to bless God as an act of adoration." It also means to bless Him, expecting to receive something. It is not a begging attitude but an expectant attitude. The scriptural connotation for *barak* is found in Psalm 72:12, 13.

• **ZAMAR** — This means "to touch the strings," and it is used concordantly with instrumental worship. It has to do with percussion, wind, or rhythm instruments, and it has a volume and downbeat to it. Examples are found in Psalm 57:8, 9 and Psalm 150.

• **TEHILLAH** — This means "to sing, and to sing praises unto the Lord." Psalm 22:3 tells us that God inhabits, or is enthroned in, the praises of His people. This is the way that God manifests Himself.

THE BOOK OF REVELATION

In the fifth chapter of the book of Revelation (as well as in other chapters) a tremendous eruption of worship is described. It is accompanied by music and singing.

In chapters 5, 14, and 15, the redeemed are described as singing and playing harps. (It appears that *all* of the redeemed of heaven will be capable of playing harps and singing.) Every time a scene in heaven unfolds, John the Revelator sees and hears tremendous rejoicing, singing, and music.

I want to reiterate that music is the ultimate vehicle for promoting the flow and anointing of the Holy Spirit. The more on fire for God that a church is, the more you hear spirited singing and worship. The more a church withdraws from God, the smaller the part music will play in that church.

STYLE

The reason music is such a vehicle for the anointing of the Holy Spirit is because it deals with man's heart instead of his intellect. And, ultimately, this is the way God deals with man. God does not deal with man's intellect. Of course, intellect is there, and many of the things of God appeal to us intellectually. But God deals primarily with man's heart — his spirit — and this is the area where music has its impact.

In view of the foregoing, there is nothing wrong with rhythm. God gave man his appreciation of rhythm. Of course, for a long time, many churches thought that any rhythmic pattern had to be ungodly or worldly. This didn't, however, in any manner whatsoever agree with Scripture.

Moses and his sister Miriam sang unto the Lord and used tambourines (a rhythmic instrument). They danced in the Spirit to the rhythmic patterns created by the tambourines. This was a time of great rejoicing as they celebrated the memorable victory of the Red Sea.

Again, in Psalm 150, David speaks of stringed instruments and cymbals. He describes a number of instruments that were then used that are similar to what we have today. And stringed instruments are generally used to create a rhythmic background.

(This in no way repudiates the great old hymns of the church that are slow and melodic, yet which serve as the very foundation of our worship before the Lord.)

CONTEMPORARY MUSIC

There is no way one can worship to modern, contemporary Christian music.

I was in a service some time back where I had no control over the music (I was only scheduled to speak).

I sat there and listened as the orchestra played "contemporary Christian music." And the people just sat there — they couldn't worship.

If they had *wanted* to worship they couldn't have. They just listened because this was all they could do.

The design and the style of the singing (which is the same as modern rock because it *is* modern rock) have other purposes altogether.

Modern rock promotes illicit sex, the drug scene, and satanism. This has fostered rebellion, disobedience, and anarchy. It brings death — both spiritual and physical.

When the people in our churches accept this type of music, it will destroy their worship and the flow and anointing of the Holy Spirit, *and it will bring death as surely as it brought death to Nadab and Abihu.* Why? Because it is strange fire offered up on the altar of incense.

THE SELF-HELP PHILOSOPHIES

In a revival crusade in a major city, I sat in my motel room and watched as a television preacher extolled the gospel of prosperity and riches.

I had heard him on and off for some months and his message never did bear witness with my spirit.

Yes, God does work to prosper His people. God takes no delight in poverty. But the things that were being said that day (and which are being promoted to Pentecostal people throughout the nation) created an adverse reaction in my spirit.

"You can get rich." "You can be successful." Success seminars, prosperity seminars — the list goes on. And for a certainty it all sounds very enticing and attractive and produces a large following. It promises riches, and money has always been a great drawing card.

There in my motel room, I asked the Lord, "What's wrong with this? It doesn't bear witness with my spirit. I know You take no delight in poverty — that poverty is actually of Satan. But why am I grieved in my spirit when I hear this?"

THE LORD SPOKE THESE WORDS TO ME

"Every message or doctrine propagated by My people must produce a greater love for Jesus Christ." In other words, the end result of every message, effort, sermon, or song must be to draw the listener closer to Jesus Christ. The listener should be encouraged to become more like Jesus Christ and demonstrate a greater consecration to Christ. "However," He said, "this modern prosperity teaching does not produce individuals with a greater desire to emulate Me. They leave prosperity services with another goal — a lust to amass wealth."

Yes, Jesus Christ is talked about, the Word of God is used, and Jesus Christ is used. But that's just the trouble — He is used. Christ is seen as nothing more than an instrument to be used in delivering the product that the listener is seeking.

I was discussing these problems with a pastor friend. The conversation, quite naturally, focused on preachers who almost constantly stress the prosperity message.

Ironically, the message doesn't direct emphasis toward God, and it doesn't elevate Jesus Christ. As a result, the gullible people following this philosophy will not grow wealthy, they will probably be separated from what little money they might have.

On the other hand, those who accept the message promoting faith in God's Word, believing God to meet every need according to His riches in glory but with the eventual goal of becoming Christlike, will ultimately receive more material blessings — if that matters.

MORE ABOUT CHRISTIAN HUMANISM

You see, according to the Word of God, the Christian perspective should always place God at the center. Man is on the outside striving to move inward toward God. God is eternally at the epicenter, and everything revolves around Him.

However, when this is distorted, man propels himself toward the center and God is pushed to the periphery. God remains in the picture but He no longer retains His proper place in respect to man.

THE "FAITH" MINISTRY

I happen to believe that the faith message propagated in the last few years has great potential for edifying the body of Christ. It has helped preachers to believe God for great things. I personally thank God for the great teachers of faith (according to the Word of God) who have been a blessing to the body of Christ.

However, some have taken this teaching to where God has been moved out of the center and man has gradually elevated himself to the place of God (II Thes. 2:3, 4). Perhaps this has been done unintentionally, but the end result is the same.

Too many individuals have seen loved ones die through misplaced faith. Their failure might be attributed to improper interpretation, but the fact is that certain individuals, due to incorrect teaching, *have exalted themselves and thus diminished God.*

CHRISTIAN PSYCHOLOGY

It is only since World War II that psychology has infiltrated our seminaries. Prior to this, few theological schools offered counseling courses based on psychology. But by the '50s almost all did, and over 80 percent were offering additional psychology courses.

In his book, *Psychology as Religion: The Cult of Self-Worship,* Paul Vitz, a psychology professor at New York University, said:

> Psychology as a religion exists . . . in great strength throughout the United States . . . [It] is deeply anti-

Christian . . . [yet] is extensively supported by schools, universities, and social programs financed by taxes collected from Christians. . . .

Then he went on to say:

But for the first time, the *destructive logic* of this *secular humanism* is beginning to be understood.

Carl Rogers has stated that psychotherapy is the fastest growing area in the social sciences. And now in the 1980s, psychology has attained the status of a neomessiah whose scientific pretensions are relieving consciences of obedience to God.

Martin L. Gross had this to say in *The Psychological Society:*

Psychology sits at the very center of contemporary society as an international colossus whose ranks number in the hundreds of thousands . . .

Its experimental animals are an obliging, even grateful human race. We live in a civilization in which, as never before, man is preoccupied with self . . .

As the Protestant ethic has weakened in Western society, the confused citizen has turned to the only alternative he knows: the psychological expert who claims there is a new scientific standard of behavior to replace fading traditions. . . .

Mouthing the holy name of science, the psychological expert claims to know all. This new truth is fed to us continuously from birth to the grave.

With so many preachers now taking psychology courses and almost *all* of the Christian Bible colleges and universities offering them, this pseudoscience has infiltrated the church.

Pastors and other spiritual leaders have accepted the claim that it is scientific and "neutral." It is not neutral, however. Psychology and psychotherapy are based on evolution, atheism, and secular humanism. They are actually a religion within themselves. In other words, *Christianity and modern-day psychology are irreconcilable religious systems.* This impossible melding, "Christian psychology," creates an unequal yoke that brings into the church the seductive influence of secular psychology.

As we mentioned a moment ago, and we concur totally with him, Martin L. Gross stated that man is preoccupied with self.

I watched a so-called Christian television program the other day and a prominent TV preacher was saying, *"The way to glorify God is to glorify self. We must love ourselves."* As I listened, I thought it rather strange that he propagated this humanistic gospel, when Jesus said:

> *"If any man will come after me, let him deny himself [deny self], and take up his cross, and follow me. For whosoever will save his life shall lose it: and whosoever will lose his life for my sake shall find it"* (Matt. 16:24, 25).

Sad to say, as the television preacher spoke these words, he was surrounded by applauding Pentecostal preachers. God help us.

FALSE PROPHETS

> *"Beware of false prophets, which come to you in sheep's clothing, but inwardly they are ravening wolves. Ye shall know them by their fruits. Do men gather grapes of thorns, or figs of thistles? Even so every good tree bringeth forth*

good fruit; but a corrupt tree bringeth forth evil
fruit. A good tree cannot bring forth evil fruit,
neither can a corrupt tree bring forth good fruit.
Every tree that bringeth not forth good fruit is
hewn down, and cast into the fire. Wherefore by
their fruits ye shall know them" (Matt. 7:15-20).

When we think of false prophets today, we think
of the strange and the bizarre — the gurus from India
who call themselves messiahs, or others of similar ilk.
However, this is not what we are warned of in Scripture.

It describes individuals disguised in sheep's clothing.
In other words, they would look "like the real thing." They
would say all the right words — it would seem plausible,
palatable, and pleasant. But Jesus said that inwardly they
are ravening wolves.

I listen to these false prophets as they appear on Pentecostal television programs and, sad to say, the crowd
doesn't recognize them for what they are. It would seem
that even the elect could be deceived.

On a Pentecostal program not long ago, a particular
"spiritual" teacher demeaned the power of God and upheld
humanism by telling the people, *"Whatever god you start*
with is satisfactory — be it the Muslim god, the Hindu god,
the Buddhist god, or the Christian God. It's a good start,
and you can build from there."

He was speaking of people being set free from alcohol.

Someone stood in the audience and mentioned the
power of God to deliver the oppressed. The teacher admitted this was possible but said it was highly unlikely.

And then the host of this Pentecostal program turned,
held up this man's book, and recommended it to those
viewing the program.

"And if the blind lead the blind, both shall
fall into the ditch" (Matt. 15:14).

I have felt strongly led of late to encourage our people to return to the altar. (And, of course, when I say altar, I'm not referring to some specific altar. I mean making an altar of our hearts wherever we might be — whether it's at the front of a church, a prayer room, or just out under a tree somewhere.)

The altar where God Almighty can touch us and the Holy Spirit can move on us is our *only* answer. And I hasten to say this:

It's not one among many answers. It's not just *an* answer that may work for me while something else will work for others. *It is* the *answer.*

God is still at the center, and He must always be our focal point. Man is on the periphery. His only hope is God. All these pseudo "helps" that we seek are as false as Satan. If we accept them, we are sowing unto the flesh and we will reap corruption. We're sowing to the wind and reaping the whirlwind.

ANYTHING IS ACCEPTED TODAY

The gospel of the hour is, *"Do not offend."* Everyone is accepted for *"what he is."* Every message is judged by *"take the good in it and leave the rest alone."* This is a prescription for *disaster.*

In our Pentecostal humanism, we have adopted the (rock) music of the world. We are accepting "another gospel" which the great Paul warned against (Gal. 1:8, 9). It is Pentecostal humanism, pure and simple, and it will destroy us.

We must go back to the Bible and to the altar. That's the only way. There's no other hope.

God is our true source. He's the one who gave us the power. He's the one who has blessed us. He's the one who meets our every need.

Total sustenance comes from Him. If we don't turn from our errant ways we will go the way of the denominations. Unfortunately, we're already halfway down that path.

CHAPTER 13

CHRISTIAN ROCK AND ROLL

 As I write this, I hold in my hands the Christian publication of a prominent American church. An article within this periodical extols the virtues of a certain "Christian" rock and roll group.

This publication compares this group with such well-known but secular groups as the Grateful Dead, Styx, and others. It then goes on to state that "rock" is the group's specialty, and focuses particularly on one specific two-hour concert described as including singing, dancing, and "rejoicing in the spirit." In the course of the author's laudatory account of this group's Christian influence, he prominently features their opinion that the *type* of music makes little difference as long as "the lyrics are compatible with Christian teaching."

The article goes on to state that this group's concerts basically draw the same *type* of young people that are attracted to *secular* rock concerts — but that their music provides a *positive alternative*, thus further concluding that rock music may well be brought into churches to draw

225

young people away from the things of the world . . . and into the things of God.

Further into the interview, this group suggests that their competition comes not from Christian bands, but from the secular rock groups — a few of which are specifically noted.

In describing their concerts, and the image they project, they boast of their light-and-sound presentation, which they consider unsurpassed by any secular rock show. They also speak of the devotional time they hold on their bus and their time of sharing together every morning as they travel. They are not, according to this interview, trying to be a secular rock group, but are — and want to remain — a *Christian* rock group!

They suggest that contemporary Christian music is booming and is fast reaching the point where it will sell at a level comparable to — or even beyond — that of many secular groups. They feel that their music — along with other Christian rock groups — can compete head-to-head with the rock offerings of regular secular groups in non-Christian stores and record shops across the nation.

Many youngsters, they report, who are familiar with their group buy their albums and wear their T-shirts, yet do not profess any association with Christianity. They explain this by saying, "They just like our music."

They consider themselves to be "missionaries — trying to learn the language of the people that they are trying to reach." They describe how the Lord gives them their music, stating that they sing the song, "God Gave Rock 'n' Roll to You." Finally, they say that God gives music to man as a gift and that He wants that music to glorify *Him*.

I have done my best to remain unbiased and objective in relating the attitudes toward contemporary Christian music — actually rock and roll — that are presented here. Now let us take a closer look at what all this implies.

MUSIC A POWERFUL INFLUENCE

Somebody observed (insightfully) that music is the great leveler. It crosses all barriers within all cultures. It has even been said that the power of music is second only to that of the preached gospel of Jesus Christ. There is a great deal of truth in both of these statements. Music *is* a compelling influence, and music *can* play a dominant role in the presentation of the gospel of Jesus Christ.

The Bible is literally *filled* with music. We read in Exodus 15 of Moses and the children of Israel singing a song unto the Lord — and that song is then given verbatim within the Word of God. The song praises the great victory wrought by God at the Red Sea — and recounts how Miriam, the prophetess and sister of Moses and Aaron, took timbrel in hand to lead the women in a time of great rejoicing (verse 20).

Many people may not realize it, but the collection of Psalms (many written by David) was the world's first songbook. The people of Israel were, in fact, the first to praise God in music and song. David is referred to as *"the sweet psalmist of Israel"* (II Sam. 23:1).

In the book of Revelation, we are given a vision of the redeemed singing and playing harps, and it appears that *all* the redeemed of heaven will be capable of playing harps and singing (see Rev. 5, 14, and 15).

The book of Revelation is actually one of the greatest books of worship in the entirety of the Word of God. Basically every time the scene in heaven unfolded to John the Revelator, tremendous rejoicing, singing, and music were recorded.

MUSICAL INSTRUMENTS ARE OF GOD

To sing with accompaniment is a command of the Word of God. I believe that the following statements from

both Testaments demonstrate scriptural approval on the use
of musical instruments while worshiping the Lord.

- Musical instruments were used by prophets when
  prophesying by the Holy Spirit (I Sam. 10:5; I Chr.
  25:1-7).
- David used instruments of music to quiet the spirit
  of King Saul (I Sam. 16:16-23).
- The righteous are commanded to use instruments of
  music in their worship (Psa. 33:1-5; 81:1-5; 98:4-9;
  147:7; 149:1-4; 150:1-6).
- In the Old Testament, it was actually a law of God to
  use musical instruments (Psa. 81:1-4; II Chr. 29:25).
- When dedicated to God, musical instruments were
  called holy (Num. 31:6).
- God's glory came down when instruments accompanied singing (II Chr. 5:11-14) — and this still
  happens today.
- Musical instruments will be used in the reign of the
  Messiah (Psa. 87:7).
- Fifty-five Psalms of worship were dedicated to the
  chief musician. It was only when Israel *misused* them
  — to commit sin — that any rebuke was made (Psa.
  132:2; Amos 6:5).
- We are told that in heaven twenty-four elders and four
  angelic beings play harps (Rev. 5:8).
- In heaven the 144,000 Jews also will play harps (Rev.
  14:1-5).
- In heaven all the tribulation saints will play harps
  (Rev. 15:2).
- The New Testament commands the use of musical
  instruments in the church. Saints are commanded to
  make melody in their hearts with psalms, hymns,
  and spiritual songs (Eph. 5:19; Col. 3:16).
- The Greek word for "psalms" in these passages is
  psalmos, which means a set piece of music, a sacred

song, to be accompanied with the harp or other instrument.

- The Greek word for "psalms" in James 5:13 is *psallo*, which means "to twitch or twang, or to play on a stringed instrument." *Psallo* also means to celebrate divine worship with music and singing. This is likewise the meaning of the Hebrew words *zamir* and *zamar* translated "psalms" in I Chronicles 16:9; Psalms 95:2; 105:2.

So we have many Scriptures within the Word of God approving and associating musical instruments with the act of worship.

LUCIFER IN CHARGE OF HEAVEN'S MUSIC?

In Ezekiel we read of the creation of Lucifer (which was long before his fall, at which time he became evil and carnate).

> *". . . the workmanship of thy tabrets and of thy pipes was prepared in thee in the day that thou wast created"* (Ezek. 28:13).

Many Bible scholars feel this pertains to the tremendous lyrical talents that God gave Lucifer.

In the book of Isaiah he is called *"Lucifer, son of the morning"* (Isa. 14:12).

When we link *"the morning stars [as they] sang together"* and *"all the sons of God shout[ing] for joy"* (Job 38:7), we realize that Lucifer was possibly the director of the great choirs of heaven, literally leading them in songs of praise and glory when God made the world.

MUSICAL HISTORY

Before Jesus was born into this world to live among men — and later to die and rise again — most music was written in the minor chords. All the great psalms, originated by the psalmist David for worship, were set basically in minor chords. (It should be noted here that the majority of music from other parts of the world of that day was demonic in origin and had little or no melodic flow.)

After the death and resurrection of the Lord Jesus Christ, music gradually changed from the minor to the major chords, and only then was its full potential realized. It was as if Jesus' life, death, and resurrection opened up the hearts of men to a higher level of worship — thus the progression from the minor to the major chords.

Most modern music, sacred or otherwise, flows with a constant melodic line and stems from the Judeo-Christian concept of worship of God.

If we look at the nations of the world that do not worship the Lord today (or that worship in a distorted or erroneous manner — for example, Buddhism, Hinduism, Islam, etc.) we find that their music has a strange and eerie sound that is disturbing to the Western ear.

In Cairo, Egypt, I went out to walk and pray just before dark. During the walk I could hear the eerie wail of the Muslims as they worshiped and prayed. There was no melody to the music, it was simply a recurring pattern suggesting despair and darkness. There was no joy or victory. (There is, of course, no joy or victory in false worship.)

From this level of misguided worship, we can follow the further degeneration of musical form until we find it at its ultimate base level — as represented in Africa (and other parts of the world) — which is attributable to *demonic* worship.

It seems apparent that music (as we know it in Western culture) stems from the Judeo-Christian principle and was intended originally for worshiping God. Satan, being the primary master of musical knowledge, has subverted all this, however. With his tremendous talents, given to him by God at his creation, he has used music as an insidious tool to enslave hundreds of millions to drugs, alcohol, illicit sex, and other types of sordid bondage.

From the small amount of information provided, I believe we can see that the whole world has been *influenced* by music — stemming either from Judeo-Christian worship, or from Satan. The important point I want to establish is that music is a *powerful* tool — whether in the realm of the gospel or in the realm of darkness.

I SPEAK WITH SOME QUALIFICATIONS

I have sold over 15 million albums in the thirty-one years we have been trying to lift up the Lord Jesus Christ through music. Our albums continue to sell at the rate of about 500,000 a year.

I began recording even before stereo was perfected. We would record the album in mono, and everything had to be right on the first taping. The engineers had to have everything set up flawlessly because there was no way to change or improve a record once it was cut. But then came two-track, four-track, eight, and on to sixteen, and thirty-two. Today, of course, the technical advances within the recording industry are awesome to behold.

Throughout this time I have watched as the Lord has blessed our records and used our music to touch the hearts and lives of literally *millions* of people. We give Him *all* the glory.

So I like to think I know *a little bit* about the kind of music God would have us deliver to the people. I also hope

I have learned, over the years, something about the manner in which music can *influence* those exposed to it.

When it comes to a discussion of different *types* of music, some people confuse taste in music with spiritual direction. This, naturally, is incorrect.

Some people are greatly blessed by a George Beverly Shea type of song. Others prefer something of the Bill Gaither variety. Still others want a little more "feeling" or "exuberance" and will select a Dallas Holm version. Irrespective of the specific direction any of these may take, it does not mean necessarily that one is more spiritual than another. Each serves its place in the great work of God.

So, yes, tastes will vary within the format of gospel, or sacred, music. With this in mind, we should never try to project that *our* tastes are uniquely pleasing to God, or that *our* preference is the only suitable music for the whole spectrum of practicing Christians.

I recall an incident involving A. N. Trotter.

The service had just ended. Many hundreds of people were present at the camp meeting. The pianist proceeded to play the invitational hymn. An invitational hymn of this nature — as the Spirit of God moves — would ordinarily be something in the nature of "Just As I Am" or "Why Not Tonight?" But much to everyone's surprise, the brother started playing the uptempo version of "We Shall See the King":

> There's a blessed time that's coming, coming soon,
> It may be evening, morning, night, or noon.
> The wedding of the Bride, united with the Groom,
> We shall see the King when He comes.

For a brief moment the crowd sat there stunned. This type of song just was not *used* for an altar call! However, it was not the pianist, it was not the evangelist who was in charge of that particular moment — it was God! If *He* had not been directing that altar service, it would have ended in disaster. The Spirit of God fell like rain over the assemblage, and scores of people responded to the altar call — as God used *that* song to touch the hearts and lives of many people.

We must *never* try to box God in so as to make *Him* conform to *our* tastes or desires. God works in any way He chooses or desires.

THE HOLY SPIRIT MUST DEFINE THE LIMITS ON WHAT IS OR IS NOT GOOD GOSPEL MUSIC

I have had at least a modicum of experience in regard to gospel music — and also in the moving and the leading of the Holy Spirit. But I would react with trepidation if someone were to tell *me* that I had to define the standards of what is or is not gospel music. I think *anyone* would have difficulty doing this.

I personally feel that every singer, performer, artist, or musician who names the name of Jesus Christ must ask himself repeatedly:

- Is this the direction that the Lord wants?
- Is this the kind of music that the Lord wants played?
- Can the Holy Spirit bless this music?
- Can the Holy Spirit anoint this music?

Only then can we — each for our particular ministries — come to a satisfactory conclusion as to what God wants for *us*. I cannot set the standard for another person, nor can he for me. And I hasten to add that this is not something that can be done once and for all. It involves a continuing process — a seeking of the Lord's face for every song we sing or play, how we sing or play that particular song, the combination of chords to be used, and the kind of rhythms to be included — even the instrumentation to be used — in each individual song. Have we, in our effort to reach the crowd, *crossed over* from that which is pleasing to God to that which is *not* pleasing to Him? This can happen easily.

Many times in playing a song, I have sensed that the Holy Spirit would have me to change the type of "fills" I would be using. Perhaps they were not compatible with His way. Even though the particular "sound" might would please the crowd, I have sensed that it was not what He wanted for that service or occasion.

Countless times I have changed an arrangement that our band had put together for the telecast — simply because I felt it did not minister as it was conceived originally. Any Christian music that does not encourage worship and praise, or elicit a sense of joy, *must* be changed.

Of course, I am not suggesting that I am infallible in this area — but I *am* saying that I try to make every effort to follow the guiding and the leading of the Holy Spirit.

Although I do not aspire to set the standards respecting gospel music (deferring as always to the Holy Spirit in this area), I feel it is incumbent upon me to speak of *course* and *direction*.

On the one hand, no one can tell me, as a minister of the gospel, what to preach. But, on the other hand, I must *always* be aware of the fact that eternal souls will be hindered or helped according to what they hear me preach. The same applies to gospel music.

Now let us view this in a little more detail.

CONTEMPORARY CHRISTIAN MUSIC

When contemporary Christian music made its debut, I wrote an article on it in the July 1980 issue of *The Evangelist*. I felt then (as I feel now) that even though the word "contemporary" is difficult to define within the Christian concept, it does imply conformity with today's worldly standards.

What does that suggest specifically?

An effort to come as close as possible to rock and roll without actually using the specific name. I felt this was wrong then, and I feel it is wrong now.

I see now that Christian contemporary music enthusiasts are beginning to call their music by what it really is — rock and roll. So let us, therefore, *look* at the words "rock and roll."

When rock started back in the '50s, it was a far cry from what it is today. The term was actually coined by Alan Freed and was street slang with sexual connotations. This within itself denoted nothing but wickedness.

However, as far as the music was concerned, '50s rock was little different from some of the music that had been played in some church services over the years. I know this may sound strange to some people, but it is true, nonetheless.

This music was basically written and played in four-four time with double time used on some songs. If a person could go back to the old Billy Sunday crusades (some seventy-five to eighty years ago) with the great choirs led by Homer Rodeheaver — he would hear basically the same rhythm patterns. It would not have the same impact, simply because they did not have the electrical instrumentation and amplification that we do now, but the rhythm patterns were the same.

People by the thousands would clap their hands and sing "Brighten the Corner Where You Are" or "When We All Get to Heaven" — and enjoy themselves immensely in the Lord. In many full-gospel churches, the same type of musical worship was carried on and has been at least *part* of the success of the great Pentecostal form of worship. It should be added, however, that rock and roll — as was offered by the world — was evil then, just as it is now, *simply because of the direction it was taking.* It then led millions astray, and it has *since* led tens of millions astray — into the worst destruction a person could imagine.

So to think that a piano or an organ delivering mournful sounds is supposed to demonstrate spirituality is wishful thinking at best — and gross error at worst. In some of this type of music, I actually believe oppressive spirits are working. And please understand, I am not demeaning particular kinds of instrumentation or the *lack* of certain kinds of instrumentation. I am speaking about music that by and large elicits no praise, worship, or joy in the Lord. Irrespective of the rhythmic patterns — whether they be slow or fast — they must be touched by God and anointed by the Holy Spirit.

But it must also be remembered that there is nothing intrinsically wrong with using rhythm in our singing in church. As previously mentioned, Moses and his sister, Miriam, sang unto the Lord and used tambourines. They actually danced in the Spirit to the rhythmic patterns created by those tambourines. This was a time of tremendous joy as they celebrated the great victory at the Red Sea. There was absolutely *nothing wrong* with what they were doing. In fact, it was very right.

In Psalm 150 (with the preceding Psalms leading up to this) David spoke of stringed instruments. He talked about cymbals. He spoke of all the instruments of worship used then that are similar to what we use today — without, of course, the electrification.

The great Israelite choirs — under the leadership of David, and afterward as long as the Lord was moving in Israel — were markedly *vigorous* in their worship. I am sure they were little different from the great choirs in some of our churches today. They all elicited praise, worship, and ministry to the Lord. All kinds of rhythmic patterns were used and God blessed them.

So rhythm, within itself, is not wrong. It is only when it is used incorrectly that the problem arises.

"Rock and roll" has *degenerated* from what it was in the '50s, down through acid rock, punk rock, and now new-wave rock. It has in the past few years become so vulgar, so obscene, and so utterly degraded that there is absolutely nothing good that can be said about it. In fact, to the contrary, Satan is using it to destroy an entire generation of young people.

Rock and roll is a prominent influence in the promotion of drugs, alcohol, illicit sex, and Satan worship. It is one of the most destructive forces active in this nation and the world today. It is literally entrapping and destroying the hearts and lives of multiplied millions of children.

It seems inconceivable that any group that considers itself Christian could accept the rock and roll designation — especially when they consider the horror imposed on an entire generation by this music.

Scripture tells us:

> *"For it is a shame even to speak of those things which are done of them in secret"* (Eph. 5:12).

> *"And be not conformed to this world: but be ye transformed by the renewing of your mind, that ye may prove what is that good, and acceptable, and perfect, will of God"* (Rom. 12:2).

I am not questioning the motives of these Christian groups, but I do question their direction. I feel the end result will be catastrophic.

Does anyone really feel that he can be used of the Lord and have the Holy Spirit anointing on his efforts dressed as a punk or acid rocker? Can a person serve the Lord while strobe lights augment the demonic patterns of a rhythmic rock-and-roll beat? Realizing that rock and roll was birthed in hell and instigated by Satan for only one purpose — *"to steal, and to kill, and to destroy"* (John 10:10) — can we believe that these diametrically opposed elements can be reconciled?

The other night I happened to chance upon a noted female gospel singer on television. She was dressed in skintight leather pants. Lights were flashing behind her as the Christian rock band played. They were dressed as most rock performers dress — in an odd assortment of weird costumes.

I wondered, "What kind of testimony does this lend? What kind of image does it project?" It was fairly obvious that there was nothing "Christian" about it.

"THE TYPE OF MUSIC DOESN'T MATTER, IT'S THE WORDS THAT COUNT"

This is one of the biggest cop-outs of all time. It is the pat excuse given by these people for their choice of format. They try to make us believe that, irrespective of chord progression or rhythm, irrespective of scene or setting, if the words give even vague reference to the gospel, anything is acceptable. They belie their own statement, however.

The entire setting deifies rock — not the Lord Jesus Christ. As a result, the observer hears few of the words — if any. His mind absorbs only what he sees and hears — and by that I mean the music.

This is what it is all about.

Basically, in secular rock music, the words are not heard — they cannot be understood over the all-pervading din of high-intensity sound equipment. And, sad to say, when they *are* heard, a person quickly realizes they are better left unheard.

Be that as it may, however, the entire picture is satanic in nature. To use the excuse that the words are the key feature ignores the nature of the problem.

The *style* of the music (if anyone knows anything about music) has always been as important as the lyrics. *The way in which it is presented influences the effect of what is said.*

Whenever a person thinks of the weird sounds of Islam, or the rhythmic beat of African tom-toms, he immediately recognizes that music *sets a mood,* that there is an underlying spirit to that music. And it is this spirit that has made rock and roll music so powerful and compelling. It is also this spirit that has made rock stars into demigods to an entire generation of young people. (And I might add, it is this spirit that has made the stars multimillionaires.) So for a person to suggest that the kind of music does not matter is to totally ignore the obvious *nature* of the whole rock and roll scene.

EXPLOITATION OR DEVELOPMENT?

The excuse used today by Christian rock groups is that this is just another *tool* to reach young people. The question must then be asked, however, "*Are* the young people being reached?" I do not think they are. There is a possibility that they are being *influenced,* but I do not think they are being *reached* for the Lord Jesus Christ.

You see, it is easy for a preacher to *exploit* his adherents instead of *developing* them. Sad to say, this is done almost continually. People are manipulated, used, and exploited. I could describe 101 different ways in which this is done, but suffice to say that it *is* done.

Christian rock and roll and secular rock and roll are indistinguishable. I cannot help believing that young people are being *exploited* instead of *developed*. Giving a Christian "Christian" rock to wean him away from drugs is like giving a drug addict methadone. Most would have to admit that this program has not worked; the individual remains in bondage. Likewise, any effort to appease the rock and roll lust in the hearts of young people by giving them a pseudo rock and roll is exploitation at its worst.

Yes, there is a tremendous attraction in rock and roll. The throb, the power of the beat, the tremendous energy generated by the light and sound all have a tremendous drawing power. So the question is: Should we accept and foster this to *attract* young people?

The answer could be compared to that of a Catholic parish a short time ago that established a bar in their church to serve their parishioners. Their excuse was that they could accommodate them in a *healthy* environment — as opposed to their going to a local saloon. In the same vein, if we accept rock and roll into the church to *reach the young people*, will it draw a crowd? Of course, and a great deal of young people would approve. But is it developing these young people for Christ? Is it leading them toward a Godly, consecrated life? I think the answer is obvious.

"JESUS CHRIST CAME TO EARTH TO BECOME LIKE MAN, SO WE SHOULD BECOME LIKE THE WORLD TO WIN THE WORLD TO JESUS CHRIST"

This statement borders on blasphemy. Yes, Jesus Christ *did* become man, but He never engaged in the sin and failure of mankind. It is an abomination even to *think* of such a thing! He . . .

". . . *did no sin, neither was guile found in his mouth*" (I Pet. 2:22).

He walked pure and clean all of His earthly life and ministry.

The problem with hard-core contemporary Christian music is that it strives to make Christ acceptable to men rather than men acceptable to Christ. It attempts to lower the Lord Jesus to *mankind's* base level — rather than elevating man to *God's* highest level.

We are not trying to make Christ acceptable to men. It is our business to bring men to the Lord Jesus Christ and to let Him change them from their old sinful, sordid ways. *This* is the intent and message of the gospel.

MONEY

I would not accuse any Christian rock performer of being in it for the money. I do not question the motives of anyone — unless his intentions become obvious and apparent. But, at the same time, we all realize that young people buy a huge volume of records. If someone concentrates on records indistinguishable from secular rock groups, however, we *may* assume that commercial motives are involved.

It would take an incredible gullibility to believe that young people are buying these records for their Christian message. There are better ways to eat a meal than out of a garbage can! In our hearts we must know they are buying this kind of music because it satisfies their craving for the sordid, the unclean, and the fleshly. Many young people *use* this kind of music because their parents will accept it on the premise that it is Christian music.

That is the reason the group referred to at the beginning of this chapter said their competition was not Christian but secular rock groups. They are certainly correct in that assessment. A great deal of potential profit is available here, and I shudder at the thought of the young souls that are to be jeopardized while traveling down this path.

AND FINALLY . . .

Any music played for the glory of God — irrespective of where or how it is played — should be chosen in light of the Word of God. Would our music be at home with Moses and Miriam on the shores of the Red Sea? Would it be acceptable to David and the great choirs of Israel, who literally set the standard for worship through music? Would it demonstrate the praise, worship, and ministry that is recorded as the book of Revelation describes the great musical ensembles of heaven?

We have to ask ourselves these questions, and we have to answer them. Music is an awesome force and when used properly can be a compelling influence.

I do not know how many young people this particular group (referred to at the beginning of this chapter) is leading to Jesus Christ. But in the final analysis, I am concerned that it may not be many; and of those who *are* placed on a certain pathway, I am concerned for those who may be led astray.

I wonder just how much of the contemporary rock music played over many Christian radio stations glorifies God. I wonder how many churches are truly giving their young people the solid Rock of the gospel when they feed them Christian rock and roll.

I am aware that there is a natural generation gap where tastes are concerned — especially in the area of music. As a general statement, however, the young are more easily captivated by the superficial and the gaudy. This is no doubt normal, and we who have had more experience must be careful that we lead these young people in the right direction — lest they be lost in the church as well as in the world.

A person may not draw as big a crowd if the strobe lights are left off, and he may not sell as many records if he does not project this image. Acceptance by the youth of today may come a great deal harder, but is that not the way the gospel has always been?

Jesus said:

"Enter ye in at the strait gate: for wide is the gate, and broad is the way, that leadeth to destruction, and many there be which go in thereat: Because strait is the gate, and narrow is the way, which leadeth unto life, and few there be that find it" (Matt. 7:13, 14).

If we do not at least point in the right direction, how many less will there be who might have found the way, but end up lost because of our failure to guide them to *"the way, the truth, and the life"* (John 14:6)?

CHAPTER 14

SERIOUS WEAKNESSES IN THE PENTECOSTAL MESSAGE

 In the midst of this great move of God, there are dark clouds on the horizon.

Some weeks ago, in taping segments for "A Study in the Word," one of the members on the panel was Ray Trask, President of the Jimmy Swaggart Bible College and former Director of the Missions Department. Ray is a missionary with some twenty-three years experience in the Far East. Between programs we were discussing various subjects, some of which centered on the Holy Spirit. Off camera, Brother Trask told me of an experience in Indonesia.

God had delivered many souls there — a tremendous harvest. The work is literally *exploding* in that great nation.

Some missionaries of another (non-Pentecostal) fellowship came to see him. In the course of their conversation the non-Pentecostal missionaries mentioned the tremendous results he — Brother Trask — and others were seeing in souls saved, while they were seeing only handfuls saved. This was, of course, very disheartening for them and they wanted to know what was wrong.

He said, simply, "Gentlemen, it's the Holy Spirit." That was about all he said on the subject. He didn't try to expound or explain further, he didn't try to promote the Pentecostal position, he just told them that the difference in their results was the difference in their relationship with the Holy Spirit.

In the ensuing weeks, one by one they started revealing to him how they were setting aside time to seek God for the moving and operation of the Holy Spirit in *their* lives. Very little (if anything) had been said about speaking in tongues. Still, one by one, as they received the infilling of the Holy Spirit, they invariably *did* speak with other tongues as the Spirit of God gave the utterance. However, that isn't the point of this discussion.

The point is this:

Ray Trask gave them the correct and *only* answer. The Holy Spirit *is* the source of all Christian power. Without the Holy Spirit in our hearts and lives, very little is going to be accomplished in regard to any ministry or in the work of God in general!

I DO NOT EXTOL THE
VIRTUES OF ANY DENOMINATION

The things I am about to say are certainly not intended as a public relations effort on behalf of any specific denomination or fellowship. I don't believe God is unduly impressed with any individual sect. I feel He loves *all* people, whoever they may be and wherever they may be, *if they are honestly reaching out toward Him.*

The things I intend to say will be solely to extol the virtues and the powers of the Holy Spirit within a person's life as that person attempts to work for God. The infilling of (or baptism in) the Holy Spirit is not a denomination; it's not a fellowship; it's not a group, or body, of people. It's an experience that comes from God and is readily available to any believer — whoever that individual may be.

Now let's retrace our steps momentarily as we restate one part of the preceding paragraph. As is recorded in Acts 1:4-8, the baptism in the Holy Spirit is not simply available, it is actually *commanded* for the believer! Jesus told those gathered in Jerusalem that they should *not* depart, but *"wait for the promise of the Father."* Of course, it was in Jerusalem that they were *"all in one place"* on the Feast of Pentecost, and what happened there was fulfillment of a number of Old Testament prophecies. This was why they were commanded to abide in Jerusalem until such a time. In Acts 1:8 Jesus told them exactly what would happen: *"But ye shall receive power, after that the Holy Ghost is come upon you."*

He commanded that they receive this infilling because He knew that without it they would have been ineffectual and incapable of performing the tasks that lay ahead. (And I hasten to add that *with* the infilling of the Holy Spirit they turned the world of that day upside down. By the end of the first hundred years after the advent of Christ, the entire civilized world of that time had been by and large evangelized. And all this — in large part — accomplished by individuals with little formal training. It was simply a result of their having been with Jesus — and then having been baptized in the Holy Spirit.)

Simon Peter was a markedly different man after his Pentecostal experience. The same could be said for all the disciples, actually. Hardly a day goes by that we don't see a television commercial extolling the virtues of the "energizer" battery. It's supposedly superior, more powerful, and longer lasting. Well, the Holy Spirit, promised to the Early Church that day by Jesus, wasn't just an energizer — He was a *transformer!* And, praise the Lord, He's still an energizer and transformer today — if we will each one just allow Him to plug Himself into *our* life.

Today ministries touching people throughout the world for Jesus Christ are ministries empowered by the Holy Spirit. They represent organizations and individuals who have been literally *baptized* in the Holy Spirit. I just couldn't be any more dogmatic on this subject. The baptism in the Holy Spirit is an absolute *must.*

With the Holy Spirit — somehow — our flaws, inconsistencies, and idiosyncrasies are overcome. Tremendous accomplishments result. To be sure, in most cases the vessel is weak (and in *all* cases unworthy) — yet the anointing oil that flows from this flawed vessel accomplishes a work for God.

Without Him, despite all of our abilities, education, money, talents, or efforts, all will prove to be in vain.

THE LATTER RAIN

The move of God taking place in the world today is strictly a Holy Spirit move (as, I believe, can be said of *every* move of God throughout the ages). The Pentecostal message is the message of the hour, the message that is getting *results.* Everything else is being inexorably pushed into the background.

In country after country throughout the world, the majority of Christians (outside of Catholics) are Pentecostal. As mentioned, Spirit-filled missionaries are winning souls in numbers that would have been considered impossible just a short time ago. By and large, the churches in America that are growing and influencing lives are full-gospel, Spirit-filled, or Pentecostal churches (all of which are simply different *names* for the same phenomenon). This is the message of power, the message of the anointing. It is, in the final analysis, *the* message that gets results.

As promised in His Word (Acts 2:17), God has supplied the *light* represented by the mighty infilling of the Holy Spirit. And those who choose not to walk in that light are gradually being pushed aside. Again, I emphasize: It's not a church, it's not a denomination, it's not even a fellowship. It's far more. It's an experience given, and even *commanded,* by God. Why is He so insistent that we accept this great gift? Because it is the only way we can attain the power needed to counteract the forces of darkness trying to *prevent* God's goals from being realized (Acts 1:8).

Should Jesus tarry His coming, the next few years are going to see a revival of unprecedented proportions. At the same time, there will be great catastrophes in the world as tremendous problems face all of civilization. Still, in the very midst of all this, Spirit-filled churches are going to grow larger than ever before — to an extent that would have been considered impossible just a short time ago.

Millions are going to be brought into the kingdom of God — saved by the blood of Jesus — as the result of an enveloping move of the Holy Spirit that's going to change this planet. I believe hundreds of thousands (perhaps even millions) of Catholics are already coming to a saving knowledge of Jesus Christ. I also believe that millions behind the Iron Curtain are going to find Jesus as their Saviour.

I believe that today's entire panoply of national and international events is setting the stage for this last great move of God. And make no mistake about it, the driving force behind all this is the power of the Holy Spirit. This is the source of growth, it is the source of life, it is the source of all power.

However, there are ominous clouds on the horizon. And *this* is what I want to discuss. Satan is working overtime to stop the inexorable march of events that will usher in this great last-day harvest. And Satan, always subtle, is most effective when burrowing from within — and he is doing this today with marked success.

The matters we will address here touch only the tip of the iceberg. We will no doubt miss many important elements because they are presently known only to God. But, at the same time, these are issues that are obvious, and which do demand exposure. I fear, in bringing these matters to public attention, we will strike sparks. But that is no excuse for remaining silent. I do not feel that I have an alternative; I believe God has directed me to write this, and I therefore *will* do it!

TOO MUCH FAITH IN HIGHER EDUCATION

I was in Los Angeles the other day in the 300 block of Azusa Street where the great power of the Holy Spirit fell first at the turn of the Century. In Los Angeles, Houston, Topeka, Winnipeg, and even in far-away China there was a great and simultaneous explosion of the mighty power of an Almighty God as He started to touch the hearts and lives of hungry souls. This was the *beginning* of the fulfillment of the great second chapter of Acts where the Lord promises to *"pour out of my Spirit upon all flesh"* (Acts 2:17 and Joel 2:28-32).

By and large, the majority of the people who experienced the great infilling of the Holy Spirit at this time were of the lower economic and social classes. They were largely uneducated. Because of this, the (perhaps) natural reaction of the establishment churches was to view the phenomenon with derision. It was passed off as a fad, as an expression of fanaticism. They were called Holy Rollers and other derogatory names.

Isn't it interesting? At the *first* outpouring of the Holy Spirit in Jerusalem, it wasn't the respected social classes or representatives of the church hierarchy who were chosen of God to serve as the cutting edge of His great revival. It was an unimpressive, unlettered group of simple folk from the fringes of "accepted" society who received this great gift. Only later did a few of the "upper crust" come to yield their lives to the influence of God's Holy Spirit.

> *"Now when they saw the boldness of Peter and John, and perceived that they were unlearned and ignorant men, they marvelled; and they took knowledge of them, that they had been with Jesus"* (Acts 4:13).

And today, during this *latest* outpouring of God's Spirit? Once again, God has chosen to reach down into a segment of society where there is *"no form nor comeliness . . . no beauty that we should desire"* them (Isa. 53:2).

Look at the setting for the beginnings of this "latter rain." You'll see no universities, no important names, no great cathedrals involved. Only *ordinary* people who trusted God and who had the courage to stand on His Word.

As this movement exploded, it overflowed into the more "respectable" religious areas and soon a thirst for establishment education began to intrude. Today a tremendous thrust toward ever-higher education has become the order of the day within Pentecostal circles.

Now I'm certainly not opposed to higher education, but I can't help wonder if this reach for higher education can't be *detrimental* to the flow and moving of the Holy Spirit. Today we see theological universities and even seminaries that have totally turned their backs on God. They preach secular humanism and openly scoff at God's Word. They are clearly *"teachers, having itching ears"* (II Tim. 4:3).

And I have to wonder how light and darkness can mix; how oil and water can be combined. I wonder what God thinks in regard to the bringing of heathenistic Philistines into the Holy of Holies.

I don't seek to judge anyone, but I'm alarmed when it seems that some (if not all) of the Pentecostal fellowships are suddenly promoting ever-higher education. Apparently some think this is the answer to all problems. In truth, I'm afraid it holds no answers at all.

Is there something inherently wrong with higher education? Certainly not. God places no premium on ignorance. But it can become *very* wrong if we start to turn to *it* instead of the Holy Spirit.

The other day one of our students here at the Jimmy Swaggart Bible College was quizzed by a pastor who discovered that she had attended another Pentecostal school previously. She was asked for her reaction.

"The major difference I can see is this," she said. "At the other school, if one tended to be spiritual, he stood out as some type of oddball. Here, if you *aren't* spiritually oriented, you stand out as some type of oddball."

I considered this very excellent answer a compliment to our school. At the same time, I don't want to leave the inference that *all* Pentecostal schools encourage the attitude of her former school. They certainly don't. However, I'm afraid the possibility exists that more and more are slipping into this mold each year.

I want to emphasize, God didn't use our Pentecostal forefathers *because* they had no education; He used them *despite* this fact. But I'm concerned that He *could* use them more effectively in their untutored condition because many looked upon their education as a *source* of any ability (real or imagined) to meet the problems of the world. You see, it's easy to get your eyes off God and to start to depend on something else.

I posed this question to one of our preachers: Isn't the knowledge of the Holy Word of God the *highest*, the *ultimate*, education?

> *"Thus saith the Lord, Let not the wise man glory in his wisdom, neither let the mighty man glory in his might, let not the rich man glory in his riches: But let him that glorieth glory in this, that he understandeth and knoweth me, that I am the Lord which exercise lovingkindness, judgment, and righteousness, in the earth: for in these things I delight, saith the Lord"* (Jer. 9:23, 24).

In other words, if a man is thoroughly versed in the Word, isn't that the highest attainment one might aspire to? If we are operating in the power of the Holy Spirit and armed with a deep knowledge of the Word of God, will our capabilities be augmented by *worldly* knowledge? I think not. I'm concerned that the Word of God is assuming a more and more *minor* role in many lives while higher education becomes more and more exalted.

Most of the so-called "mainline" denominations have traveled this road, and I believe this is a major factor in their downfall. So shouldn't we consider this question: *Must we follow in their path?*

EVANGELISM

Show me a church or a fellowship that is aflame with the power of God and I'll show you a fellowship or an effort that is rich in evangelists and in evangelism.

The old-fashioned, circuit-riding Methodist preachers were evangelists. Methodist evangelists were known for their strength and power. Today they are a dying breed. Sad to say, in Baptist circles it is much the same story. When it comes to Pentecostal circles, God forbid, but we are beginning to find ourselves in the same position.

When Frances and I first started in evangelism in 1958, there was a goodly number of capable evangelists within the fellowship we ministered in. It would seem today that the number has diminished almost to the point of extinction. Oh, there are still a few good evangelists left, but precious few.

Some say the days of long, protracted meetings are past, that our culture will no longer accommodate this type situation.

I'm certain these factors have played a part in creating the conditions that now prevail. At the same time, however, I feel it's not a healthy sign. I believe it goes much deeper than the "culture" or "times." I think we're not producing evangelists because the ground has, in some cases, become fallow and the climate is no longer suitable for the development of individuals called of God for this field.

What produces evangelists? A total dependence on the Holy Spirit in an atmosphere that flows with the power of the Holy Spirit, great altar services with people weeping before God, and with the Holy Spirit accomplishing His work in hearts and lives.

Without evangelism, the church dies. Oh, I realize that evangelists have never been given much credit in Pentecostal circles, and that's an odd thing, really, because the great Pentecostal move has been largely spearheaded by evangelists.

Pastors will say, "We would have revivals but there are not any good evangelists."

And, of course, the answer to that is, when the church comes back to total dependence on God, *then* it will produce evangelists. When there are no more evangelists, there will be no more spirit, no fire, no power. The great altar calls will wane and die.

Today in Pentecostal churches we have degenerated into seminars such as "How to Succeed in Life," "How to Be a Winner," and many similar types of foolishness. Where are the God-called, Spirit-filled evangelists who thundered the grace and glory of God, who provided a climate where the Spirit of God could move while altars filled with the hungry and the repentant?

If we lose this — and we *are* starting to lose it — all of those who have their doctorates will not help us. Our big churches will not help us. As C.M. Ward said a long time ago: The evangelist rides point; he's the clean-up hitter. He's ultimately the man who scares the devil back to hell and hell out of the devil.

THE BEHAVIORAL SCIENCES

Today the church has become little more than a referral bureau.

- The church refers the drunk (the *sick,* if you please) to Alcoholics Anonymous.
- The church refers the emotionally disturbed to the counselor.
- The church refers the troubled marriage to the seminar.
- The church refers the insane to the psychiatric ward.
- The church refers the sick to a medical service.
- The church refers the neurotic to a therapist.

Today the well-educated preacher has either a major or a minor in psychology or sociology. I believe, from what we're seeing, that this just might be the worst thing that could have happened to our preachers, our churches, and our people. Modern-day psychology, as taught by universities, is based on secular humanism, evolution, and atheism. When papered over with a thin veneer of the Word of God, this unsavory stew suddenly becomes "Christian counseling." In truth, it is little more than "Christian humanism," and one can't help but wonder whether this isn't the greatest Trojan horse of all.

Modern-day psychology, striving to cure humanity of all its inherent problems, is like a communist economy — it simply will not do the job! It gives us acceptance in the eyes of the world when we include it within the range of our church services and functions.

The well-rounded church was once a center of *prayerful* activity — the prayer meeting was the order of the day with men and women calling on God. But today? The prayer meeting has degenerated into some type of semi-seminar with precious little (if any) prayer included.

I recall preaching a camp meeting with A.A. Wilson years ago. He told about the great church God helped him build in Kansas City. He laid the credit for that church's success to its prayer room. He said the police once knocked on the door and said a complaint had been filed.

They said it came from the family whose house backed on the church property. When asked the reason for the complaint, they mentioned the prayer room specifically. "It sounds," they said, "like a maternity ward."

They didn't know what it was, but the loud pleading and crying of souls calling out to God were the very secret of A.A. Wilson's church — and of his ministry.

But we've changed horses today. Now the center of church activity revolves around the counselor. Great churches have great counseling centers. All members are encouraged to meet with the counselors. There, on a one-on-one basis, they root out and solve all the parishioners' problems. Presumably, they talk them to death.

You see, there's always been something in the mind of man that compels him to accomplish everything by *himself*. We want to save ourselves — or at least be contributors *toward* our salvation. We just can't accept the simple fact that Jesus paid it all — *in full!*

In the same vein, we want to *help* ourselves. We feel that somehow *we* have the answers to our problems. We surely must be smart enough to solve our problems — so we try, and we try, and we *try*. To legitimize it, we add all types of degrees to our names, we put signs on our doors, and it certainly looks impressive. But in the final analysis the heart is still left lonely and empty. Why? Because, ladies and gentlemen, *we just can't do it by ourselves!* You see, whenever we meet with something we don't understand, we want to change it. Even as Pentecostals, we don't really understand the power of God. It is what built us, it is what formed us into what we are today, it is our whole basic substance and underpinning. Still, we don't really understand it.

It's a mystery to the human heart and mind. No matter how consecrated and dedicated to God we might be, no matter how the Spirit of God can deal with us and move within our lives, we still can't *comprehend* the true breadth of God's abilities.

Some time back, at Family Worship Center in Baton Rouge, the Spirit of God moved mightily during the Sunday service. It was one of those times when the Christians present, along with the unsaved, rose unbidden from their seats and, prompted only by the Holy Spirit, made their way down toward the altar. The Holy Spirit, having anointed His Word, used it to penetrate to the deepest core of the human heart. Sin, unconfessed, was brought to the surface. The Holy Spirit went immediately to the core of all problems. He never misses.

How well I remember the sight. Many of those present, men and women alike, were lying prone on the floor, their bodies heaving in sobs as the Spirit of God moved within them. I had no idea what their problems were, but God knew — and He took care of them! But, you see, we don't understand this — and above all, we have nothing to do with it. Perhaps this somehow offends us.

And now today, even in our Pentecostal circles, we're having our seminars on the home. We're finding out all about having a happy home and how to raise perfect children. And yet we have more divorces and wayward children than ever before.

We have seminars which, in all reality, are little more than expanded counseling sessions — advising people on how to overcome their frustrations and fears. It all *sounds* great. We go through all the right motions . . . but I wonder how many real *results* are produced.

The other day I had a young man write me a very angry letter. Even though he was a full-gospel preacher, he ridiculed the altar of prayer. "What good can it do?" he asked. He assured me in his letter that a pill was his answer. A "Christian psychologist" had provided the prescription for this pill that was solving all his problems.

First of all, I'm not so sure there *is* such a thing as a Christian psychologist. I suspect that the two words may be mutually incompatible. There are Christians and there are psychologists — but I'm not at all sure the two can be combined. Oh, I know that statement will be laughed at, but I still wonder.

Secondly, I wonder when we're going to learn that pills are *never* the answer. It would seem that we should have had enough experience with chemical solutions to life's problems, enough "better living through chemistry."

But still we go right on, looking for the next great pill or substance that will *really* lift the load from off our shoulders.

And, finally, the very thing this young man ridiculed, the old-fashioned prayer service — pouring it out before God, asking His help, asking the Holy Spirit to cleanse our hearts and lives — is the only *answer.*

However, our Pentecostal churches are falling into this same trap. Today the behavioral science people have taken the place of the Holy Spirit. And as the Holy Spirit steps aside and watches what's taking place, I wonder what *He* thinks. I think the answer to this is fairly obvious in the precious *little* results we're seeing as our churches accept more and more of the methods of the world.

MUSIC

Music has always been a very important and integral part of the delivery of the great Pentecostal message. The closer people come to God, the more they want to sing about it. Ours is a singing salvation. Someone said a long time ago that when a church loses its evangelists it loses its way. So, too, when a church ceases to be a singing church, it loses its way. Salvation produces singing. Music is a living part of the move of God. It has always *been* that way and it always will *be* that way.

Therefore, I'm disturbed and somewhat embarrassed by much of what passes for Christian music within the Pentecostal movement today. I'm even *more* concerned because it is the Pentecostal movement that is largely responsible for the introduction and promotion of contemporary Christian music. This has further led to the so-called "Christian rock and roll" which is a diabolical force undermining Christianity from within.

I want you to pause and think about the following words by Augustus M. Toplady:

> Whilst I draw this fleeting breath,
> When my eyelids close in death,
> When I soar through tracks unknown,
> See Thee on Thy judgment throne,
> Rock of Ages, cleft for me,
> Let me hide myself in Thee.

Now roll *these* words around on your tongue. They're from *Never Felt Better* by Brian Belew and Kris Klingensmith (ASCAP — Lexicon Music, 1983).

> But we've never felt better,
> Straight for the sky, baby, do it or die,
> Never better,
> And it's okay to be this way
> Cause rock and roll is here to stay.

Or how about these from *No Compromise* by Brian Clark (BMI — Moona Music, 1984)?

> Jesus met the devil and the desert winds did blow;
> He said, "If you be the Son of God,
> Take a rock — and make him roll."

Consider these "religious" lyrics from *Radio* by Darrell Mansfield and Dennis Carothers (BMI — Doulos Publishing, 1983).

> I'll never stop playing that rock 'n roll,
> I've got a message that must be told;
> He is the rock and He makes me roll,
> I don't care if I ever make the radio.

Compare these examples and I think you'll begin to sense what is happening. So-called Christian radio stations are blasting out contemporary "Christian" music that is indistinguishable from worldly rock. Hard-rock addicts who tune in accidentally have been known to call in to request particular rock recordings and they are surprised when told that it is a Christian station.

Music is a powerful and influential expression of the message God has given us. And I can't help but think this is one of the symptoms of decay infecting the Pentecostal movement and that there *are* clouds on the horizon.

I sat at a table the other day with two Baptist brethren, discussing the great move of God all over the world. And with chagrin I had to admit that much of the contemporary and rock and roll "Christian" music of today stems from Pentecostal artists and Pentecostal churches.

I was told recently that most of the Pentecostal churches oppose my stand on this subject. "You don't care about the young people," they say.

Maybe the *real* truth is that I care too much! My family (Jerry Lee Lewis in particular) helped start rock and roll, so perhaps I have better insight than most in this area. Under the guise of Christianity it produces no better results *within* the church than it does in the world.

A young Pentecostal youth director reported this recently:

In a skating rink full of young Pentecostals, the loud-speakers on the wall were blaring contemporary Christian rock that couldn't be distinguished from secular rock and roll. He watched the behavior and temperaments of the young people as they grew noticeably more hostile week to week.

He then changed the music to a more traditional Pentecostal type and watched as the general conduct again changed — this time to one of cooperation and harmony.

This was an unplanned experiment, but even as an admitted advocate of contemporary Christian music, he had to admit that it did exert an influence that was *not* Christian in character.

I turned on the TV the other day and a so-called Christian program was on the air. Contemporary music (that was little or no different from the rock variety blasted out over MTV) was filling the background. Young people were dancing to this music. Oh, no, it wasn't dancing in the Spirit, this was called "interpretive dancing." And all this in a Pentecostal church.

To be sure, it was cloaked in high-sounding religious phraseology, interpreting the feelings of the inner man in the spirit. But *what* spirit?

Did this reflect the great Israelite choirs of the Old Testament? How so? I wonder if it wouldn't be considered blasphemy to compare what I saw on TV with the great Psalms of David or Asaph as they were sung by the great choirs in Israel so long ago.

Satan has *always* tried to subvert the church by intruding the world into it. I wonder if he hasn't succeeded more than we might choose to admit.

MISSIONS

Jesus said, *"Go ye into all the world, and preach the gospel to every creature"* (Mark 16:15). This is God's mandate to the church, and it is not an *option*, it is a *command*. (I will hasten to say this: The great Pentecostal movements have been in the forefront of taking this gospel of Jesus Christ to a lost and dying world. The staggering and truly *astounding* results can only have come because of the impact of the Holy Spirit. Yet there are danger signals here as well.)

Think about this: This one single ministry (Jimmy Swaggart Ministries) gives more to foreign missions than any one of the great Pentecostal fellowships, with one exception, and that is the Assemblies of God. We help build Bible schools and schools for the children, as well as churches. We also help support the missionaries, the printing of literature, and the airing of television programming in foreign languages.

I believe that one of the reasons God has so abundantly blessed this Ministry is because of our efforts to take the gospel to those who've never had the opportunity to hear it. I believe that the reason God has blessed the great Pentecostal movement as a whole is its emphasis on taking this great message to those who must hear it — most for the *first time*. Still, we're not doing enough — and efforts are being made to curtail even what little *is* being done.

We hear statements such as, "We need it here more than they need it over there" or "We must take care of our own before we bother with those over there." The *fact* is that if we don't carry out the Great Commission of Jesus Christ, we will wither on the vine and *die*.

A major reason the Holy Spirit is being poured out upon this dying world is to help carry out the Great Commission. If we fail in this, we will one day answer to God. Certainly we will not be judged guiltless for lack of knowledge or the ways and means wherewith to carry that knowledge.

MINISTRY

In the midst of this great move of God all over the world there is another dark cloud on the horizon. This is the fact that we are beginning to have even more unwholesome elements infiltrating the Pentecostal fellowship.

I sat one day and watched a Christian television variety program. An individual was being praised and acclaimed by the program's host as a prime example of spirituality. In truth, he was anything *but*. His life was a *mockery* of everything that is decent and holy.

A short time ago I watched another television show where another evangelist was held up to the American public as a model of holiness. If he is, one can't help but wonder if God has changed His mind about homosexuality.

Of course, we all know God hasn't. But the sad thing is that we sometimes refuse to believe what is crystal clear before our eyes. How many pastors of Pentecostal and full-gospel churches put individuals of questionable repute behind their pulpits — simply because they draw crowds? And then they *call* it revival.

In this age of high-pressure hype and salesmanship, must we stoop to such level and expose our trusting flocks to unwholesome elements, just for the sake of drawing a crowd?

Or perhaps it's the "Gospel of Love," which in truth radiates little or *no* love.

In other words, we are to accept *anything* that comes along under the guise of ministry — and ignore what happens to the people who come under such influences. Make no mistake about it, the spirits of these individuals produce nothing but tragedy in the hearts of those they influence. Sheep are truly being delivered to the wolves.

And God knows — in the midst of the great Pentecostal message — get-rich-quick schemes and prosperity promotions abound. How is the cross affected when "preachers of the gospel" tell the people that Jesus died to make them rich?

What is the end result when believers are told that if they give a *certain* amount God will send even more back to them? This is nothing more than a spiritual slot machine, a Las Vegas betting parlor — the difference being that while you supposedly can't *lose,* you cannot in fact *win.*

I wonder what the Apostle Paul would have thought, as he wrote to Timothy from a damp, dark prison cell, had he heard some of what passes for the gospel today. Oh, yes, prosperity *is* a part of the gospel, but only a *part* — certainly it is not the whole message. Far from it.

Evangelist after evangelist and preacher after preacher have regaled their listeners with confident statements of "God told me" — and then gone on to speak of the great riches that were to be poured out on those who would practice the proper incantations. Of course, this is a compelling gospel. Who *doesn't* want to be rich?

I sit and watch television and I listen to what is being said. I read pamphlets, papers, and books. And I can't help but think of the millions in the world who are dying without God and the hundreds of millions who have never heard the name of Jesus Christ — the great majority of whom will be cast into eternal darkness and burn in hell forever. And I then see millions of dollars being spent for television time to extol the virtue of "Christian Seminars," "How To Claim Your Blessing From God," and "How To Guarantee Financial Success."

Some time ago I was talking with an eighty-one-year-old man. He had listened to a particular television evangelist for many years. In all those years of listening, he and his wife had seldom missed a telecast. Neither of them knew how to be saved; neither one knew anything about salvation; neither one knew anything about Jesus Christ. Thousands of hours of television time and all they had heard was "How To Be A Success Through God."

All this is plastered over with a vague veneer of spirituality. Scriptures are sprinkled throughout the platitudes that say *nothing* to the listeners. But the hearts that weep and hunger for a living Saviour and delivery from bondage? They listen in vain!

LISTEN TO ME FOR
JUST ONE MORE MOMENT

If by chance you're still with me, I beg of you not to judge the oil and the wine by the flawed vessel delivering it. All of us desperately need prayer, but the Holy Spirit is real and He is perfect. God help us that we do not allow the greatest message in the history of the world to be cheapened and distorted by sleazy appeals to personal greed.

Two thousand years ago a blind beggar cried out, *"O thou son of David."*

Millions of blind beggars are *still* crying out. All of our worldly ways, all of our talents and abilities can't slake the thirst of one such thirsty soul.

Only Jesus can, and if we fail to introduce Jesus to a dying world we have utterly *failed* in what God has set before us to do.

CHAPTER 15

THE MOST DANGEROUS HOUR FOR THE CHURCH

THE OFFICE OF THE PROPHET

Within our present worldly society, it is perilous practice indeed to align oneself with the prophets of God. In the broader perspective, of course, this has *always* been a dangerous position to hold. Most people rebel at hearing the cold, hard facts of any situation, and God is not given to platitudes, sugar coatings, or half truths. Therefore, those who attempt to deliver His Word, exactly as He gives it to *be* delivered, are prone to find themselves ostracized, vilified, (and sometimes even crucified).

Those seeking worldly acclaim and recognition would do well to shun the position of messenger of God. The world heaps little praise (or reward) on those who hold up a mirror to their sins and shortcomings. Unfortunately, the Lord does, from time to time, single out individuals and direct them to present such messages publicly — which are always true, current, and necessary for the moment. I believe the Lord has given me such a message, and I intend to deliver it.

I accept the responsibility with a humble heart, but with full knowledge of the results that invariably befall the messenger. I *already* have experienced the consequences of following the course God has charted for me. I fully expect that there will be more trials in the future. Parallel with these, however, comes a sense of accomplishment and that exquisite sense of security that can only be experienced when a person knows he's trying to operate within the will of God.

A PRAYER OF CONSECRATION

In 1982, God spoke to me in unmistakable terms and gave me some tremendously important insights into this Ministry and into the work of God as a whole. I was praying at the time, and I remember particularly the tremendous feeling of anointing that permeated the experience.

God began speaking to my heart, and a feeling of lassitude seemed to descend on me. Then He told me He was going to require of me that I deliver certain words to the Catholic church, to the Protestant denominations, and to the Pentecostal churches.

At that time He only gave me an inkling of what He would eventually deliver. He asked if I would deliver the message He was just *beginning* to unfold to me. Of course, my first thought was an immediate "yes." But then He told me this:

"Powerful forces will oppose you — not only on the religious scene, but in the secular world as well. The message I want you to proclaim will not set well in the hearts and lives of millions. Are you willing to *pay the price?*"

I'll never forget that moment. It was like a mild electric current putting my whole being on edge. And then He told me what the price *could* be.

"Are you willing to *lose* your whole Ministry as you know it today? The buildings I've helped you build? The outreach that touches the world? The largest television network on the face of the earth? Are you willing to give up the college (which was, at that moment, just in the planning stage)?"

It all flashed before my eyes. In my spirit I could see my life completely changed. I could see everything gone — the dreams collapsed, the Ministry dissolved, and all we had built over those last twenty years shattered as if it had never existed. It seemed like the weight of the world was upon me. I sobbed almost uncontrollably. It was as if my heart would break.

I then prayed a prayer of consecration: "Yes, Lord, I *will* say what You want me to say and I'll do what You want me to do. If we lose everything, I will still do it. If Frances and I have to go back to pulling a U-haul trailer and going from one country church to another, I'll do it."

Please understand, that prayer didn't come easily. I fully knew the heartbreak it could cause. Then God spoke further.

He said, "If you *will* obey me, I will stand by you. I will protect the work *and* Ministry. But you must do what I've told you! At the same time, you must be willing to pay any price I ask!" And then He added this:

"Not only will the Catholic church and the different denominations attack you violently, but your *own* will turn against you as well."

Again, I felt as if my heart would break. Even though it hurt, I wasn't surprised at the reaction from the Catholic church and, for that matter, the modern denominations.

That could almost be *expected*. But it *did* hurt to think that *"my own"* would turn against me.

THE MONTHS THAT FOLLOWED

Almost from that moment, I began to see God's warnings come to pass. First of all, He started to pour into my heart all He wanted brought before the people. It was strong and powerful, and it was obviously anointed. I felt like I knew that God was directing me. But at the same time, I also knew that if it *wasn't* God, this new direction would literally mean the *destruction* of everything we had built up over the past twenty-five years. Then it happened—exactly as the Holy Spirit had said that it would. The storm in all its fury broke about our heads.

The full power and might of the secular news media ripped into us with every weapon at their disposal — newspapers, television, and magazines. None of them weak, local efforts; I'm talking about the world's most powerful periodicals, newspapers, networks, and stations zeroing in on us. The onslaught was terrific.

We were in a crusade in Guatemala City, Guatemala, when a particular incident occurred. Satan, with all his fury, tried to have our program thrown off several stations. At two o'clock in the morning, just before the crusade was to begin, I was seeking God under a heavy burden when the Spirit of the Lord suddenly spoke to me. He said: "You have obeyed me and have not feared that the television stations would be lost. Therefore, I will set an angel as a sentinel at each station. And if some are so evil that they *persist* in following the dictates of the evil one to where they ban your programs from their station, they will be plunging themselves into destruction. And I will give you a *new* station in the same area to replace the original one, but with an even better time slot and a better audience. My message *will* be delivered to the people and to the world."

We've seen the Lord do just this, time and time again, since that night. In the few cases where we were dropped from stations, we have either been reinstated in our old spots or the Lord has given us a better hour and station in the same market area. It has been exactly as the Spirit of God promised. The angels *are* standing sentinel.

The Lord has further told me that He's going to use the telecast to touch the whole world. And He will use it because of the anointing of the Holy Spirit that flows upon it and within it.

Oh, yes, with an unbridled hatred such as few might expect, the Catholic church did exactly as the Lord said. But behind all those billowing clouds of black anger, thousands upon thousands of Catholics are coming to a saving knowledge of the Lord Jesus Christ. And for this we give all the praise and all the glory to God.

We are seeing a move of God among the denominationals relative to the Holy Spirit, especially among the people, but in small degrees respecting the leadership.

I made the statement some time back that there seemed to be a greater hunger for God among Catholics than among Protestants. I think from the results we're seeing today, this statement may have been too mild.

At least efforts to reach the minds and hearts of Catholics have elicited anger — which is a reaction that demonstrates interest. Among the Protestant denominations? Massive indifference. Could this mean that Catholics *do* have a concern for their relationship with God (although misguided and misdirected) while the modern Protestant denominations don't really *care?* That is a frightening thought, to be sure, but one that must be entertained.

I THOUGHT WE WOULD ESCAPE
THE LAST WARNING THE LORD GAVE US

The Lord told me that my own would turn against me. I felt that this, somehow, could not happen. And it looked for a time that it wouldn't. But then the Lord started to deliver what He wanted me to pass on to the denominational and Pentecostal worlds. I will outline it here just as the Spirit of God has given it to me.

Starting in the late '50s, building during the '60s, and gathering strength through the '70s, the Spirit of God has fallen in an unprecedented way on the denominational world. Hundreds of thousands (maybe even millions) of Baptists, Methodists, Presbyterians, etc. have been brought into the fullness of the Holy Spirit. But even though these were glorious times, with God's Holy Spirit actively knocking on the door, the entire superstructure of the denominational churches (their pastors and leaders) has almost without exception battled violently against the flow and moving of the Holy Spirit.

God further told me this: "There are still, despite the general impression one receives, many within the upper levels of the denominations who genuinely love Jesus Christ. They are true Christians in every way. But they are growing old. And once they are called home, *there will be no one coming along to take their places!"*

God has honored, and will continue to honor, their ministries to the greatest extent He can. He will do this for His own good and sufficient reasons. But once they're gone, no one will be raised up to fill the gap. And at this point the denominational structure will almost totally turn its back on God. To be honest, they are precariously close to this point right now. But soon they will almost *totally* deny the faith once delivered unto the saints.

Does this mean that it's *wrong* for a person to belong to a denominational church? Not at all. Does it mean that denominationalism, within itself, is wrong? Again, no, that's not what we're saying — and that's not what God is saying. It just means that the denominational world has, by and large, rejected the Holy Spirit. They've made no bones about this. "We don't want any part of it," they say. They've relegated it to the past with the apostles. They say it's not for us today, it's from the devil, or any number of variations on these basic statements. Whenever light is given, and that light is rejected, there is almost inevitably a general spiritual decline. Jesus phrased it so beautifully and so aptly. If only the leaders of the denominational churches would turn to John 3:19, pray to God for enlightenment, and then read: *"And this is the condemnation, that light is come into the world, and men loved darkness rather than light."*

Ah, *there's* the condemnation! When it's available and men obstinately *reject* it, where shall they turn for salvation? To secular humanism? To the brotherhood of man? To liberalism? Anywhere, it would seem, but to a *childlike faith* in God Almighty.

A short time ago I watched the most powerful denomination in the Protestant world in their conclave in Dallas. They are irrevocably split right down the middle. About half of them already have slipped into total spiritual depravity. And even though the other half struggles and tries to hold up the teaching of the Word of God, it is obviously a futile effort. By and large, they have denied the working and moving of the Holy Spirit. As previously stated, when the last few stalwarts of this group are gone, there will be none to take their place.

God is pouring out of His Spirit upon all flesh, but if it is rejected there is nothing left but spiritual disintegration. As a result, you can watch and you will see a continuing decline in the spiritual orientation of these groups. We are already at a point of blatant denial of the Word of God, the inerrancy of Scripture, and the power of God. And now, if the Lord tarries, one can't help but wonder how much *further* they'll sink.

In the early '60s, I preached a series of camp meetings with A.N. Trotter, one of the greatest men of God I've ever had the privilege of knowing. He had a profound impact upon my ministry. He made this statement to me one day: "Brother Swaggart, the Pentecostal fellowships have gone so far down the road of backsliding that it's already too late. They won't make it back."

I'll be frank with you. At that time, I didn't understand what he meant. Then (in the '60s) it seemed to me that the spiritual world was on a roll; there was no place to go but up. If I'd been forced to comment on his statement I would have had to say (in honesty) that I didn't believe him.

He was seeing things that were too subtle for me, in my youthful enthusiasm, to perceive. But he was right.

The Pentecostal message is unquestionably the message of the hour. It's the message of power and love that God is using to take His Word to a world that's lost its way. It is the *only* vehicle that God is using effectively to get His work accomplished today. Oh, this doesn't mean that people outside of the Pentecostal fold can't be saved or that other lives can't be touched. Certainly they can. But as a whole, it's the power of the Holy Spirit that's accomplishing things. Without this, precious little will be done.

Please note, I'm not extolling the virtues of any particular fellowship, movement, or denomination. I am extolling the power of the Holy Spirit.

Today is Pentecostalism's finest hour. Inroads are being made as never before. Its great messages (that Jesus saves, that Jesus baptizes in the Holy Spirit, that Jesus heals, and that Jesus is coming again) are girdling the globe at an *unprecedented* rate. However, even in the midst of all these glad tidings, there are ominous clouds gathering on the horizon.

THE LEADERSHIP OF THE BASIC PENTECOSTAL FELLOWSHIPS IS MORIBUND AND DIRECTIONLESS

By and large, the leadership structures of the major Pentecostal bodies are political in nature — instead of spiritual. They are providing little sense of direction or practical guidance. Their structures have become almost totally political, to the point where there is almost no room for anything spiritual. Now, when I say "political" I'm not speaking of government, I'm talking about religious politics. How do I know this?

The leadership of the major Pentecostal fellowships (and there are exceptions, albeit few) refuses to take a stand on *anything*. Consequently, the only movements of the living God that believe in and promote this great outpouring of the Holy Spirit are rudderless and directionless. There's nothing coming forth but the "sound of silence." Tragically, if any position *is* established, it's almost inevitably the *wrong* position.

I think the thing that hurt the most was the reaction of the majority of my own Pentecostal brethren in regard to our ongoing discussion with our Catholic friends. In effect, their reaction was this: Don't do anything to upset them. We want to win their approval. It's not politically *expedient* to start pointing out spots and wrinkles. We desire fellowship, so don't examine *doctrines*. Don't tell them what's wrong, you'll get their backs up.

Others seemed ashamed or embarrassed at the messages we were preaching over television. The bridges they were building to the denominational world and to the Catholic church were being undermined. I spoke to one dear brother, many years my senior, and said to him, "The bridges you're trying to build to the denominational churches are useless. God has long since forsaken that house. You're building roads to a once-great city that has degenerated into a massive spiritual slum."

I am going to say something here that might sound strange coming from me, since I am a television evangelist, but it needs to be said.

TODAY, TELEVISION MINISTRIES ARE PROVIDING THE LEADERSHIP WITHIN THE PENTECOSTAL WORLD

And to be completely frank, this is *not* a favorable development. Television ministries should serve as a supplement, a tool, an assistance to the local churches. They cannot take the place of God-ordained local (and national) leadership. But, when the leadership is flabby, indecisive, and directionless, something *must* step in to fill the vacuum. The powerful element of television has by now largely taken over this function. Because of this, it has become the most dangerous hour of the church.

For the most part, "Christian" television is now setting standards that are spiritually weaker and more disoriented than the local churches or the Pentecostal leadership. Oh, to be sure, television is a powerful tool; so powerful, in fact, that most people think that if a preacher is on television, he automatically becomes an unimpeachable authority on all matters, spiritual and theological. Sad to say, this is generally *far* from the truth.

There is always a divisive force lurking within the church that seeks to change its direction. God believes in excellence; this force accepts mediocrity. God promotes virtue; this force accepts human fallibility. God accepts only morality; this force points to man's "animal nature."

What is this force? Certainly the Christian purist would point to Satan, but those who exalt this "higher" viewpoint would point with pride to their humanitarian orientation. "We must," they would say, "demythify the church. We must make it interface with today's reality. We must bring the church down to where the average man can feel *comfortable* with it." Tragically, we're just about there.

It takes strong leadership to bring the masses to a spiritual standard of consecration and holiness. When that leadership is lacking, the people will inevitably revert back to worldliness, impurity, and even ungodliness. (Read Exodus 32:1-7.)

When one reads the Old Testament and reviews the reigns of the kings of Judah and Israel, he sees that every time a Godly king was on the throne, the people were inspired toward Godliness. The moment a wicked king assumed the throne, the people eagerly followed him down the road toward spiritual (and often national) destruction. The same thing is happening today in the Pentecostal church.

Sad to say, the average Christian does very little innovative thinking. The Lord referred repeatedly to His people as sheep. And He didn't utter these words carelessly. He *knew* that sheep need strong and intelligent leadership. Lacking this, they follow anything or anyone who stands before them. Slaughterhouses utilize a "Judas goat" to lead sheep down the ramps that take them to their destruction. Do we have Judas goats in our midst today?

I recently tuned to a Christian program. The host was talking about a Christian nightclub. It all sounded spiritual and uplifting. Yet it will help lead the church into spiritual decline because hundreds of thousands will say, "They're doing it so it must be all right."

I watched another Christian telecast. The star of one of today's top situation comedies was on the program. His own show is about as smutty and lascivious as anything on the air today. Every traditional value is lampooned and ridiculed. The last time I chanced upon it, it was extolling and glorifying the "virtues" of the homosexual life-style. But on this Christian show, the star (and purveyor of all this filth) was presented as a model for the nation. Oh, he used all the right words. He talked about being "born again." Still, no mention was made of denouncing this ungodly life-style. He was fully accepted as a Christian *despite* his promotion of everything that is ungodly.

We see this time and time again today. Role models, even in the Pentecostal world, are now athletes, movie stars, Nashville entertainers — and anyone else who has any type of notoriety or fame. Now let me say a word about this:

Of course, at times these people do get saved, and we thank God for this. We should love them, pray for them, and do everything we can to direct them toward the proper paths. But if they insist on continuing in a life-style that totally repudiates everything that is Godly, we should by no means *sanction* their misguided life-styles by featuring them on our television programs.

We may try to absolve ourselves by protesting that we don't approve of *all* they do. But the moment we put them in our pulpits or on our programs, we *are* telling the world that we see nothing wrong with their life-style, we accept what they do at face value, and we consider them to be acceptable examples for all Christians to follow.

And what does this do? It opens the door for an entire generation of young people to head off in a direction that is totally *opposite* to Godliness. And they are going this way by the millions. Our youth are *lost*. And Christian television, to a great measure, is the *cause* of this tragic situation.

Years ago, one of the most popular names in the entertainment world (and in Christendom) was with me. We were on our way to a meeting that night. He told me this: "Yes, I'm singing in nightclubs and I'm going to continue to do so." He persisted in this path, and this course has caused untold tens of thousands of young people to be led astray and lost.

By and large, Christian television *is* setting a standard. Unfortunately, in most cases it's not the standard of the Word of God. Christian television is promoting "Christian psychologists" and "Christian rock and roll." Now I know what rock and roll is, I know what psychology is, and I know what Christianity is. And I do *not* believe that either of these can be combined with Christianity. The terms are so inconsistent that they make no more sense than if we referred to "Christian prostitution" or "Christian child abuse."

It is Christian television that is extolling "Power of Positive Thinking" seminars — which are little more than a Band-Aid over the terrible cancer of sin. They also promote "Get-Rich-Quick" schemes that have no foundation whatsoever in Christian principles.

I feel ashamed that so much of "Christian" television programming is Pentecostal in orientation, and that *these* are, by and large, the very ones who are *most* out of line with God's principles.

THIS IS THE MOST DANGEROUS HOUR THE CHURCH HAS EVER KNOWN

Yet this should be our finest hour. This is the moment of the greatest worldwide offensive the Holy Spirit has ever initiated. God is getting ready, I believe, to pour out His Spirit in a manner never seen before.

I believe millions are going to be ushered into the Kingdom. And yet, Satan has done well in sowing his seeds of dissension and obstruction. He has confused and weakened the impact of the two greatest messages ever delivered to mankind — those of salvation through the blood of Jesus and the mighty power of the Holy Spirit.

I was preaching recently in New Haven, Connecticut, and God said to me, "Tell the people this: You must draw close to Me. You must stay in My Word. You must understand the flow and the moving of the Holy Spirit. If you don't, you will be deceived by what *appears* to be of God, that *sounds* like it's of God, but in reality is *not* of God."

Millions will be led astray — into spiritual weakness, spiritual incapacitation, and even backsliding — simply because they were not able to discern the difference between the true and the false.

This *can* be the church's finest hour. Or it can be the church's most dangerous hour. I'm afraid *both* doors are open to us. Which one will we choose to walk through? God help us!

CHAPTER 16

THE NEED OF THE MODERN-DAY CHURCH

 "But ye shall receive power, after that the Holy Ghost is come upon you: and ye shall be witnesses unto me both in Jerusalem, and in all Judaea, and in Samaria, and unto the uttermost part of the earth" (Acts 1:8).

It has been thirty-one years now since I first preached this great gospel of Jesus Christ. Frances and I started our ministry when Donnie was just a baby. Our early years were a constant succession of meetings, going from one church to another doing evangelistic work.

Then, in 1968, the Lord told me to go on the air. January 1, 1969, marked the first radio program for the Campmeeting Hour. Believe me, it was a most humble beginning. We started on one station in Atlanta, Georgia, and in the next few weeks expanded it to include Houston and then Minneapolis.

These were *trying* times. I'll never forget the first time that we completely ran out of money — and it didn't take

281

long! I grew so discouraged that I wrote our few stations and told them that the Campmeeting Hour would be canceled. I could see no way to stay on.

I shall forever remember those days. I happened to be in Louisville, Kentucky, preaching a meeting for Reverend Waymon Rodgers at Evangel Tabernacle. Frances wasn't with me at this particular meeting. I was staying in the local Holiday Inn, and it turned out to be a night that would be etched indelibly on my mind.

I couldn't sleep, so about three or four o'clock in the morning I began to seek the Lord in prayer. The Spirit of God started to move strongly on my soul. I remember lying on the floor on my face, sobbing before God, when the Holy Spirit spoke to my heart and told me what I was to do — or more accurately, what I was *not* to do. He said, "It's not *my* will that you cancel the Campmeeting Hour; I will make a way."

I would re-live that moment many times. For even though there was no immediate specific indication of change, in a very few days our whole situation improved *dramatically*. God used the program mightily until we were on over six hundred stations worldwide on a daily basis with one of the largest religious audiences in the *world*. Shortly thereafter we began our television ministry.

THE ADVENT OF TELEVISION

As soon as God put us on television, the Ministry literally exploded. Oh, there were battles — such battles that I couldn't even begin to recount them — and they aren't over yet. But nothing is worth having if it isn't worth fighting for. So we fought, and we're continuing to fight today. And as we have fought the powers of darkness, the Lord has used — and continues to use — this Ministry in a tremendous way. Of course we give Him the glory.

I guess I've said all this to point up one fact: For the last thirty-plus years, I've not only *watched* the mainstream of religious life but have been immersed in it as well. And I've seen appalling *deterioration* — as well as a mighty outpouring of God's Holy Spirit. I will explain.

I've seen some three decades of God's moving of the Spirit. I've also watched some of the mightiest denominations in the history of the world weaken and crumble. I've seen others (to which the world gave little credence) blossom and expand into great forces in the spiritual arena.

THREE TRUTHS

I want to deal with three specifics here. I want to talk first about the scriptural truth of the baptism in the Holy Spirit. Then I want to address myself to a church world that has by and large denied the reality of this great experience from God. Finally, I want to discuss the dangers facing the church world that has accepted this great experience.

1. THE SCRIPTURAL TRUTH OF THE BAPTISM IN THE HOLY SPIRIT

I heard a preacher say something once that I have never forgotten. He stated that if a preacher, church, or fellowship (or an entire denomination, for that matter) can determine the way in which the river of God is flowing — and then get into that current — they'll flow along with the Holy Spirit and receive God's blessings. He continued on to say, however, that multiplied millions are trying to row their boats in a dry riverbed. In other words, the Holy Spirit *once* flowed in the very direction they're going — but it's not the direction God wants them traveling *now*. That brother delivered a great truth.

I believe the mighty outpouring of the Holy Spirit in these last days is the Lord's final, great movement for the world as we know it. It is transdenominational. It has nothing to do with particular creeds or doctrines but is the biblical route that should be universally followed by *everyone* who has accepted the Lord Jesus Christ as Saviour.

So briefly I want to review what I believe is the scriptural truth in regard to God's direction and flow in this day in which we are living.

The baptism in the Holy Spirit is not received at conversion. I realize many churches teach that the Holy Spirit is *received* at conversion and that after this there is nothing more to be experienced. They are half right. The Holy Spirit *is* received at conversion. In fact, there is nothing that we receive from God that is *not* delivered through the agency of the Holy Spirit. Everything comes *from* God, *through* Jesus Christ, *by* the Holy Spirit.

We believe, however, that the *baptism* in the Holy Spirit is a totally separate (and subsequent) experience that can come only *after* salvation and that it is given to endow the Christian with power for service according to Acts 1:8.

I believe the baptism in the Holy Spirit is always accompanied by speaking with other tongues. Herein is the source of the great controversy today. Still, I feel it is absolutely scriptural and undeniable if one will only make a proper search of Scripture. Acts 2:4 is abundantly clear and specific. Acts 10:45,46 further develops this foundation. Acts 8 and 9, while not specifically mentioning tongues, strongly *imply* that tongues were involved in these situations also. Then Acts 19:1-6 reinforces it all.

If you haven't received the Holy Spirit with the evidence of speaking with other tongues, you haven't

received the baptism in the Holy Spirit! I realize this is a strong statement, but I feel God would have me deliver it just as I believe it. I feel there is a definite biblical basis for this view, and we have explained it in the preceding section.

However (and I want to make this very clear), no one should *seek* tongues. The tongues will come automatically. (And incidentally, these tongues are *languages*. They are not gibberish, incoherent babble, or meaningless chatter. They are languages known somewhere in the world but not by the speaker.)

These three statements are the basis for a great division between the churches that feel strongly *either* way on the issue. I don't believe I can put it any simpler. It is probably the most controversial spiritual subject in the world today. And still, at the same time, it seems that the moving of the Holy Spirit upon the general church world has by and large finished its course, or at least is about to change its direction. That doesn't mean God won't *continue* to fill believers. He will do so until the rapture and even after the rapture. But I do feel strongly that the great tidal force of the Holy Spirit movement has begun to change directions. It's almost as if those who *would* receive have received — while those who would *reject* have rejected the experience. (And it should be noted here that the Holy Spirit will never impose Himself on anyone.) And now I want to look at the second imperative.

2. THE CHURCH WORLD THAT HAS DENIED THE BAPTISM IN THE HOLY SPIRIT

The church world that has denied the power of the Holy Spirit has by and large gone into total apostasy or modernism. Some time ago, one of the largest Protestant denominations met in a special session to finalize what they have been debating for several years — whether they would ordain homosexuals. When denominations sink this low, there is nothing left — they have totally turned their backs on the precepts of God. They have gone into apostasy.

Most of the established Protestant denominations are so spiritually bankrupt that they have little or no knowledge of God. Most of the millions of people who attend these churches do not even know what the born-again experience is. Now please don't misunderstand. This is *not* a blanket indictment. There *are* exceptions, and we thank God for them. But as a whole there are few left.

Thousands of ordained "ministers of God" are supporting socialistic, modernistic causes. "Liberation" theology is being taught and preached. That means church people are working with rebels and terrorists to overthrow properly constituted governments. Communistic doctrines are preached from behind pulpits. Terrorist activities are not only condoned, but they are encouraged and supported financially. All of this in the name of a social gospel and because the church has denied — and thus lost — the true power of Pentecost: power endued by the Holy Spirit.

Even those who have not sunk into gross modernism drift without power. In many circles the word "church" has little or no meaning today. It is an exercise in, and an expression of, futility. The Lord Jesus Christ put it graphically when He addressed the church at Sardis in Revelation 3:1: " . . . *thou hast a name that thou livest, and art dead.*"

This is the situation of all too many church leaders and members today: they are dead but they don't know it. The Holy Spirit has been ignored or even openly rejected, and thus they have ended up spiritually dead.

Many of the fundamentalists are in total disarray today. Some twenty years ago the fundamentalists comprised the largest churches in the United States. The majority of these were Godly men who loved the Lord Jesus Christ. They were seeking to win souls, and they believed God. Yet, strange as it may seem, these individuals who were laboring to live clean lives and to present a picture of separation from the world *rejected* — almost to a man — the legitimacy of the Holy Spirit outpouring. What is perhaps *more* tragic, they did so with outrage and even hatred. As a result, perhaps, in the last fifteen years I have seen the fundamentalist movement plunge largely into disarray. And even though God is still blessing their efforts, after a fashion, they aren't what they *once* were, nor are they what they might have been *had they accepted the Holy Spirit outpouring.*

No, the movement will not die, and I pray it doesn't because there are some great men associated with it. But it is not what it once was, and there is a reason. I believe the fundamentalists have lost their solidarity and their direction because of this stance they have taken on the baptism in the Holy Spirit.

Now am I suggesting that God is wreaking vengeance on these denominations? God forbid. What I *am* suggesting, however, as was mentioned at the beginning of this chapter, is that they are trying to row their boats in a riverbed where the water has ceased to flow. Now let's look at the other side.

3. THE CHURCH WORLD THAT HAS ACCEPTED THE BAPTISM IN THE HOLY SPIRIT

Isn't it interesting that the various Pentecostal fellowships have grown immensely in the last few decades — churches that were on the wrong side of the tracks, hardly afforded passing notice by the mainstream religious forces of the world — and today are the Lord's main heralders of the great message of salvation by grace. Couple this with the good news of power through the baptism in the Holy Spirit, and it's no wonder this force has girdled the globe to the point where the largest church in the city is more often than not a *Pentecostal* church.

Why is it that the missionary work of the Pentecostal movement has touched *millions* until there is no effort in the world today that can even remotely *approach* what God is doing in the foreign field by way of the great Pentecostal message?

The answer has to be the baptism in the Holy Spirit. It has to be the acceptance of what we discussed in the first point of this chapter. This is the way God is moving today, the direction the river is flowing, and the area where the power is falling. This is Pentecostal power!

And once more I emphasize, when I use the term "Pentecostal power" it is *not* meant to imply some particular denomination, fellowship, or association. This is an experience for all people of all churches. In other words, every believer should be filled with the Holy Spirit if he or she is to travel in the direction of the Lord's flow and work *effectively* in the Lord's vineyard. Anyone committed to "going with God" had better ask the Holy Spirit to enter his life and to serve as his road map.

DANGER FLAGS ARE FLYING

Unfortunately, danger flags are flying. A few years back, a preacher asked me what I saw as the future direction of the Pentecostal churches. This was my answer to him:

Our churches must remain Pentecostal; this is the crying need of the hour. If we lose this, we've lost our reason for being. There have been Holy Spirit outpourings in the past, and they have inevitably ended up degenerating into denominations as the participants lost their early zeal and turned from Jesus and the Holy Spirit to *men* for direction. This is happening within the Pentecostal/Charismatic movement today, and as surely as God allowed it to happen in the past, He will allow it again — if *we* insist on forsaking *His* guidance for the security of an organized structure. The Holy Spirit will *not* work within a structure not of His making. So we must be on the alert for the intrusion of man-made structures into our direct relationship with God. Else we are going to find *ourselves* trying to row a boat in a dry riverbed.

What are some of the signs that should be putting us on the alert? Many of our Pentecostal leaders are emphasizing higher education. Now, don't misunderstand — God places no premium on ignorance. But at the same time, our strength is not the seminary; our strength is not the doctorate. Our strength is not in the number of degrees our preachers might have. *Our* strength lies in the flow and direction and outpouring of the Holy Spirit as we allow Him proper place in our services.

The Holy Spirit covers a multitude of sins. In other words, *we all make a lot of mistakes!* We walk when we should be running, we run when we should walk, and sometimes we mistake *our* inner promptings for those of the Holy Spirit. But despite all this, the anointing of the Holy Spirit covers us and gives us victory. Still, old-fashioned, Holy Spirit revival is demeaned and ridiculed in many Pentecostal circles.

Where does the problem lie? We have "come of age." Our churches are as big and as "successful" as all the others now; we are suddenly finding ourselves on the *right* side of the track. Our preachers are well-educated. We know how to suppress our natural enthusiasm until we fit right into a "proper" image of today's Christian. But what concerns me, in order to protect all this (which has been totally supplied to us *by* the Holy Spirit), will we retreat on all fronts until we preach a gospel that has been watered down so that it is no longer gospel at *all?* Will we so retreat from our convictions that we will try to cover the barrenness of our souls with a little "speaking in tongues"?

In a giant meeting some time ago, a preacher friend of mine (a great man of God) asked all the Pentecostal preachers present (and the audience numbered in the thousands) to stand to their feet if they could say they were *totally* opposed to alcohol in every form. Quite a number of the preachers did *not* stand. Is this a portent of the future for the Pentecostal movement? God forbid!

In an increasing number of churches, the old-fashioned mourner's bench has given way to the counselor's couch. We've substituted psychoanalysis for the power of the Holy Spirit. And as this happens, our churches are being flooded with divorce, broken homes, twisted lives, perversion, and dreams turned to nightmares. What's happening?

The answer is simple. If we don't have true Holy Spirit revival in our Pentecostal churches, we will lose all that we now have. We must not forget that this has all been given to us *by* the Holy Spirit. If we forget, we, as Samson of old, *"wist not that the Lord was departed from him* [us]" (Judges 16:20).

I BELIEVE THIS

I believe that *one* of the reasons for God's ordering me to build a Bible college is that young men and women must know the power of God firsthand! Young ministers must realize that the power of the Holy Spirit is not *one* of God's answers, it's His *only* answer!

I am deeply concerned that we have a generation of young people coming up in our Pentecostal churches who really don't know what the Pentecostal experience *is.* We've streamlined it, we've refined it, we've organized it to death.

Without question, our Pentecostal forefathers made mistakes, but the power of the Holy Spirit *covered* their mistakes. There are certainly a lot of things we need, but there's one thing we can't do *without* — and that's the power of the Holy Spirit.

My mother finished only the sixth grade. By today's standard she wouldn't be considered an educated woman. But she was filled with the Holy Spirit, she lived and breathed the Lord Jesus Christ; she knew the Word of God. So perhaps in the true sense, she was supremely educated.

You see, she came from a poor sharecropper's family and as such had no social status. But she knew the King of kings and the Lord of lords — and I'm not at all sure but what that isn't the greatest social status of all.

Mama never knew a lot of the "advantages" that we feel we need to get this great job done for the Lord Jesus Christ. But she was filled with the Holy Spirit — and I mean *filled* — so perhaps she had the greatest tool of all.

When my mother died, there were literally hundreds and hundreds of men, women, boys, and girls — those who had been snatched from the burning because of her life— who filed past her casket for a last moment of contact with her. Their faces were wet with tears. Men who had been drunkards were now sober, homes that had been broken were now united, lives that had been wasted in debauchery and perversion had been brought into harmony with the Lord Jesus Christ. The line seemed to never stop.

Her life was a microcosm of what the church should be today: a life guided, directed, empowered, and anointed by the Holy Spirit. Without this we are doomed to be little more than chaff driven before the wind.

One hundred religious persons knit into a unity by careful organization do not constitute the church any more than eleven dead men make a football team. The prerequisite is life, always. (A.W. Tozer)

And that life is the Holy Spirit. (Jimmy Swaggart)

"I indeed baptize you with water; but one mightier than I cometh, the latchet of whose shoes I am not worthy to unloose: he shall baptize you with the Holy Ghost and with fire: Whose fan is in his hand, and he will throughly purge his floor, and will gather the wheat into his garner; but the chaff he will burn with fire unquenchable" (John the Baptist [Luke 3:16, 17]).

CHAPTER 17

THE BEHAVIORAL SCIENCES: PSYCHOLOGY, SOCIOLOGY, AND PSYCHIATRY

Picture if you will what might appear to be a strange scene. (Assuming, of course, that you have never actually seen — or participated in — such an event.)

Many are kneeling, some are standing, others are sitting, while still others might be *lying* on the floor. Hands are raised. Some are weeping, some are laughing, some are praying silently. The one common element is that most have been touched by God!

From where you stand, off to one side watching and listening, you might not understand what is taking place —

293

especially if you are among the uninitiated. It would certainly sound strange to your ears.

Some are groaning, some sobbing, some praying aloud — and as the sounds join together and assail your ears, they do nothing to satisfy your questions.

I suppose one might say, in all honesty, that it would not be a pretty picture. The locations might vary. It could be at the front of a church (although this is becoming less and less common). It might be in a prayer room, or it could be a solitary figure kneeling by his bed at home.

Wherever this might occur, what we're describing is an old-fashioned altar service or a "praying through" session — where people touch God and God touches them. The only compliment one might pay one of these sessions is, "It works!"

THE ONLY SOLUTION

I believe what I've described (which some of you will readily recognize while others won't even have heard of) is basically the only solution to the problems besetting mankind today. I realize that we don't hear much about it anymore, and I know it has been "phased out" of most churches. I am also aware that we have substituted the earthly, carnal, humanistic "behavioral sciences" of psychology, sociology, and psychiatry for this former practice of "praying through" to God's will. But Satan is merely playing one more massive trick on the church of the living God. And unless we come back to those old-fashioned altar services where men meet Jesus at Calvary, we are playing once more into his hands.

In honest altar services or private prayer meetings, the work of the Holy Spirit functions in the heart and life of the believer. Here the individual comes clean with God and lays his difficulties and problems before the Lord, weeping them through at Calvary as the individual goes to the *Source*. And once again, I realize I'm using a term that's outdated and old-fashioned, but I believe "praying through" is a solution that still works for people today.

WE'VE CHANGED

The term "praying through" is now derided in many religious circles. Even well-meaning Pentecostals have stated that "it's not for us today; it's a waste of time. Nowadays, all we have to do is 'name it and claim it' or 'believe it and receive it.' "

Admittedly, it doesn't take God *very much* time to accomplish a thing, but we often forget one important cog in the wheel — the human element. It takes us finite human beings a *long* time to get things right. A lot of work has to be done by the Holy Spirit before we're *ready* to receive the things we need from God. Above all, millions of Christians are today asking for things they don't need, perhaps don't even want, and which certainly in no way involve the will of God for the individuals concerned. (All of this, a result of today's tendency to not bother with "praying through" on all matters.)

When I was a boy, the old-fashioned altar service was what the entire meeting led up to, what it was all about. And, yes, it was ridiculed and laughed at in many circles even then. But there seemed to be far fewer nervous breakdowns within the church community in those days. There were fewer divorces, and clearly, there were fewer lives shattered by the powers of darkness. There appeared to be less bondage. Maybe I'm mistaken in that, but I think not.

The greatest psychiatric team in the world is still Jesus Christ and the Holy Spirit. The greatest book on psychology is the holy Word of God. It is, to be honest with you, the only *true* book in the world on psychology.

WHAT ARE WE DOING NOW?

We have traded these old-fashioned altar services (if we ever had them) for the social sciences. Our preachers are majoring in psychology and getting their degrees in sociology. Although this brings them the respect of the *world,* one can't help wondering how much good it does in spiritual matters.

I'm going to say some things I think will shock some of you, but I believe they need to be said.

Today the people in our churches are suffering more nervous breakdowns, more divorces, more twisted and wrecked lives than ever before in the history of the church. And yet we have more trained psychiatrists. What's wrong? Why aren't our carnal, Philistine ways *reducing* these unfortunate statistics?

The problem is that all too many of our preachers today are receiving their education in secular schools which, in reality, have turned their backs on God. Our colleges and universities *used* to exist for the purpose of training young people to develop a disciplined mind and to learn how to study. Such discipline would lead to useful and fulfilled lives. It would help solve some of the problems of the day, and those so trained could be counted upon to become useful servants to God and their fellowman.

This no longer seems to be the purpose of higher education. Colleges and universities seem to exist today for the sole purpose of subsidizing their professors' unfettered search for whatever it is they happen to view as "truth." One man has said that it seems students are now little more than a necessary evil, little more than a means of paying the freight on the professors' eternal quest for esoteric knowledge.

As a matter of fact, no one is considered to be truly educated today unless he believes that there is no such thing as absolute truth (and by extension, of course, the whole Bible is thus thrown into question — and disrepute). Even the word "moral" is a "dirty word" today in most educated circles.

A meeting was conducted a while back where hundreds of college and university presidents agreed that nothing is absolutely right and nothing is absolutely wrong — and of this they are absolutely sure! Of course, I am absolutely sure that they are absolutely wrong!

One professor said that colleges are educating people away from their common sense — and they're certainly educating them away from the Bible, which is the only *true* source of education the world has ever known.

Sad to say, multiplied thousands of preachers have fallen for the secular way of helping individuals. Consequently, I wonder if anyone *is* being helped. And, even further, I wonder how many are being *harmed?* You see, it has been truly said that the greatest problem facing this country today is not ignorance; it's believing things *which aren't true!*

It would seem that all of the religious, political, psychological, and sociological systems of today are based on philosophies and presuppositions. And if these preconceived ideas are false, then all doctrines and ideologies based *upon* them are false. Following such ideas will produce frustration, confusion, and the ultimate disintegration of any society or element that tries to accommodate them. I'm concerned that this has now been pulled over into the church as well. In fact, I *know* it has been adapted into the church. This is sad, but it is true.

Most of the modern-day psychology is based on the foolish assumptions of one Sigmund Freud — a man who was painfully insecure, who couldn't stand to have anyone look at him, and who had a markedly abnormal life, even to including a perverted relationship with his mother.

To compensate for his own hangups he came up with all kinds of ridiculous assertions. For instance, he made sex a purely biological function and removed it from the realm of morality. The bottom line of such reasoning is that homosexuality (or any other type of perversion) isn't considered immoral. We, on the other hand, believe that man has a will, and that man is responsible for what he decides to do within that free will.

The Bible contains over 2,000 verses suggesting that man is born with a free will. However, a man can commit an act so many times that it becomes an ingrained habit. This habit eventually becomes his nature and the man ends up a slave to his nature (under bondage to his *acquired* nature). True, Jesus came to break such bondage, but never forget: God holds man responsible for the choices that rule his habits and thus, eventually, his nature. In other words, man makes the choices — not his environment, not chance, not fate. Man can be *influenced* to sin, but he can't be *caused* to sin. And influence is never an *irresistible* force one can't refuse.

A person can have reasons for sinning and still not sin. A man can say "yes" or "no" to a good influence — and can resist or yield to a bad influence. Consequently, the problem lies in the heart of man and not within his environment.

Sociologists would tell us that a man's problems are caused by his environment — failing to recognize that they are caused instead by an evil heart that has sinned against God (which is the result of the fall).

That's what the statement means, "Man is a product of his society." Under this type of thinking, society is responsible for everything man does. But does God agree? No! God says that *man* alone is responsible for his actions; not society and not environment. Man's freedom from responsibility is the gospel of sociology — which makes secular humanism its religion.

I maintain that the Bible is the only true book of preventive psychology ever written. Unfortunately, the church is forgetting this. The church, once again, needs to recall the difference between weakness and disease. It is impossible to reason with disease. You can't talk a person out of a case of smallpox. And — if mental problems are sicknesses (as liberal thinkers try to convince us they are), then why try talking to a psychiatrist at a $70-an-hour rate? This is also what we try to do with alcoholics. We refer to alcoholism as a disease, when in reality it is a *sin*.

A disease is, by actual definition, an abnormal condition within an organism, as a consequence of infection or malfunction, which impairs the normal physiological activity. So what's the point of all this? The point is that counseling won't change a disease or sickness.

COUNSELING

Now, let's for a moment look at the word "counseling." This has become the mainstay of efforts to help most people within our churches today. It used to be that the preaching of the gospel performed this task. It used to be that altar services, where God was dealing with individuals as we outlined at the beginning of this chapter, were the key to mental health. No more. Counseling is now the great thruway that leads all to help and healing — be it pastoral or clinical counseling. In many of the larger churches, extensive *staffs* of trained psychologists are utilized to keep their parishioners healthy and happy.

SECULAR HUMANISM

Where does all this psychological *mumbo-jumbo* come from? This entire program, which the church has little by little come to accept, stems directly from secular humanism. And secular humanism is, of course, the most *in*humane philosophy ever concocted on our Lord's earth. It has, in fact, become *the religion of sociology.* Its basic tenet is that humanism looks at man as the basic building block of everything, and builds upon man a world (and cosmic) view and philosophy which relentlessly proceed to eliminate God in any divine dimension.

Secular humanism is the summation of all that is anti-God. Actually, communism is merely secular humanism within a political format. Sociologists tell us that man can find happiness by merely seeking it. But we know happiness can only be achieved by serving one's fellowman and by voluntarily losing one's life for Christ's sake, subsequently serving Him.

So the point I'm making is this: Our preachers who have majored in psychology or sociology and are trying to counsel people from this perspective will be noneffective at best and harmful at worst.

I believe the so-called behavioral sciences (psychology, sociology, and psychiatry) are totally humanistic in content, with a foundation of inherent worldliness that denies God and the Bible, that does not recognize the cause of man's difficulties, and certainly does not know the cure. In essence, it only majors in *effects.*

I'm little interested in anyone who tells me how I act when I already *know* how I act — but I don't know *why* I act like I act or who can keep me from acting like I act. Consequently, any church or preacher who plans to help people by such methods will produce few long-lasting results. The answer must come back to what I originally pointed out — honest prayer and seeking of God's face. Unfortunately, this isn't "popular" today.

IS IT POSSIBLE TO MERGE
BIBLICAL AND CLINICAL COUNSELING?

Is it possible to unite the Ark of the Covenant and Baal? Is it possible to join the Levitical priesthood with the Philistines in the service of the temple? Can one use worldly means to attain spiritual results?

You see, youthful teachers are being spewed out of colleges today completely brainwashed in humanistic principles. The majority of these young people, sad to say, have lost their faith in God. They may persist in some type of religious *orientation* (in name only) or they may even adopt some "fringe" type of Christianity. Their system of *values,* however, is one totally at odds with the traditional Judeo-Christian concept. The foundation is so-called Christian humanism and the end result is destruction. But thousands of preachers, even well-meaning ones, are coming out of schools filled with this so-called "Christian humanism."

Those so trained are inclined to impose this on their congregation, thinking this is the "help" that is needed. Such "preachers of the gospel" (and one must wonder which gospel) are attempting an impossible feat of surgery: to graft secular humanistic beliefs onto those of the Bible. This will never work.

I have listened to psychologists and sociologists expound on the principles of their secular humanistic train-ing and have watched them then tack on some obscure Scripture reference, thinking they will thus add an element of righteousness to what they're promoting.

Some might well ask, "Are you stating that *all* psy-chologists, sociologists, and psychiatrists are of little use to individuals in the area of problem-solving?" That's *exactly* what I'm saying. They are of little use and are probably of great *harm.* I'll even go further than that.

302 *Spiritual High Treason*

I believe that the Christian psychologist, if he seeks to heal people from a *humanistic* philosophy, is doomed to failure. He may have reams of worldly credentials, but the end result will be *failure*. Once again, no matter how sincere the individual may be, he's still trying to paper over worldly philosophies with the Word of God, and *this will not work!*

FROM ACTUAL EXPERIENCE

I was talking to a man who has an earned doctorate, an extremely well-educated individual in these areas. He told me that for some time he had tried to help people by using a system of humanistic philosophy. As head of the counseling department of a large church, he had spent hours talking with people, apparently to no avail.

He went on to say that he came to the conclusion that he was helping no one. But when he changed his methods and got the counselees down on their knees and made them realize that Satan, sin, or a selfish heart was the cause of their problems, the results changed drastically. They began to realize, as he did, that only God could help them, and He could help immediately.

This man told me that they began to realize that God's power was able to break the bonds and chains of sin. He said that only when he watched them kneel in prayer with their faces bathed in tears and with the Spirit of God working in their lives was he able to see results in his work.

Thank God he did see it, because *this* is the answer. It would seem our "uneducated forefathers" were more educated than we know. The old-fashioned principles of the Bible worked then and they work now. Actually, they are virtually the *only* principles that will ever work in man's behavioral abnormalities.

WHAT ABOUT PASTORAL COUNSELING?

Limited pastoral counseling can certainly be helpful — if based directly on the Word of God with the *power*
of God as its obvious source. However, I heard A.N.
Trotter say something once that I never forgot. To be
completely honest, I didn't fully understand it then, but it's
now coming more sharply into focus.

In essence, he said that preachers who sit for hours
counseling individuals, soaking up one sordid story after
another (of adultery, triangles, fornication, and every other
type of perversion that exists) are not only failing to help
these individuals, they are *actually harming themselves!*

He went on to say that this eventually soaks into the
preacher's subconscious, and it has to have an ultimate,
long-term effect of evil upon that preacher. Then, he added,
if individuals can't be pulled up out of the filth by the
powerful and anointed preaching of the Word of God,
there's little that can be done for them through personal
counseling.

Basically, the majority of individuals — even some
Christians — aren't willing to depend on God's Word as
delivered through preaching. They want to have someone
on whom they can place responsibility (blame) for any
advice they will accept. The problem is basically that
people don't want deliverance from their problems — they
want people who can be saddled with part of the *blame* for
the problem. One of the truest statements ever made was
this: "When people come asking for advice, they seldom
want to hear the *truth,* they just want to receive support for
what they've already decided!"

And so it is with "helpful advice" for problems. People
seek counseling for one of two reasons: either to *evade*
personal responsibility — or to *impose* responsibility on
others. This is much easier than consecrating your life to

God and doing what you already know it takes to get the problem solved. Is it any wonder then that we have the excess of counseling that we have today?

And how did A.N. Trotter state it so long ago? He said if people will come to church and be faithful, if they're attending the right kind of church where the Word of God is preached in power and the fullness of the Spirit, if they will endeavor to walk before God with all of their hearts in deep consecration — the old song will remain true. You can *"Take your burdens to the Lord and leave them there."*

I realize that may sound simplistic and old-fashioned. But once again I say what I said at the beginning of this chapter: About the only good thing you can say about it is, "It works!"

WHAT ABOUT MARRIAGE COUNSELING SEMINARS?

Here again, if a husband and wife will study the Word of God and believe God to help them in their weaknesses (whatever these weaknesses might be), the problem can be solved through the Bible and at an altar in prayer. I may sound completely out in left field, but I know I'm right.

About the only good in marriage seminars is that for the few days (or hours) they're in session, they keep the attention of the participants diverted. Here they are given elements of information already revealed in the Word of God had they taken a little time to study and dig them out. Then the couple sets out to live a prescribed formula outlined by the marriage counselor. This may produce an honest effort or it may not. But what we are doing is attempting to treat the *symptoms* — rather than treating the problem.

I maintain that there would be no need for marriage counseling if husbands and wives would live for God, if they would walk in paths of righteousness, and if they would attempt to abide by the Word of God and pray their problems through. However, we all know that sometimes one or both parties *will not do this.* If they won't, a counseling session won't change anything! An old-fashioned *revival* will change the situation if the Spirit of God is allowed to work in the hearts and lives of the individuals.

You see, the word "counsel" is a strong word in the Bible. Proverbs 11:14 tells us *"Where no counsel is, the people fall: but in the multitude of counsellors there is safety."*

But the type of counsel spoken of here is not the type of counseling generally promoted today. The word counsel simply means *advice.* Modern counseling is, of course, "professional guidance of the individual by utilizing psychological methods in collecting case history and using various techniques of the personal interview in testing interest and aptitudes." *This* is where we go wrong.

The absolute and correct method is biblical; the Bible is literally full of good advice. It is the greatest book of advice there is. Advice runs all the way through it, from Genesis to Revelation. It is actually *the* book of advice.

However, modern clinical counseling, which has riddled most so-called "pastoral counseling" today, actually stems from a foundation of secular humanism, not regarding God or the true cause of man's problems — which is man himself.

As a result, in most marriage seminars, humanistic techniques are used — with almost universally unsuccessful results. If they are as successful as some proponents claim, one can't help but wonder why divorce rates are the highest they've ever been in history.

BACK TO GOD AND BACK TO THE ALTAR

Maybe I'm old-fashioned. Maybe my methods don't fit in with the modern way. To be frank, I'm glad. I never intended that they should. I have no desire to make them fit.

If we'd just get back to the good old-fashioned altar services where men weep and cry before God, where the Holy Spirit has an opportunity to search our hearts. Here we can dig down, define, and voice to God our faults, and wait for Him to offer His services to heal and set us free. If only we'd get back to that old-fashioned "praying through" we might be surprised at how well it works and what great psychology it really is.

All kinds of ideas are being tried today, but they're all doomed to failure without God. And again I must emphasize that we can't take the world's ungodly, humanistic, God-denying methods and try to pack them in on the Word of God and the ways of God. The two will never mix.

I'll close this chapter by saying this: I believe that psychoanalysis, or even clinical psychology, is attractive to those who wish to be relieved of their responsibility and, because of this simple and unvarnished fact, it does more harm than good. I believe that psychoanalysis is basically a hoax and maybe the biggest hoax ever played on humanity.

Harry Conn, in his book, *The Four Trojan Horses of Humanism,* said:

> One of the most thrilling truths of Christianity is this: Whatever deficiencies we may have had in our heredity, environment, and training, if we will choose to turn from our selfish ways, seek and find the Lord in true conversion, we will get a new Father who will help and love us. The Spirit of God will dwell in us (which is a welcome change in our inner environment) and teach us His ways. We then

have the power to change our environment for good and become a part of the solution to the world's problems.

What can I add to this except, "Amen!"

CHAPTER 18

BIBLICAL COUNSELING

INDEPENDENT BAPTISTS

When Frances and I began our evangelistic ministry in the late '50s, the Independent Baptist churches were the largest, most active, and fastest growing of all the churches in the United States. To the best of my knowledge, the list of the top ten churches in membership (and even the top one hundred) was comprised largely of Independent Baptist churches — with the Southern Baptists also occupying a prominent position on these lists.

Regrettably, in the last several years, membership growth in most Independent Baptist churches has slowed down considerably, and has even come to a grinding halt in many. There has been a noticeable decline in the membership of many Southern Baptist churches as well. This is a truly shocking situation because the Baptists are a tremendous force for good in this country.

On our way to California some time ago, Frances and I boarded an American Airlines flight. As we took our seats, a brother joined us and introduced himself. He was a well-known and respected Independent Baptist evangelist.

During our conversation, I asked, "Why has your church's growth stopped, and why is there even a decline in membership in some areas?"

His answer surprised me because it was so totally unexpected. He said that the cause of the great growth was evangelism. In other words, he said, it was a matter of soul-winning. He said the consuming passion of just about all the church's pastors was win souls, win souls, and then go on out and win *more* souls.

This evangelist said the people were taught to win souls, and they were exhorted from the pulpit to win souls. The majority of pastors had great burdens for souls, and this concern was transmitted from the pulpits to the congregations. As a result, multiplied hundreds of thousands were brought into the saving knowledge of the King of kings and Lord of lords. This was the secret behind the tremendous growth, he said. But he sadly added that many of the Independent Baptist churches no longer concern themselves with soul-winning.

Several years ago, he lamented, Christian counseling took over as the new superhighway to church expansion. Soul-winning all but stopped. Church after church allowed its soul-winning efforts to languish as it concentrated instead on "Christian counseling." Suddenly, psychology was in vogue and generally regarded as *the* way to go. He said the church believed that counseling would make problems go away and draw people to the churches.

"We thought," he continued, "that the main difficulty was a lack of self-esteem and once this was corrected, the problems would disappear."

He went on to say that today the churches are flooded with seminars on self-esteem, marriage workshops, inner healing, alcoholism, and the like. This is why the churches are dying today, he concluded.

He then went on to single out one of the greatest Independent Baptist churches in America.

This church, he noted, used to routinely carry a membership roll of five thousand. Today it is down to about three thousand — and declining. This evangelist said the pastor there told him the other day, "If we don't get back to winning souls, my church is going to die."

PENTECOSTAL AND CHARISMATIC CHURCHES

The spectacular growth in Pentecostal and Charismatic churches began in the middle '70s, and there were solid reasons for such growth. A great outpouring of the Holy Spirit had taken place all over the nation and around the world. People were hungry for God. Due to coast-to-coast Christian television programming and the genuinely spine-tingling services being held in Pentecostal and Charismatic churches, searching people began to flock to them and were abundantly fed.

At that time, in fact, many of our churches adopted the soul-winning programs and techniques of our Independent and Southern Baptist brothers. As a result, the Pentecostal and Charismatic churches began to grow explosively — until today the largest churches in the nation are, to a great extent, Pentecostal and Charismatic. These include the Assemblies of God, Church of God, Foursquare, Word of Faith, Independent, and others.

However, having attained this desirable position, we are beginning to fall into the same trap that so recently betrayed our Independent Baptist brothers. And if we continue down this road, we will suffer spiritual death as surely as they are suffering it now.

WE DO NOT QUESTION MOTIVES

I have absolutely no reservations about the motives of counselors (psychologists, etc.). I do not question their

312 Spiritual High Treason

commitment to be of genuine help to the people they serve. There is no amount of money that can compensate a person for sitting down, hour after hour, assuming the burdens of others. This comes only through a deep and abiding dedication to helping your fellowman. So I want to emphasize that I have no mental reservations whatsoever as to the commitment and dedication of such men. I must, however, question their *direction*.

The other day, I was speaking with one of my associates. We discussed a specific church, one which I have always considered a great church. I fear it's now showing signs of deterioration, just as many churches and ministries — and even entire denominations and fellowships — are doing. They expend a tremendous amount of energy and display great activity. In many cases, impressive results ensue. But one must look *beyond* this to the end results of the path they're pursuing.

The church we were discussing will, if Jesus tarries, lead its membership farther and farther *away* from God's way. It's like a runner. He may be the fastest person in the race. His conditioning and techniques may be beyond criticism. But if he's headed in the wrong direction, he's never going to show up at the finish line.

And that's what's happening as our Pentecostal and Charismatic churches fall — by the thousands — for the false lure of the siren named "psychology." Little by little (but inexorably) they abandon God's guidance as prescribed in His Word. And even though they might still be enjoying growth, they will shortly find this reversed as spiritual death sets in. Why? Because there's really only one way to build the kingdom of God. This way, as we've said repeatedly, is by preaching and teaching the Word of God.

"Go ye therefore, and teach all nations,
baptizing them in the name of the Father, and of

*the Son, and of the Holy Ghost: Teaching them
to observe all things whatsoever I have commanded you: and, lo, I am with you alway, even
unto the end of the world"* (Matt. 28:19, 20).

Actually, the fifth word in this Scripture might better
have been translated "preach to." The Greek word *mathe-
teuo* — which is here translated "teach" — connotes the
making of disciples, or the enrollment of pupils. In other
words, the intent is to suggest "preaching to."

So Jesus, in His last commandment to all who would
ever follow Him on this earth, tells us to preach the gospel
to all nations and to teach them all the things He commanded in His Word. *If one deserts this prescribed method
of God, the end result will be spiritual death.*

There is no life, other than that which we receive from
God. Counseling, psychology, and psychotherapy are
nothing more than Freudianism — which boils down,
simply and elementally, to *humanism.* And, of course, it is
impossible to take that which is conceived in the world and
reconcile it to the things of God.

IS THERE ROOM FOR
"ONE-ON-ONE" COUNSELING?

Certainly there is. There are innumerable people who
need sensible, rational counsel. In fact, the word translated
throughout the Bible as "counsel" is more properly read as
"advice" or "advise."

*"Hearken now unto my voice, I will give thee
counsel [advice]"* (Exo. 18:19).

"Where no counsel [advice] is, the people

fall: but in the multitude of counsellors [advisors] there is safety" (Prov. 11:14).

Many similar Scriptures could be quoted, and these all refer to the sage advice required, from time to time, by all of us. But you will search the Bible in vain for any reference to "counsel," where the meaning is anything other than practical, commonsensical, personal guidance. There is no inference anywhere of structured programs to control or organize one's spiritual orientation. The Lord and His Word are, quite clearly and simply, the sole authority in this area.

"And the children of Israel arose, and went up to the house of God, and asked counsel of God, and said, Which of us shall go up first to the battle . . ." (Judg. 20:18).

"In whom also we have obtained an inheritance, being predestinated according to the purpose of him who worketh all things after the counsel of his own will" (Eph. 1:11).

At Family Worship Center here in Baton Rouge, we have two counselors for a church that averages over 6,000. The vast majority of those who seek counsel are people from *outside* the church — while the overwhelming percentage of the members have their needs met directly by the ministry and the altar. And I maintain that's *still* the way it should be!

THE MINISTRY OF THE WORD

In church after church, preaching is becoming the forgotten element in members' relationship and communication with God. Even teaching is becoming subverted and distorted as it gives way to counseling sessions, marriage workshops, and an almost endless shopping list of similar substitutes.

If the pastor of the church knows the Word of God (and he should, or he shouldn't be there) and if he habitually finds refreshment in communication with God, he will meet the needs of the people *without* any need for faddish expediencies. Sooner or later, just about every problem we ever face as individuals will be addressed from the pulpit — *if* the preacher is attuned to the Spirit of God and His promptings. (Here, of course, it might be pointed out that those who habitually *miss* services should not count on this prescription for curing their spiritual ills.)

I study the Word of God constantly. I would like to think that I spend about half my time praying. Still, virtually every time I listen to a preacher preach the Word of God under the anointing of the Holy Spirit, I hear some word given that the Holy Spirit uses to counsel me. A question will be answered, a need will be met, a fresh vista in the Word of God will be opened where there were only rote words before.

Often there will be a moving of the Spirit that cannot be explained or even defined. But at that moment a great need will be met within my heart and life. A word of faith will come, instruction from the Holy Spirit will be delivered, or the power of God will throw back the powers of darkness.

Please read the following Scripture carefully.

"Now when the sun was setting, all they that had any sick with divers diseases brought them unto him; and he laid his hands on every one of them, and healed them. And devils also came out of many, crying out, and saying, Thou art Christ the Son of God. And he rebuking them

> *suffered them not to speak: for they knew that he was Christ"* (Luke 4:40, 41).

There is something tremendously important here that we should take particular notice of. It concerns what the Pentecostal churches once *had* (and some few still *have*). There are many incidents mentioned in the Bible where Jesus *discerned* evil spirits and cast them out. But in this passage there is *no* indication that He took particular note of any devils, nor that He ordered any out. Still, the Bible states that they *came out.* It says specifically that He "healed the sick" — the departure of the demons was more of a side effect.

Now if Jesus did not discern them and command them, why did they come out? Why didn't they just lurk stealthily in their hosts, hoping they were undetected and might so remain? *The obvious reason for their noisy departure was the anointing of the Holy Spirit.*

Most of our preachers today seem total strangers to the anointing, which makes one wonder. Is the anointing absent because they're not *aware* of it, or is it absent because they don't actively *seek* it? In any event, when the teacher is teaching or the preacher is preaching and a heavy anointing falls, problems will be solved in the hearts and lives of the listeners. They may fail to understand what's happening, and the preacher may fail to discern it, but satanic strongholds that have long dominated hearts *will be thrown down in that moment* — just because Satan can't *stand* being in the tangible presence of the Holy Spirit.

Holy Spirit anointing breaks the yoke. If this anointing were more common in today's services, we would find less need for counseling. The yoke would be routinely broken as the Word of God is preached with power — under the anointing of the Holy Spirit.

This is God's method; this is God's way. Satan can deal with our intelligence, he can handle our abilities or our education, and he is not hindered by beautiful buildings or by sweet-singing voices, but he is absolutely *shattered* by the anointing of the Holy Spirit.

But God doesn't carelessly strew His Holy Spirit anointing about. The preacher's life must be a life of prayer and consecration. He must literally abide in the Word. He cannot be so strung out with wild and fruitless windmill tilting that he has no time for communion with God.

Of course, the congregation is an important factor, too. When the people know their pastor is spending time in prayer and the Word, they will not *expect* him to dissipate time and energy in the pursuit of other endeavors, as important as they may be. And, of course, when people's problems are solved during services, far less individual ministry is called for.

This is really why we go to church in the first place. Oh, to be sure, hospital visitation is important. Attending certain functions is important. *Many* things are important, but these all pale to insignificance when compared to the importance of a pastor who is attuned to God. And, as we've said and will continue to say, when all these factors come together, needs will be met by the Holy Spirit and there will be little need for formal programs directed at mass-produced solutions.

WHEN WE COUNSEL, HOW SHOULD WE COUNSEL?

I have a dear friend who has a doctorate in psychology. For some time he headed the counseling department of a large Assemblies of God church. The people came in droves and, to all appearances, he was a resounding success. But was he really? *He* said it was the most frustrating experience of his life. He dealt with these people according to the psychological principles he had learned in seminary.

He said he did not remember seeing a single individual who he believed was helped by God in one of these counseling sessions. It finally reached the point that he called out to God and asked what to do.

So from that point on, when people came to him, my friend stopped explaining away or excusing their sins as "mistakes" or "mendacities." Instead, he took what was, for him, a new tact — but, yet, a proven way.

"You have sinned," he would tell them (if the person had sinned). "Let's get on our knees and ask God for forgiveness and cleansing."

Suddenly, there was permanent victory instead of a long succession of improvements and relapses, advances and retreats. Now, in place of the former litany of excuses and justifications, the Holy Spirit would move in and there would be conviction. Hopeless cases (under his former methods) were suddenly solved.

"Howbeit when he, the Spirit of truth, is come,
he will guide you into all truth" (John 16:13).

As we've stated, there must be genuine love, warmth, and compassion in the heart of the individual who serves in the role of counselor. The person with whom he is dealing must feel and accept this love. Then, *the only textbook or system needed is the Holy Bible.* It has the answer for every spiritual problem anyone will ever face.

"According as his divine power hath given
unto us all things that pertain unto life and
godliness, through the knowledge of him that
hath called us to glory and virtue: Whereby are
given unto us exceeding great and precious

*promises: that by these ye might be partakers of
the divine nature, having escaped the corruption
that is in the world through lust"* (II Pet. 1:3, 4).

If the minister isn't convinced in his heart that the Word
of God truly holds the answers to all human problems, it is
a situation in which he should, quite simply, find employ-
ment in some other field. The preacher who settles in under
such conditions is, when all the justifications and excuses
are put aside, clearly a man who is true to neither himself
nor the people he serves. He must know — and believe —
the Word. And the only way he will come to know the Word
is by long and diligent study.

*"Study to shew thyself approved unto God, a
workman that needeth not to be ashamed, rightly
dividing the word of truth. But shun profane and vain
babblings: for they will increase unto more ungodliness"* (II Tim. 2:15, 16).

In these two verses we are told, in effect, to know the
Word of God and to shun the psychological way. At this
point, the subject should be directed to his knees. Then we
can allow the Holy Spirit to be true to His Word, and He
will deal with that person's heart and life. It really doesn't
matter what the problem might be, the solution *will* appear.

"A STUDY IN THE WORD"

Some time back, on a segment of our daily telecast, "A
Study in the Word," we taught a short series on the terrible
problem of incest. The mail literally flooded our offices.

On the program we simply outlined the difficulty and
then delivered the Word of God:

"For if ye forgive men their trespasses, your heavenly Father will also forgive you: But if ye forgive not men their trespasses, neither will your Father forgive your trespasses" (Matt. 6:14, 15).

In this very complex problem, we simply gave them the Word of God and told those who had been victims, *"You must forgive the person who has wronged you. There is no other way."*

We received scores of letters from individuals who told of their lives being wrecked, of spending countless hours with psychologists and psychiatrists, and all to no avail. Then they heard the telecast, and they got down on their knees and poured it all out to God. They begged the Lord to forgive them for their unforgiveness and anger against those who had wronged them. This was extremely difficult to do, but they reported almost unanimously that they felt peace for the first time in their lives.

Others told of calling a stepfather, an uncle, or some other relative and telling them that they forgave them.

No, there is nothing in the Bible that commands us to continue associating with anyone who is troubled — or especially anyone who is innately evil. But the command is there, and we must forgive if we are ever to receive help.

The letters overwhelmingly described victory after victory, and all because the people had done it God's way. And, amazingly, it was all completed in a few minutes' time. When we do something God's way, it's always surprising how *simple* it can be.

The other night at Family Worship Center, following the service, a large crowd had gathered around the altar to pray. Frances felt led to kneel beside a particular young lady. As she ministered to her, the fact came out that she had been molested as a child and that the memory of the incident remained as a cloud hanging over her. She hated the person who had done it, she hated men, and she hated herself.

Hearing this, Frances told her, "Honey, you're going to have to turn this over to the Lord and ask forgiveness for harboring this hatred. And you're going to have to forgive that person who did this to you."

When Frances said this, the girl looked at her in shock. She had never heard such a suggestion before, despite the fact that she had, over the years, discussed the situation with a number of therapists, counselors, and psychologists.

I'd like to say it was easy from there on, but it wasn't. The pain had been there too long to be dispelled in a moment. But as they talked, it all began to hit home. And then, suddenly, it seemed as if a torrent was released. "Lord, I forgive them," she said, and immediately, true healing was hers.

And there it was. An affliction that *years* of man's efforts couldn't dispel disappeared in a moment when the Holy Spirit was allowed sway. Today that young lady is free, and it's all because she did it the Bible way.

This is something every minister should keep in mind. You can ramble on all day long, but you can't talk victory into someone. It only comes by getting down on your face before God, coming clean, and letting Jesus take over.

There's an old song that says it:

> Give up and let Jesus take over,
> And He will make a way for you.

And what if the troubled person doesn't *want* to come clean with God and pray the matter through? Then, unfortunately, there is nothing you can do and there's nothing God can do. At that point, you might as well terminate the counseling session.

CAN PROVEN PSYCHOLOGICAL METHODS BE
USED IN COUNSELING?

Quite simply, no!

The only way a psychologist or a psychiatrist — or one with a degree in counseling — can be of help is by starting out with a complete *rejection* of all accepted psychological "systems" and "methods" and turn instead to total reliance on God and His Word. Psychological methods are of the world, and they will not work.

"But how about this? I'll admit that ninety-five percent of psychology is bunk. But it does have *some* truth, doesn't it?"

No, unfortunately, it doesn't have *any* truth. What we might mistake for truth is little more than a matter of observing reality. You see, psychological methods do observe (and admit) reality, but reality isn't necessarily a synonym for truth. Let me explain:

Take some of the implements of the dark arts: tarot cards, crystal balls, and ouija boards, for example. In the right hands these can be made to "work," and work to a terrifying degree — whether or not you might have personally witnessed such a performance. But can we call this *truth?*

And then there's drug addiction. Watch a heroin addict push a broken-off medicine dropper into a scarred vein. Watch him work the bulb and then sink back with glazed eyes into a state of dreamlike euphoria. Certainly, this is reality at its seamy worst. *But is it truth?*

Psychology (or psychiatry, or therapeutic counseling, or whatever name you prefer) *has* collected a number of facts, and they do describe reality. But are they God's truth? I submit that they are not. *Only Jesus Christ is truth* — as manifested in His person and in His Word.

This is the greatest threat to the great Pentecostal and Charismatic movements today. *We are trying to graft psychology's basically false methods onto God's truth. This can't be done!*

If a little emotional or behavioral progress is made in "therapeutic" sessions, it will no doubt be because some little truth from God's Word found its way into the session. But it must be realized that such progress will be temporary at best. The long-range result will almost inevitably be harmful to the subject's spiritual condition because the overall direction will be *away* from God's true ways.

CAN THIS SITUATION BE TURNED AROUND?

With God, of course, all things are possible. But, to be painfully honest, I'm not optimistic.

The psychological route is appealing. It's "modern," it's "scientific," and it's "socially acceptable." While it is, in truth, little more than shamanism or witchcraft, it is this aura of respectability that will do us in.

It seems that the church has always craved acceptance by the world. The ways of God are, as a general statement, a curse to the world. The world has never understood them, no doubt because the world doesn't *want* to understand them. They make fun of spiritual things, which are a target for their ridicule and derision.

There is, of course, a little area within everyone that craves acceptance — and the less we are in tune with God, the more susceptible we are to this worldly need for social acceptance. There has always been something of a stigma attached to the true Pentecostal way. One of the easiest ways to minimize this stigma is to mask it with the trappings of science — *as represented by psychological methods.*

Today the Charismatic and Pentecostal communities are, by and large, totally committed to this false way. Every

Bible college I'm aware of is now teaching psychological counseling. More and more are continuing on to obtain advanced degrees in this false art. If any dare speak out against it, they are branded as misanthropes and anachronisms — throwbacks to the old days of "witch burning."

Purely and simply, the psychological route must be rejected for what it is — a house built on sand. You can't join Freud, Adler, and Maslow with Moses, David, Joshua, Stephen, and Paul. There are just too many antagonisms between their principles.

IS THERE A PLACE FOR INNER HEALING SESSIONS OR MARRIAGE SEMINARS?

By and large, no. "Inner healing" or "healing of the memories" sessions — even though thinly papered over with Scriptures — have their roots firmly set in the sand of psychology.

Marriage seminars? If those I've seen are typical, it's more a matter of silliness than danger. When we first started Family Worship Center, we had an individual in who had a reputation as an "expert" in the area of marriage seminars. He spent the major part of his time with us trying to solve the great "toilet paper crisis" that he sees as today's greatest threat to marriage! According to his observations, the majority of marital difficulties have their roots in differences over the proper way to unroll toilet tissue — and he sees his life as a crusade to finally settle this problem. Really, I'm serious.

So we invited another one. He used Barbie dolls as examples of "good" and "bad" marriages.

Just the other day I was reading about one of the most successful marriage experts. His basic contribution to science is to have husbands and wives stare fixedly into each other's eyes for as long as fifteen minutes. Basically, this is his "method." I suspect there are just about as many methods as there are marriage counselors, and I also have a vague suspicion that most (or all) of them make as much sense as the ones we've encountered.

If married couples faithfully attend a good Pentecostal church, put themselves under the ministry of a Godly, Holy Spirit-filled pastor, and live by the Word — their marriage will be sound. It's just that simple.

I like what Evangelist Don Brankel said. It was many years ago, when he had just started out as pastor of his first church. He was not himself married at this time. He was, in fact, just a kid who suddenly looked around and found himself pastor of a church. And, inevitably, some came to him for marriage counseling. What could he, drawing from personal experiences, tell them?

His answer was better than all of the psychological double-talk and mumbo-jumbo that's being passed out today. "Get saved, get Listerine, and get filled with the Holy Ghost," were his immortal words.

I have had many problems in my own life and ministry. Some have been disturbing to the point where I wondered if I could go on. However, I have never turned to a man or woman for a solution. I have always gone directly to God.

Sometimes the answers did not come as quickly as I might have liked, but in such cases it wasn't the Lord's fault; it was because Jimmy Swaggart was a "hard study." But little by little, the answers did come, and over the years, all my "insoluble" problems have been solved.

I am absolutely convinced that, had I gone to individuals (noble as their motives might have been), this Ministry would not exist today. When it comes to spiritual problems, if you go to man, you will get man's solutions. If you go to God, you will get God's.

As Joshua said so long ago . . .

" . . . as for me and my house, we will serve the Lord" (Josh. 24:15).

BIBLIOGRAPHY

Jay E. Adams, *The Biblical View of Self-Esteem, Self-Love and Self-Image,* (Harvest House, 1986).

Martin and Deidre Bobgan, *The Psychological Way/The Spiritual Way,* (Bethany House Fellowship, 1979).

Harry Conn, *The Four Trojan Horses of Humanism,* (Mott Media, 1982).

Martin Gross, *The Psychological Society,* (Random House, 1978).

William Kirk Kilpatrick, *Psychological Seduction,* (Thomas Nelson, 1983).

Bruce Narramore, *You're Someone Special,* (Zondervan, 1984).

Jacob Needleman, "Psychiatry and the Sacred" in *Consciousness: Brain, States of Awareness and Mysticism,* (Harper and Row, 1979).

Earl Paulk, *Satan Unmasked,* (K-Dimension, 1985).

Earl Paulk, *The Wounded Body of Christ,* (K-Dimension, 1985).

Pat Robertson, *The Secret Kingdom,* (Thomas Nelson, 1982).

Robert Schuller, *Self-Esteem: The New Reformation,* (Word, 1982).